The Genius of Genesis

The Genius of Genesis

A Psychoanalyst and Rabbi Examines the
First Book of the Bible

Dennis G. Shulman

iUniverse, Inc.
New York Lincoln Shanghai

The Genius of Genesis
A Psychoanalyst and Rabbi Examines the First Book of the Bible

iUniverse, Inc.

For information address:
iUniverse, Inc.
2021 Pine Lake Road, Suite 100
Lincoln, NE 68512
www.iuniverse.com

ISBN: 0-595-28025-0 (pbk)
ISBN: 0-595-74720-5 (cloth)

Printed in the United States of America

To Pamela Tropper, my wife and soulmate

Wherever Pam is, that place is Eden

Contents

At the time that our teacher Moses lived, there was a king who was an expert in phys-iognomy, the ancient art of discerning character from facial structure and features. This king had heard for many years of the extraordinary accomplishments of this Moses who had not only won freedom for his people from the powerful Pharaoh, led his people in their hurried exodus from Egypt, promulgated and administered a set of moral teachings with justice and wisdom, but also continued to lead his people in their protracted and circuitous wanderings in the desert. To this king, there was no leader alive in all the lands like this Moses.

The king decided to study Moses' face in order to understand his exceptional char-acter. That very day, the king ordered an artist into the wilderness to find and paint the great Moses.

Weeks later, the artist returned and with pride revealed to the king and his many courtiers his portrait of Moses. The king, after scrutinizing the painting and then con-sulting with the wise men of the kingdom, was shaking with rage. "We know that this cannot be the great Moses that I have heard about for so many years," the king bel-lowed. "This face reveals a character of profound evil—a man dominated by lust, arrogance and adultery." The king, feeling betrayed by the artist's attempt to deceive the king and humiliate him in his own court, ordered that the painter be put to death at sunrise.

The king was then determined to find Moses himself so that he could look upon his glorious face. The royal retinue set out into the wilderness and, after many trying days, found Moses and the children of Israel in their camp.

Gazing upon Moses' face, the king was exceedingly distressed.

"Moses," the king said, "Your face reveals a character of great evil. How can this be?"

Moses carefully considered the question and replied, "Because my greatness, O King, is not in my nature, but in that I struggle against it."

After some long moments of shared and contemplative silence, Moses then contin-ued, "It is only that man who struggles against his nature that can be considered great, for it is only he who has true free choice."

1

A Psychoanalytic Journey to the Sacred

The real foundation of a man's inquiry does not strike a person at all.—And this means: we fail to be struck by what, once seen, is most striking and most powerful.

—*Ludwig Josef Johann Wittgenstein*

As the first man and woman leave the Garden, I am with them. Because the ancient voice of the text speaks to me, I feel their longing to go back, their guilt and shame about what they have just done, their fears about the future. I feel their anxiety about whether their Creator, their Father, their God is still with them, and still loves them. I feel their panic quickly rise as they recognize that this no-longer-so-cozy world might not make life possible for them or their children.

As Abraham walks silently up the mountain to sacrifice his son, I am with him. I ask the same questions he asks. Should I obey the dictates of my God and my principles, or is there a higher good that involves the sanctity of human life? Can I be Abraham if I refuse to listen to the God I revere and lead others to know and worship? Can I be Abraham if my beloved God that I worship demands human blood for His adoration?

As Jacob wrestles throughout the long dark night, I am with him. I know how he struggles with himself and his history. I sweat with him as he glares at his own betrayal of his father and brother. I sweat with him as he witnesses, full-face, his character, naked and base. Then, the next morning, I weep as he and his brother weep—brothers at last.

My goal in this book is to bring you right next to me on this pilgrimage into the psychological wisdom literature that is Genesis. For this journey, it is Adam and Eve, Abraham, Isaac, Jacob and his children, and even God who serve as guides. It is my fervent hope that, by examining the narratives and heroes of Genesis, we will, by journey's end, find *ourselves*.

This book is the love child of my mind and heart. It is an offspring of my self as a clinical psychologist and psychoanalyst living in twenty-first century America, and my self as a Jew living within an ancient history and tradition. This book's conception was not the product of impulse, but rather reflects a lengthy process, an idea that evolved, more often than not, without my conscious awareness. Like the joyous couple who has just given birth, it is my hope that this literary love child will be blessed with the *best* of each of its parents—have the best of the present and the past, the best of the secular and the religious, and the best of contemporary psychology and ancient wisdom.

Why this book?

Ten years ago, when I prepared the first of countless public lectures and classes to come on the relationship between psychology and the Bible, I was completely unaware of the journey on which I was about to embark. That day, seated in my psychotherapy office, as I organized my notes on the psychology of the binding of Isaac, I had only the slightest inkling of the power that this subject and other biblical subjects and their myriad derivatives would have over me personally, and on my work and thinking as a psychoanalyst. Until that day, I was a serious student of psychology and psychoanalysis, and only a casual student of religion. What I studied in the Bible class I attended at my synagogue on some Saturday mornings, I generally understood as a psychologist—interpreting the biblical text the way I might interpret a patient's dream, seeing the Torah verse within the constricted purview of my contemporary psychoanalytic theory, making little effort to appreciate the scholars and faithful who had energetically struggled with the same verses since they were first chanted more than two thousand years ago.

After that first psychology-Bible lecture, I was hooked. Something in the intersection of the psychological and the biblical fascinated and disturbed me. I found myself reading everything I could about the history of the biblical text. I found myself scrutinizing and contemplating the convergent and divergent ways in which various commentators interpreted a line of Torah. I found myself studying and considering Jewish, Christian and Muslim sages who struggled to make sense of a biblical narrative within their religious tradition and their sociocultural and historical context. I found myself marveling at the way my scholar ancestors, from all three monotheistic traditions, responded with conceptual creativity and acute senses to seemingly-minor inconsistencies and distant subterranean rumblings in the sacred text. I found myself preoccupied with understanding the biblical mind, and the thousands of minds that examined the Canon for guidance and inspiration. I found myself troubled, and sometimes sleepless, thinking about the "negative tradition" within the bible—Lot offering his daughters to an enraged mob in Sodom, Moses ordering the genocide of the Midianites, God killing the Israelite rebels and their families. I found myself captivated by my spiritual predecessors' striving to find meaning and beauty in the ancient.

My religious studies led me to see an arrogance in psychoanalysis that I had not so clearly seen before. Sigmund Freud, a proud heir to the intellectual revolution of the nineteenth century, understood religion as representing all things backward-looking, dogmatic and close-minded. Science, for Freud, on the contrary, was open-minded and modern. Freud and the majority of Freudians made a great effort to distinguish psychoanalysis, their infant "science," from religious practice and belief.[1] With religious study, I became troubled by the assumption and the belief that psychoanalysis, only a youthful player on the field of human transformation, a mere one hundred years old, holds itself out as unique. It strikes me as ironic that a discipline, whose basic discoveries involves placing the individual within his context, asserting that each individual is profoundly influenced by his history, and can only be understood within his history, claims to be a brand new discovery, a discipline without context. For Freud and the vast majority of his followers, psychoanalysis was most definitely *not to be* associated with religion.

That first psychology-Bible lecture led me on the road which I am now traveling—to understand psychotherapy and psychoanalysis as a discipline within the long-standing and well-established wisdom tradition of Western religion.

My religious studies also had impact on the clinical situation. I began to hear the biblical in my patients' narratives. I heard the echo of Judah, one of Jacob's sons, in my patient Seth. For years, he carried the oppressive weight of an extramarital affair that not only puzzled, but sickened him. Like Judah, who was instrumental in selling his young brother into slavery in Egypt, Seth suffered. Both Judah and Seth had to face themselves and those they had betrayed and hurt in order to find peace in their lives.

In my patient Janet, I heard the echo of idolatry, both appreciated as intensely seductive and vehemently condemned in the pages of the Bible. Janet, feeling empty and devoid of value, fell in love with a long list of powerful men who she idealized, submitted to and resented. Marriages, again and again, disintegrated. Janet each time would end up hating the idol/husband who could not maintain his godly position and make Janet feel safe. Repeatedly, Janet found herself abandoned by her deity. This sad woman was left alone to face herself and her emptiness—impelling her to seek yet another idol to worship.

In my patient Neil, I heard the echo of the wrathful and capricious God. encountered in the Book of Numbers. So terrified of the unanticipated attack—the taxi who might swerve into his lane, the bus driver who might lose consciousness, the elevator cable that might give way—that he lived a life in which he controlled the angry gods by interring himself within his apartment. Neil's world, like that of the Israelites in the wilderness, was rife with terror, unpredictability and superstition.

In my patient Joan, I heard the echo of Mount Moriah, where Abraham prepared a fiery sacrificial altar for his son. A woman with three young children, Joan felt driven to find "love's blissful union" with a man. Each time Joan found herself in a relationship, she rationalized her abandonment of her children by asserting that this was ultimately in their best interest, and even serving a higher spiritual purpose for them and for her.

In each of my patients who were becoming more whole, I heard the echo of the marching feet of the children of Israel who so long and unhappily wandered through the desert of Sinai. In the psychoanalysis, with each step away from their idiosyncratic constrictions and their personal pharaohs and Egypts, my patients' unfamiliar turf of the future became more terrifying. As well, their nostalgia for the old and familiar became more palpable. Like the Israelites in the Torah, the journey from Egypt to our Promised Land is dangerous, protracted and circuitous.

Beyond the compelling ancient narratives that reverberate with contemporary human voices, over the past ten years of my expanding scholarly interests and vision, I discovered that the religious can offer much of what I found lacking in the psychological. The glory of psychoanalysis is that it provides a space in which the nuance can be explored and examined. Each dream image, fantasy, memory, association, and relationship past and present is subject of the psychoanalytic inquiry within the analyst-patient couple. In this clinical process, individuality is understood and revered. The individual is not only the subject of the psychoanalytic inquiry, but also its goal. The aim of psychoanalysis is an integrated and self-aware *individual*.

The religious viewpoint offers us something different. The individual in the sacred text is certainly important—Abraham, Rebecca, Joseph, Moses, Cyrus, Mary, Pilate, Peter, Muhammad—but he or she is not the goal of the inquiry. In the religious, the individual always dwells within the intricately-woven nest of community and the Divine. In the Hebrew and Christian Bibles and Koran, each individual is an instrument of God's plan or purpose, or an obstacle to it. Each individual is profoundly affected by the spiritual successes or failings of the previous generations. Similarly, the choices made by each individual in one generation makes a deep mark on the lives his children and grandchildren will live. In the sacred texts, and not from the psychoanalytic, I discovered that each individual has a greater purpose beyond himself, that each individual's life must be viewed within an expansive and sweeping multigenerational landscape involving heaven and earth.

Even Sigmund Freud conceded that religion and its ritual practices served a socially useful function. In one of the earliest papers in which he characterized religion as psychopathology, as reflecting a public obsessive compulsion, Freud understood that religion was a positive force in aiding the individual in his struggle with socially-destructive ambitions. Freud wrote, "The formation of a religion too seems to be based on the suppression and renunciation of certain instinctual impulses. These impulses however are not, as in the neuroses, exclusively components of the sexual instinct. They are self-seeking, socially-harmful instincts [that religious ritual defends against]."[2]

Understandings as to how people change are a preoccupation of both the religious and the psychological points of view. I began to see how religious theories of transformation can deepen psychological perspectives. The focus of psychoanalysis is insight. Its assumption is that if the patient were able to make the unconscious conscious, to become aware of what has been hidden, yet dominating, that transformation of behavior and character would flow naturally from this new awareness. In this psychoanalytic model of change, insight is king, and action an after-thought.

My inquiry into the Bible and its implicit theories of how people change, encased within the ancient narratives, revealed that the sacred text, like the psychoanalyst, does appreciate the importance of insight. However, for the biblical, insight is not the endpoint of human transformation, but rather a significant stop on the way to it. Judah does not only have to recognize that he has wronged his daughter-in-law Tamar, but also has to confess his sin publicly and make amends to her. Jacob does not only have to wrestle with himself all through the night, but, as the sun rises, has to face the brother he betrayed twenty years before. Joseph's brothers do not only have to know and experience their guilt for their murderous impulses and scheme, but have to demonstrate to Joseph and themselves that they have changed. They will be severely tested. Will they again betray Jacob's favorite son (this time Benjamin)? Even God, after blotting out almost all life on the planet He had lovingly created only six chapters before, not only regrets the Flood, but also makes reparation. God resolves never again to destroy the world, and sends a rainbow to remind Him of this promise. For the biblical heroes of transformation, insight is necessary so that action can be taken.

So far, I have focused on how the ancient can augment and extend the modern. Are there no ways in which the contemporary psychoanalytic perspective can deepen the religious?

My inquiry into the sacred text and the myriad Jewish, Christian and Muslim voices commenting on it, discovered that the Bible is read, in each case, through a clouded lens. The actual text in the Torah, in most cases, is obscured by the reader's specific theological "ax to grind." Some examples: The eating of the fruit in Eden is the act that causes mankind to fall, not referred to in the text, thereby requiring a Christ to redeem us from sin. Isaac is 37-years-old, not a lad as he is referred to in the text, when his father Abraham brings him to the slaughtering site, thereby giving Isaac a more active role in choosing this horrifying test. Esau, Isaac's older son and Jacob's brother, is more an evil figure than he is a pathetic victim of his mother's agenda and his brother's ambitions, as portrayed in the text, thereby making Jacob's deception and betrayal somewhat less morally reprehensible. For many segments of the religious community, in each of the three Abrahamic religions, the biblical text is read through the eyes of specific respected commentators with distinctive "spins" on what is written. A possible result of this process is that the biblical text may be crushed under the pressure of interpretation.

On the contrary, the power of the psychoanalytic stance is its commitment to pursue an undefended and unfiltered perception of the individual. This is precisely what motivates the analyst to suggest free association to the patient. This is the reason for psychoanalytic focus on the resistances, within the patient and the analyst—to clear away obstacles to truthful perception and apperception. It is this observation without "spin" that Freud argues is the ideal that the analyst and patient should energetically seek in the analytic situation. Freud writes, "The technique [of psychoanalysis] is a very simple one:…It consists simply in not directing one's notice to anything in particular, and in maintaining the same 'evenly suspended attention,' as I have called it, in the face of all that one hears…For as soon as anyone deliberately concentrates his attention to a certain degree, he begins to select from the material before him. One point will be fixed in his mind with particular clarity, and some other will be correspondingly disregarded; and in making this selection, he will be following his expectations or inclinations. This is precisely what must not be done…If he follows his expectations, he is in danger of never finding anything but what he already knows. And if he follows his inclinations, he will certainly falsify what he may perceive."[3]

What Freud advocated for both the patient and the analyst in the psychoanalytic situation, this "evenly suspended attention" in relation to the clinical material, this perception of the subject without prejudice, theory or agenda, I also discovered, in this past ten years of serious biblical study, to be a useful ideal when investigating the personalities and narratives included in the Torah. Yes, I learned to appreciate the sensitivity, perceptiveness and creativity of the commentaries on the biblical narrative, but also to distinguish text from comment. It was the application of the psychoanalytic stance to the biblical that made this possible.

Thus far, I have emphasized the ways in which the biblical and psychoanalytic are different. In the past decade, however, I have also discovered the remarkable convergence of these two worlds I have most of the time quite comfortably straddled. The psychoanalytic attitude toward the clinical material and the commentator's attitude toward the sacred text have much in common. I would summarize both sets of attitudes, while standing on one foot, by stating that there is no such thing as nonsense. Ben Bag Bag, a Babylonian rabbi, quoted in the *Mishnah*,[4] taught, speaking about the sacred text, "Turn it, turn it, for all is within it, and contemplate it, and grow gray and old over it, and stir not from it." In the same vein, Freud, almost two thousand years later, describing what he had learned from his neurology professor, Jean Martin Charcot, and summarizing both Freud's and Charcot's scientific method, wrote that the psychoanalytic inquiry involved looking "at the same things, again and again, until they themselves begin to speak." This single stance in relation to the sacred text/clinical material is the hallmark of the method that the contemporary psychoanalyst and the ancient biblical commentator share. It is interesting to note that Freud made this explicit early in his career as a psychoanalyst when he referred to the patient's dream as a "sacred text."[5]

What I discovered, when sitting with and listening to my patients or studying an ancient text, that the task is the same. This task always involves directing my attention so completely to the words that I can fill in the spaces between, behind, around and below the words. Sometimes, this process involves listening to the silences that are deafening, for example, Abraham rising early in the morning to sacrifice his son after receiving the command from God the night before, with no words of protest from Abraham or description of his sleepless night. Then sometimes, this process involves uncovering the disguise that lurks behind the words, for example, discerning what is meant by a specific image or association, a ladder, a dark corner, a river, a serpent, a necklace. Other times, this process involves raising questions about the consistency of the narrative or the character of the protagonists, for example, if Isaac is a wealthy man and sends his son, Jacob, away with a blessing, why is Jacob on this terrifying wilderness journey with neither possession or servant.

For me, sometimes the psychoanalyst, sometimes the biblical commentator, the method also has a shared purpose—by exploring each nuance of the material under scrutiny, no matter how seemingly trivial or irrelevant, I attempt to relate to the material, actively struggle with it, in order to discover multiple meanings within it. Whether analyzing a patient's dream or reconciling two discrepant biblical texts, I have found that it is this psychoanalytic-biblical inquiry, this energetic engagement with whatever story is being heard, that gives life to, and honors its subject and object.[6]

Most central to the project of this book, over the ten years of my becoming a serious student of religion, I have been struck by how the vital questions that the psychoanalyst, Bible, rabbi, priest, minister and imam ask are, for the most part, the same questions. Who are we? What is our nature and potential? How much of our nature is divine breath, that is, transcendent, inspirational, creative; and how much of our nature is governed by our animal histories and biological, cultural and social limitations? Do we have freedom of choice and action? What is the nature of and the restriction on this freedom? When we suffer, what helps? Is human transformation possible? If so, how do we change? What is required to make a new choice in one's life? Are there constraints on this potential for transformation? What is it that helps us find meaning in our experience and our lives?

It is these questions that are the focus of this book.

It was on September 11, 2001, as I sat in my New York City psychotherapy office, three miles north of the World Trade Center that was abruptly and eerily no more, that I decided that I had to write this book. With the smoke and dust choking my beloved city, and a gaping bleeding hole in its soul, the obscene result of religious fundamentalism, I felt the need to write what I had learned, taught and lectured for the past ten years—that in the biblical narrative lies answers to the most important and troubling contemporary questions of our lives; that *we do not have to yield this great library of psychological wisdom literature to the fundamentalists.*

It was on that day of death and devastation that I decided to capture in print my journey to the sacred. It is my burning hope and prayer that this book helps us reaffirm that our lives *do* have meaning, beauty and purpose. This is, after all, the point of the Bible, and its most compelling, lasting and cherished message. This *is* the genius of Genesis.

PART I
Who We Are

Only after this sumptuous banquet that is the earth was made ready by the Creator. Only after the sun and moon and stars were precisely placed in the heavens, the fish in the rushing seas, the animals and all manner of plants and trees on dry land, and the birds in the sky. Only then, in the final hours of His work week did God create humanity.

This creation was not only last, but also distinct from all of His other creatures in its essential nature. After all, this creature was created in God's image.

But alas, even the divine image, like the musty photograph of a beloved ancestor discovered in a forgotten attic scrapbook, fades. So now in the Garden, we find a creature who is more than a little lower than the angels, a composite character who is more dust than Divine breath, more earth than he is heaven, more fragile vessel than he is God's delegate. This creature feels the pain of loneliness and clings to his fellow creatures for comfort. This creature, more a child to his Creator than a clone of Him, disobeys God's command. This creature, this faded divine image, lies to his God and to himself and renounces all responsibility for his actions. This creature is without a moral center. As they leave Eden behind forever, God sees what He has created, and is profoundly disappointed.

From Homer to Shakespeare to Hemmingway, from Plato to Kant to Freud, from Genesis to Jeremiah to Job, wisdom literature is the study of who this creature is—at our most transcendent and at our most savage, and at all the infinite points in between. Wisdom literature examines our essence and our potential, and the complex composite that is humanity.

It is therefore here, with the question of who are we, that we begin our investigation of the psychological wisdom literature that is the Book of Genesis.

2

The Beauty and Uniqueness of "In the Beginning"

For the end of all our exploring will be to arrive where we started, and know the place for the first time.

—*T.S. Eliot*

Every millimeter of the earth we inhabit quakes with the miracle of creation. In the deepest ocean, so dark that human eyes cannot see into its depths, unnamed life swarms and teems and flourishes. In each tiny fragment of dirt or drop of water, infinite generations of creatures are born, live and die. Even encased miles beneath the most frozen of earth's lands and seas, separate from all sources of light for eons, we find diverse colonies of microbes, proving creation's irrepressible impulse and rhythm.

In response to Job's challenge, it is God's creation—this shivering, buzzing ordered sphere of life—that God depicts from the whirlwind.

> Do you hunt prey for the lioness?
> Do you satisfy her young,
> when they are crouching in their lair,
> sitting in ambush in the covert?
> Who puts prey in the raven's way,
> when her fledglings cry to God,
> wandering, aimless, without food?
> Do you know when the antelope gives birth,
> watch for the calving of the deer?
> Do you count the months they have to pass,
> know how, when their time has come,

they crouch, split open for their young,
release their newborns?
The calves thrive, grow in the wild,
then leave them, never return…
Delightful is the ostrich wing—
but is it a pinion, like stork or vulture?
She leaves her eggs on the ground,
warms them in the sand,
forgets that they could be crushed by feet,…
Yes, God deprived her of wisdom,
created her without sense;
yet when she runs up a hill
she can laugh at stallion and rider!
Do you give the stallion his strength?
Do you clothe his neck in a fearsome mane?…
Does the vulture take wing from your wisdom,
when he spreads his pinions southward?
Does the eagle soar at your bidding,
building his nest up high?—
He dwells, shelters on cliffs,
on rock crags and fastnesses.
From there he seeks food,
and his eyes peer far.[7]

Just as in creation, we see the mind of God, a complex and balanced artwork of matter and cell, of environ and organism, in the creation stories, ancient and modern, biblical and pagan, do we discover the mind of man.

We often take our biblical poem of beginning for granted. So familiar are we with its words and music. However, when we read the first account of creation found in Chapter One of the Book of Genesis with fresh eyes, we discover a text that is elegant in its language, soaring in its poetry and profound in its philosophical and theological assertions. In addition, when compared with all other creation accounts, that is, with all other cosmogonies, *Bereshit*[8] is unique in its content. Bereshit's distinction is particularly noteworthy when one compares the Genesis description with the *Enuma Elish*,[9] the cosmogonic myth of Israel's most important neighbor in the ancient Near East. From a comparison of Babylonian and Israelite cosmogonies, we can discover what sets apart the biblical from all other creation accounts.

> The *Enuma Elish*, probably composed circa 1450 BCE, describes the relationship of the gods to the world and the resulting establishment of the city of Babylon. It derives from much older Sumerian, Assyrian and Canaanite poetic traditions. The *Enuma Elish* was meant to be sung at ancient Babylonian festivals in honor of the gods. Preserved on seven tablets, approximately 150 verses on each tablet, almost this entire prose poem is extant.

The *Enuma Elish* begins with a description of an age when there was no heaven, no earth and no gods. Only two forces of nature existed during this primordial time—Apsu, the sweet water, the begetter, a male force, and Tiamat, the bitter water, a female force. It is from the merger of these two waters, these elements of nature, that the gods are created.

Conflict then ensues. "Discord broke out among the gods although they were brothers, warring and jarring in the belly of Tiamat, heaven shook, it reeled with the surge of the dance; Apsu could not silence the clamour, their behavior was bad, overbearing and proud."

Greatly distressed by the gods' (his children's) behavior, Apsu speaks to Tiamat, "Their manners revolt me, day and night without remission we suffer. My will is to destroy them, all of their kind, we shall have peace at last and we will sleep again."

Although Tiamat argues against Apsu's scheme to destroy the children, Apsu arranges the murders. Ea, the god with the most wisdom and ability to devise and execute plans, learns of Apsu's plot and kills his father, enslaves his brother gods and assumes the crown and throne. "Ea has defeated his enemies and trodden them down. Now that his triumph was completed, in deep peace he rested, in his holy palace Ea slept. Over the abyss, the distance, he built his house and shrine and there magnificently he lived with his wife."

It is from the union of Ea, the usurper, and his wife that Marduk, the god to become the ruler of all the gods and world, the most sagacious, most perfect, having been endowed with unlimited powers of vision, hearing and strength, is born.

The other gods, with the support and urging of Tiamat, wage war against Marduk and his forces. "They [Marduk's forces] jostle the ranks to match with Tiamat, day and night furiously they plot, the growling roaring rout, ready for battle, while the Old Hag, the first mother, mothers a new brood."

The Marduk forces, the gods in his camp, then appoint Marduk the supreme ruler. "We have called you here to receive the scepter, to make you king of the whole universe. When you sit down in the Synod you are the arbiter."

In a hand to hand battle, Marduk then fights and kills his own grandmother Tiamat, splitting her womb with his arrow. "The lord [Marduk] rested; he gazed at the huge body [of Tiamat], pondering how to use it, what to create from the dead carcass. He split it apart like a cockle-shell; with the upper half he constructed the arc of sky, he pulled down the bar and set a watch on the waters, so that they [the waters] should never escape...And high in the belly of Tiamat he set the zenith. He gave the moon the luster of a jewel, he gave him all the night, to mark off days, to watch by night each month the circle of a waxing waning light."

The *Enuma Elish* continues, "When all the gods in their generations were drunk with the glamour of the manhood of Marduk, when they has seen his clothing spoiled with the dust of battle, then they made their act of obedience." All the gods then proclaimed Marduk the "Great Lord of the Universe" and blessed him with peace.

Marduk then promises the gods that he will build them a great city on earth, a home of the gods, Babylon, where the gods will administer justice. Joyous, the gods declare, "This great lord was once our son, and now he is our king."

At this point in the Babylonian cosmogony, man is created. "Now that Marduk has heard what it is the gods are saying, he is moved with desire to create a work of consummate art. He told Ea the deep thought in his heart. 'Blood to blood, I join, blood to bone, I form, an original thing, its name is man.'" Marduk orders that man be formed from the blood of the leader of the rebel gods. Kingu is murdered and, from his blood, man is created.

Marduk then divides the gods, half for the heavens, and half for the earth. Dwelling places (temples) are established in Babylon for the earthly gods, and man is assigned the task of slavishly serving the deities through acts of sacrifice and worship.

The *Enuma Elish* then concludes with a feast of the gods in which they all sing praises to Marduk, "He created man, a living thing, to labor for ever, while gods go free...Let men rejoice in Marduk! The prince of the gods. Man and earth will prosper, for his rule is strong, his command is firm, none of the gods can alter his will...Let the gods speak: this was the song of Marduk who defeated Tiamat and attained sovereignty."

Although the distinctions between the Babylonian and first Genesis creation narratives are of more philosophical, theological and psychological significance, there do exist some interesting similarities in these two ancient Mesopotamian visions of cosmogony.[10] In both, the heavens and the waters are separated by the firmament. In both, water, Apsu and Tiamat in the Babylonian myth and *tehom* (rushing waters, Genesis 1:2) is a pre-creation given, that is, in both sacred texts, water is not explicitly described as being created. In both, the differentiation of day from night precedes the creation of the sun, moon and stars. In both, the creation of man is one of the final acts of Divine creativity.

The differences between the Babylonian and Israelite cosmogonic narratives are of much greater significance than are the similarities. The *Enuma Elish*, in fact, shares more of its themes with other pagan creation narratives than it does with its monotheistic neighbor.[11]

First, as seen in the *Enuma Elish*, in the beginning, there is nature, and then there are gods. In this narrative, the preexistent waters, male and female, Apsu and Tiamat, sweet and bitter, merge. From this blending of natural forces, from this primordial ooze, emerge the gods.

In creation narratives of other pagan cultures, this theme is also evident.[12] For the Egyptians, for example, before there was a world or gods, there were primeval waters. From these waters, the first god, Atum, is formed. Atum begets a pair of gods, who, in turn, parent Earth and Sky. The world is created when a god lifts Sky off of Earth.

In the Canaanite cosmogony, time, desire and mist are present before all other things. These elements give birth to Air and Wind who, together, give birth to a cosmic egg. It is from this cosmic egg that the world and the gods emanate.

In the Greek Orphic mystery cult, all was dark until Wind impregnates Night, who then lays her silver egg. From this egg, Eros hatches and sets the universe in motion.[13]

The cosmic egg symbolism also plays an important role in the creation narratives of cultures outside the ancient Near East. In the Vedic Creation Hymns of India, primordial waters hold a "golden germ," within which is contained the world and the gods.

Yehezkel Kaufmann, the preeminent biblical historian, concludes his study of pagan cosmogonies by asserting that, "...In the pagan view, the gods are not the source of all that is, nor do they transcend the universe. They are, rather, part of a realm precedent to and independent of them."[14]

Second, the pagan god who rules the world is more often than not the child or grandchild of the god who creates the world. Consequently, pagan cosmogonies are tales bloodied by divine intergenerational conflict and war. In the *Enuma Elish*, we see a graphic example of this celestial strife. Apsu and Tiamat, the primordial forces of nature, from which the gods emerge, are killed by these same gods. Apsu plans the murder of his own divine children. Instead, Ea, one of Apsu's sons, kills him and usurps his throne. Tiamat then goes to war against her son, Ea, and grandson, Marduk. In the heat of this battle, Tiamat is stabbed and killed by Marduk, and the earth and firmament are created from her bleeding corpse.

Even man, in the Babylonian cosmogony, is a creation of conflict and war. We read that man is formed from the spilled blood of Kingu, a murdered rebel god.

This pattern of intergenerational conflict and warfare is also seen in the well-known Greek creation narrative as described in the *Theogony* by Hesiod, a contemporary of Homer, 8th century BCE.[15] Cronus, the youngest of the Titans who are the children of the marriage of Heaven and Earth, kills his father, usurps his father's throne and marries his own sister, Rhea. As soon as Rhea bears children, Cronus swallows them to prevent their possible future usurpation of his divine power. When the sixth child-god, Zeus, is born, Rhea, in order to save this child's life, gives her husband a stone wrapped in swaddling clothes to swallow instead of the infant Zeus. Later, Zeus forces Cronus to regurgitate all of Zeus' siblings (Hestia, Demeter, Poseidon, Hades, Hera). A ten year war between Cronus' children and the Titans results in the consolidation of divine power in Zeus, the defeat of the titans and the exile of Cronus to the underworld.

A third feature of pagan cosmogonies is their exclusive association with a specific people or geographical region. In the *Enuma Elish*, immediately following the creation of man, Marduk establishes the city of the gods. In this cosmogonic account, it is not man that is its glorious culmination, but Babylon, with its dwelling place for the gods and its magnificent temples.

In as varied cultures as the Samoan cosmogony in which the creator god, Tagaloa, establishes his island kingdom of Fiji and Tonga, or on the Cycladian Island of Delos, the birthplace of the Greek twin gods, Apollo and Artemis, one finds a similar theme. From the earliest origins of the world, Pagan creation narratives *belong* to a single nation. It is that nation's land, cities and people who become the exclusive focus of the gods' creative attention.

Finally, in Pagan creation narratives, in the beginning, there is the story, and then there is a world. In the *Enuma Elish*, we learn in great detail who are the players (Apsu, Tiamat, Ea, Marduk) and who did what to whom *before* we learn of a world and of the creation of humanity. For each of these divine players, the more important the god, the more information is known. We know what his/her gender is. Who he likes, loves and hates. What motivates her behavior and thinking, and to whom she feels loyal.

In addition, one finds the history of the birth of the gods preceding that of the birth of the world, that is, theogony preceding cosmogony, in such varied creation accounts as those found among the people of Papua, New Guinea,[16] Mbuti

Pygmies, the San (Bushmen) of the Kalahari, the Navajo of North America, the Phoenicians in the ancient Near East and the Aborigines of Australia.[17]

As we have seen, four motifs characterize the ancient Babylonian creation narrative. These are the subordination of the gods to nature, the conflict of gods of creation with gods of social order and justice, the special association of the creation gods with a particular locality and people, and the existence of an explicit and detailed "biography" of the gods. Thematically, the *Enuma Elish* is identical with a wide variety of pagan creation narratives in the ancient Near East, as well as accounts constructed by people in distant and isolated cultures. The first chapter of Genesis is, on the contrary, a world apart.

First, when examining the Bereshit cosmogony, it is striking how loudly the first Genesis creation narrative proclaims that God, not only created nature, but also stands apart and above it. *Bereshit* asserts, "When God began to create heaven and earth...God separated the light from the darkness...God made the two great lights [the sun and the moon], the greater light to dominate the day and the lesser light to dominate the night and the stars...God made wild beasts of every kind and cattle of every kind, and all kinds of creeping things of the earth...And God [then] created humanity in His image."[18]

In Genesis, there is the sharpest of distinctions drawn, never discerned in pagan cosmogonic myths, the God alone is the *creator*, and therefore everything else in the world and in nature, without exception and ambiguity, is *creature*.

This Creator-creature distinction was challenged by a system of beliefs popular at the time of the early rabbis. Gnosticism was an influential philosophy in the Greek, Jewish, and Christian circles as well as among the later Sufi Muslims. Gnostics believed in a pervasive dualism that ruled heaven and earth. Following a primal catastrophic splitting, a primordial spiritual "big bang," God retreated into the heavenly spheres, while an evil force, the Demiurge, created the world, which serves as man's prison.[19]

The ancient rabbis conceptually parried these Gnostic theological challenges. They were greatly concerned that one might think that God did not act alone in creating the world. Interested in preserving this uniquely Jewish distinction between creator and creature, a theological pillar of monotheistic religion, the sages unequivocally asserted that no angel was created until after the first day.

"Rabbi Johanan said: They [the angels] were created on the second day...Rabbi Hanina said: They were created on the fifth day...Rabbi Luliani b. Tabri said in Rabbi Isaac's name: Whether we accept the view of Rabbi Hanina or that of Rabbi Johanan, all agree that none were created on the first day, lest you should say, Michael stretched [the world] in the south and Gabriel in the north, while the Holy One, blessed be He, measured it in the middle; [quoting Isaiah 44:24] but I am the Lord, that maketh all things; that stretched forth the heavens *alone*; that spread abroad the earth *by Myself...*"[20]

In a similar vein, Rashi (1040-1105), the most respected of redactors of rabbinic commentary on the Torah, scrutinized the Hebrew used in the seven days of creation. On all days subsequent to the first day, the text uses the ordinal, that is, "There was evening and there was morning, a *second* day," or "a *third* day," etc. However, on the first day, after separating light from darkness, the Hebrew reads, "There was evening and there was morning; *one* day." Why is the sacred text inconsistent when completing the first day? Rashi states that this is to teach us that when God created the heavens and the earth, He was one and alone, that He created our world without angelic assistance. This first day was a "day of one."[21]

Maimonides (1135-1204), Aristotelian philosopher, talmudist, biblical commentator and physician, expanding this point, chose to begin his monumental codification of Jewish law by stating, "The basic principle of all principles and the pillar of all sciences is to realize that there is a First Being that brought every existing thing into being."[22]

Therefore, what we discover in the Israelite creation narrative, unique among its many pagan counterparts, is a Creator who is the lone author of nature—not its product. The God of Bereshit's monotheism is always subject, not object.

Second, as we saw in the brief review of pagan cosmogonies, even before there was a world, there was conflict. An important trait of the pagan creation narrative is that the god who creates a world is different from, and at odds with the god who takes an interest in its creation and administers its justice, for example, Apsu *vs.* Ea, Tiamat *vs.* Marduk, Cronus *vs.* Zeus. The pagan created world is therefore born in, and emerges from war and conflict.

In Genesis Chapter One, it is God who creates the world and later, in the next chapter, who takes an interest in His children, His Adam and His Eve. It is God, the Creator, who hears the suffering of His people in Egypt and chooses to free them from their bondage. It is God, the Creator, who leads the children of Israel into the Promised Land. There is no heavenly intergenerational war between the creator and the ruler. There is no room in monotheism for such a dichotomy. The God of Genesis, Exodus, Deuteronomy, Isaiah, Proverbs and Job is one and the same.[23]

Umberto Cassuto (1883-1951), the distinguished biblical scholar and commentator, states, when describing the style and content of the first Genesis creation account, "The language is tranquil, undisturbed by polemic or dispute."[24]

When a world begins with war and conflict, as it does in the pagan cosmogonies, there is no hope for peace, but a world that begins with peace, as it does in the first Genesis narrative, can return to this blessed state. The concept of peace (*shalom*), so central a concept in Jewish philosophy, theology and liturgy, traces its origin to our first biblical text.

The importance of heavenly peace to human experience on earth is captured in the final paragraph of the "Mourner's Kaddish," recited whenever there is a minyan in a synagogue. In the "*Oseh Shalom,*" the prayer reads, "He who creates peace in His celestial heights, may He create peace for us and for all Israel."[25]

> For the classical prophets twenty-eight centuries ago, as well as Jewish philosophers in our own time, and significantly shaping Christian belief over the past two millennia, it is the return to this primordial state of peace, God's celestial heights, that will distinguish the days of the Messiah. Mordecai Kaplan, the founder of Reconstructionist Judaism) wrote, "Peace is the aim of human life to which all other aims are secondary. It is the spirit of holiness. It *is* the Messiah."[26] For Abraham Joshua Heschel and Erich Fromm,[27] it is a taste of this primordial state of peace, a glimpse into God's celestial heights, that the Jew experiences on the Shabbat.

Third, Bereshit is a creation narrative that is unique because it is universal. Until we meet Abraham for the first time in the twelfth chapter of Genesis, by tradition 1,948 years following the Creation, the biblical text is the story of *all peoples* in the known world—not Israel's alone. William Robertson Smith (1846-1894), professor of Arabic at Cambridge University and a Semitist, was greatly impressed by this aspect of the Book of Genesis. Although his scholarly and archaeological work emphasized the non-Israelite Semitic antecedents of the Israelite religion, Robertson Smith saw, in the biblical creation, no traces of Semitic influences. In no other cosmogony he studied, even among Israel's immediate neighbors did he find a creation narrative that was pan-tribal. "In only the Hebrew text does one find that God is a God of the world *before* He is a God of Israel. This universalism is not observed when examining the legends of any other Semites."[28]

Although the biblical creation text is explicitly universal in its content and theme, distinguishing it from pagan cosmogonies, some of the most influential rabbis of the past two thousand years have interpreted the text in a narrow nationalistic way.

Rabbi Isaac, who lived in Israel during the brutal Roman persecution of Jews and Christians (circa 290 CE), taught, "Why did the Holy One, blessed be He, reveal to Israel what was created on the first day and on the second day, etc.? So that the nations of the world might not taunt Israel and say to them: 'Surely, you are a nation of robbers [because you took the Promised Land from others].' But Israel can retort, '...The world and the fullness thereof belong to God [because He created it]. When He wished, He gave it to you; and when He wished, He took it from you and gave it to us.'"[29]

Both Rashi (1040-1105) and Ramban (1194-1270), the two most important biblical commentators of the Middle Ages, still greatly influential today, quote Rabbi Isaac's teaching as explanation for why the Torah begins with creation. Rashi, the acronym for Rabbi Solomon ben Isaac, was the most respected commentator on the Bible and the Talmud in his and many succeeding generations. He lived and taught in Troyes, in the Province of Champagne in northern France. The First Crusades (1095-1096 when Rashi was fifty-five years old) killed many Jews and did incalculable damage to the Jewish communities in northern France. Rashi knew personally people who died at the hands of these first Crusaders on their way to "liberate" the Holy Land from the Muslims. Ramban, the acronym for Rabbi Moses ben Nahman, was the leading biblical commentator and talmudic scholar of his generation. In 1265 at the age of seventy-one, Ramban was forced to flee his native Spain for Israel to avoid a trial by the Dominicans (with the active support of Pope Clement IV) who charged Ramban with "views that abused Christianity."

It is important to keep this historical context in mind when one evaluates these sages' particularistic interpretations of the uniquely-universalistic creation text. As we have seen, all three were living during times when Jews were exceedingly oppressed by gentiles for their religious beliefs—Isaac during one of the times of severe Roman persecution, Rashi and Ramban during the time of the Crusades, the bloodiest period for European Jews before the Shoah. Given these social circumstances, it is not surprising to observe that a radically universal text like our biblical creation narrative gets reinterpreted to comfort the suffering and bleeding faithful.

Fourth, the most remarkable aspect of the Genesis creation narrative, when comparing it to all its pagan counterparts, is not what it includes, but rather what it does not. Bereshit begins with the clause, "When God began to create heaven and earth," without ever describing who this God is, where He came from or what motivated Him in this seemingly-sudden blessed burst of creativity, this seemingly-sudden "act of infinite loving kindness."[30]

Instead, the first Genesis creation narrative describes not who God is, but rather what God does. In only ten Divine commands, nothingness is changed into somethingness, "unformed and void" (*tohu va-vohu*) shaped into a world, chaos transformed into order.

1. God said,	"Let there be light." (Genesis 1:3)
2. God said,	"Let there be an expanse in the midst of the water, that it may separate water from water." (1:6)
3. God said,	"Let the water below the sky be gathered into one area, that the dry land may appear." (1:9)
4. God said,	"Let the earth sprout vegetation: seed-bearing plants, fruit trees of every kind on earth that bear fruit with the seed in it." (1:11)
5. God said,	"Let there be lights in the expanse of the sky to separate day from night; they shall serve as signs for the set times—the days and the years; and they shall serve as lights in the expanse of the sky to shine upon the earth." (1:14-15)
6. God said,	"Let the waters bring forth swarms of living creatures, and birds that fly above the earth across the expanse of the sky." (1:20)
7. God said,	"Let the earth bring forth every kind of living creature: cattle, creeping things, and wild beasts of every kind." (1:24)
8. God said,	"Let us make humanity in our image, after our likeness. They shall rule the fish of the sea, the birds of the sky, the cattle, the whole earth, and all the creeping things that creep on earth." (1:26)
9. God said to them, [man and woman,]	"Be fertile and increase, fill the earth and master it; and rule the fish of the sea, the birds of the sky, and all the living things that creep on earth." (1:28)
10. God said,	"See, I give you every seed-bearing plant that is upon all the earth, and every tree that has seed-bearing fruit; they shall be yours for food. And to all the animals on land, to all the birds of the sky, and to everything that

creeps on earth, in which there is the breath of life, [I give] all the green plants for food." (1:29-30)

Awed by this aspect of the Genesis creation narrative, and the God who was its major playwright and actor, one of the 70 names the rabbis of the Talmud used to refer to God was, "He who spoke, and the world came into being."[31]

A Creator without theogony or biography; a Creator who is known by His actions and impact alone; a Creator who is a verb, not a noun;[32] the Creator of *Bereshit*; this Creator is without correlate or prototype in the pagan world.

A Selective Biblical Exegesis

At the beginning of (*bereshit*) God's (*Elohim*) creating the heavens and the earth, when the earth was unformed and void, and there was darkness over the surface of the deep, and God's spirit hovering over the water—God said, "Let there be light"; and there was light.[33]

And God [*Elohim*] said, "Let Us make humanity [*adam*] in Our image, according to Our likeness."…God created humanity in His image, in the image of God [*b'tzelem Elohim*] did He create it, male [*zachar*] and female [*n'kayvah*] did He create them.[34]

***Bereshit*: At the beginning of.** Although the vast majority of English translations, by both Jews and Christians,[35] choose to translate the first verse of the Torah as, "In the beginning, God created the heavens and the earth," Rashi (11th century) constructs a strong grammatical argument, citing numerous examples in the Hebrew Bible of other verses in which "*bereshit*" is used, that a more accurate translation is "In the beginning *of*…" It is Rashi's contention, echoed by Abraham ibn Ezra (12th century) and a number of modern biblical translators, that the word, "*bereshit*," is not in the absolute, but in the construct state. Biblical Hebrew, which has no word for "of" conveys possession by changing word form, for example, *devrei* not *devarim Torah* (words of Torah), *b'nei* not *ba-nim Yisroel* (sons of Israel). The Ramban (13th century) asserts, in his commentary to Genesis 1:1, that if the Torah wished to convey, "in the beginning" as an absolute, the Hebrew would have been "*barishonah*," not "*bereshit*."

What may seem like a trivial Hebrew grammatical discourse on a single word form has significant philosophical and theological implications.

The change in the understanding of the single word, "*bereshit*," transforms creation from a static process to one with motion and continuity.[36] With the "in the beginning" God created the heavens and the earth at a fixed time with a clear defined and specified origin. With "in the beginning *of*" creation of the heavens and earth are part of an ongoing continuing process. There was a God before He created the world who was perhaps involved in other things prior to choosing to turn His Divine attention to our homeland. With "in the beginning *of*," the first verse of the Torah catches God in the middle of God's story—not necessarily at the starting point. By understanding this one word in a slightly different way, we apprehend that Genesis 1:1 is the biblical account of the commencement of *our narrative journey,* but not necessarily God's.

Maimonides, in his *Guide of the Perplexed* (written in 1190), addressing the philosophical underpinnings of this biblical exegesis, wrote "I have already made it known to you that the foundation of the whole Law is the view that God has brought the world into being out of nothing *without there having been a temporal beginning.*"[37]

But what was God doing before He decided to turn His attention to creating our heavens and our earth? For the answer, we need to inquire of the midrashic imagination. Rabbi Abbahu (a sage of the third century CE), attempting to explain why the Torah repeatedly says, "God saw that this was good," taught, "The Holy One, blessed be He, went on creating worlds and destroying them until He created this one and declared, 'This one pleases me [I will keep it]; those did not please me.'"[38]

In Jewish thought, as we have seen here, creation has no beginning. But also, creation has no end either. Each morning, in the synagogue, the worshipper, before reciting the "*Shema,*" the assertion of God's oneness, prays, "To the blessed God they offer melodies; to the King, the living and eternal God...Truly, He alone performs mighty acts and creates new things,....*In His goodness, He renews the creation every day, constantly*...Blessed art Thou, O Lord, Creator of the lights.[39]

Elohim: God. There are many names of God used in the Hebrew Bible.[40] The most common ones are (a) YHWH (the "Tetragrammaton," the personal name of the God of Israel), (b) *Adonai* (a term which means "my Lords" and has been used to refer to a human master,[41] as well as a Divine one), and (c) the variations of *El* (the ancient personal name of God in the Ugaritic Canaanite language), for example, *l Elyon* (God, Most High), *El Olam* (God Everlasting), *El Shaddai* (God Almighty) and *Elohai* (most frequently found in the Book of Job) or, in the plural, *Elohim.*

The great significance Judaism endows to the Divine appellation is most clearly attested to by the talmudic Rabbis' prohibitions barring them from pronouncing or writing the biblical names of God, and their invention of alternative terms. In the Talmud and the midrashic literature, God is often referred to as, "ha-*Kadosh Baruch-Hu*" (the Holy One, blessed be He," or as "*Makom*" (literally "place") meaning "the Omnipresent."

The Kabbalists, the Jewish mystics of the 13th century, continued the talmudic-midrashic practice by developing names of God that more closely fit their religious experience, while avoiding the use of the biblical designations. The most frequently used appellatives in their literature were "*Temira de-Temirin*" (the Hidden of Hiddens), "*Attika de-Attikin*" (the Ancient of Ancients) and "*Ein Sof*" (He who is Without End).

It is *Elohim* alone who is the actor In the first Genesis creation narrative. *Elohim*, often used with the definite article, "*ha*," to mean "The God," is written over two thousand times in the Hebrew Bible. Interestingly, *Elohim* has a plural ending. Sometimes, *Elohim* is treated as a singular noun, for example in our first verse of the Torah in which the verb, "to create," is in the singular. Sometimes, even when using *Elohim* to mean Israel's one God, *Elohim* takes a plural adjective or verb, for example, "And it came to pass when God [*Elohim*] caused [plural verb] me to wander from my father's house, that I said unto her…"[42]

Also of interest to this exegesis on the first creation narrative, and the discussion of Abraham's Binding of Isaac as well (Chapter Four), *Elohim* has multiple meanings in the Hebrew Bible. *Elohim* can signify Israel's monotheistic one God; or *Elohim* can be used in the Bible to signify pagan gods or even goddesses:

> Thou shalt have no other gods [*elohim*] before me.[43]

> And Samuel spake unto all the house of Israel, saying, If ye do return unto the Lord with all your hearts, then put away the strange gods [*elohim*] and *Ashtarot* from among you, and prepare your hearts unto the Lord, and serve Him only: and He will deliver you out of the hand of the Philistines.[44]

> For all the gods [*elohim*] of the nations are idols: but the Lord made the heavens.[45]

> For Solomon went after *Ashtarot,* the goddess [*elohim*] of the Zidonians, and after Milcom the abomination of the Ammonites.[46]

YHWH, the name of God used for the first time in the second creation narrative, on the other hand, is a personal name for the God of Israel. *YHWH* is never used in the Hebrew Bible to signify gods or goddesses, and is uniformly singular.[47] For the purpose of this chapter's biblical exegesis, the focus of this section will be exclusively on *Elohim*, the "star" of our first creation text.

So who is *Elohim* in Genesis Chapter One? What is He like? *Elohim* is first and foremost the creator of the material world—lands and seas, water and sky, grass and shrubs and trees, fish and birds and creeping things, stars and moon and sun, man and woman. In relation to his creation, to his creatures, He stands gloriously above and apart.

Elohim's relationship with the world is a relationship of creative distance. We do not see *Elohim* walking among his creatures, speaking with them and admiring His own divine craftsmanship and artistry. We will hear His conversations with His creatures only in the second creation account. In this text, what we discover is an *Elohim who* announces and creates, and blesses man and woman. But this *Elohim* is a God who never touches us.

Like *Elohim's* pre-Israelite history, reflected in the diverse and seemingly-contradictory uses of the word in the Bible and the plural ending, *Elohim* in our first creation narrative, is more a God of nature, a universal Divine creative force, than a God of personal involvement or relationship.

***B'tzelem Elohim*: In the image of God.** The creation of humanity, as it is described in the first Genesis narrative, is distinct from all other creations that precede it. With all other objects of Divine creativity, creation is a one-step process. "And God said, 'Let there be light;' and there was light...And God said 'Let the water below the sky be gathered into one area, that the dry land may appear. And it was so...And God said, 'Let the earth bring forth every kind of living creature: cattle, creeping things and wild beasts of every kind.' And it was so."[48]

Like the guest at a formal reception, the human couple, however, is welcomed into the world only after it is announced. Prior to human existence in the world, we know something about what is in God's mind concerning His final creature. Only in relation to human beings do we read that God *intended* to create before we read of His actual creating. "And God said, 'Let Us[49] make humanity in Our image and according to Our likeness.'"[50]

When creating only humanity, why does God announce before He acts? The imaginative answers to this question guide us to an appreciation of how pre-"Eden man and woman are understood within the context of this first creation narrative.

Rabbi Huna, quoted in the *Genesis Rabbah*, asks why God, when creating humanity alone demonstrated "due deliberation." God, according to this midrash, wanted to make sure all that mankind might require was in place and ready, that the candles were lit, the table was set and the food was cooked, before the honored guest arrived. God, Huna taught, responding to a challenge from the angels about the creation of man, asked, "Sheep and oxen, all of them, why were they created?

Why were the fowl of the air and the fish of the sea created? A tower full of good things and no guests. What pleasure would this be for Me, the host?"[51]

In another midrash, Rabbi Hoshaya (circa 200 CE) taught that the angels were dazzled by the first human. "When the Holy One, blessed be He, created Adam, the ministering angels mistook him for a Divine being and wished to exclaim 'Holy' before him. What does this resemble? A king and a governor who sat in a chariot, and his subjects wished to say to the king, 'Domine!' [sovereign!] but they did not know which one was the king and which one was the governor."[52]

The psalmist also associates God's creation of the world in Genesis Chapter One with the glory of man.

> When I consider thy heavens, the work of thy fingers, the moon and the stars, which thou hast ordained;
>
> What is man, that thou art mindful of him? and the son of man, that thou visitest him?
>
> For thou hast made him a little lower than the angels, and hast crowned him with glory and honour.
>
> Thou madest him to have dominion over the works of thy hands; thou hast put all [things] under his feet:
>
> All sheep and oxen, yea, and the beasts of the field;
>
> The fowl of the air, and the fish of the sea, [and whatsoever] passeth through the paths of the seas.
>
> O LORD our Lord, how excellent [is] thy name in all the earth![53]

In the Bible he translated into German with Moses Mendelssohn (1780-1783), Solomon Dubno, commenting on Genesis 1:26, wrote, "Man was the crown of creation, a little lower than the angels, possessor of an immortal soul, capable of an intelligent acknowledgement of his Creator and ruling the world by dint of his wisdom. 'Let Us make man,' the Creator announced. In other words, after I have created all the foregoing for the sake of man, to supply his needs and enjoyments, let the master enter his palace."

Once the planning is completed, the provisions obtained, the finest of table-cloths, china, crystal and silver laid, and the guest announced, who is it, according to this first creation narrative, that arrives within the palace? It is "*b'tzelem Elohim*," the image of God.

Genesis 1:27 is the most radical single verse, the most clear and unambiguous assertion of ethical monotheism found in any sacred text. The verse reads, "And God said, 'Let Us make humanity in Our image, according to Our likeness.' God created humanity in His image, in the image of God did He create it, male and female did He create them." A midrash captures the exuberance of perceiving humanity as "in God's image." According to this midrash, as each man or woman walks down a road, a troop of angels leads the way, shouting, "Make way! Make way! Here comes the image of God."[54]

Umberto Cassuto, in his comment on genesis 1:27 (humanity in the image and likeness of God), aware of the pre-Israelite origins of this metaphor, asks whether the meaning of this verse, when it was composed, was physical (characteristic of paganism) or spiritual (characteristic of Israelite monotheism). Cassuto writes, "There is no doubt that the original signification of this expression in the Canaanite tongue was, judging by Babylonian usage, corporeal, in accordance with the anthropomorphic conception of the godhead among the peoples of the ancient East. Nevertheless, when we use it in modern Hebrew,…we certainly do not associate any material idea with it, but give it a purely spiritual connotation, to wit, that man, although he resembles the creatures in his physical structure, approaches God in his thought and in his conscience. It is clear, therefore, that the meaning of the phrase changed in the course of time…The question then arises: when did this change come about?" Cassuto concludes his analysis of the God image metaphor that this phrase was already understood as spiritual by those who composed this section of the first creation epic poem. For the twelfth-century Moses Maimonides and the Kantian philosopher, Hermann Cohen eight centuries later, it is through the non-corporeal, that is, through human reason that man and woman become the image of God.[55]

In the final hours of God's busy work week in this first creation narrative, God crowns His creativity by forming man and woman. Most significant, the creation of humanity in God's image is twelve chapters before there is an Abraham, twelve chapters before there is a Jew. The Genesis verse does not tell us that some human beings are made in God's image, and some are not. The Torah asserts, without any qualification, ambivalence or ambiguity, that humans, that is, *all* humans, Jew and Gentile, free and slave, whatever their color, are created in God's image.

And, in case one might conclude erroneously that humanity (*adam*) does not include women, Genesis 1:27 makes its point explicit, "…male and female, did He create them."

Interestingly, the traditional English translation of Genesis 1:27 is, "And God created *man* (not humanity) in His image, in the image of God He created *him* (not it); male and female He created them." Biblical commentators and grammarians have written that "*adam*," in addition to meaning "man" (in the narrow sense to mean only males), can also mean "humankind."[56] And yet, most English and other-language translations of this verse preserve the gendered sense of these words. This is particularly surprising because four chapters later in Genesis, describing the same creation of man and woman, *adam* clearly means humankind. The Genesis 5 text reads, "On the day that God created *adam*, He made him/it in the likeness of God. Male and female God created them. And on that day they were created, God blessed them and called *their* name '*adam*.'"[57]

Drawing on the narrow understanding of the word, "*adam*," to mean "man," not "humankind," The *Disputatio Nova*,[58] written in 1595, "proved" that women were not human. This pamphlet was popular in the seventeenth and eighteenth centuries. It was translated into many languages of Christendom. The Disputatio Nova argues, "If God wanted a woman to be human, like Adam, He would not have used the singular, saying: I want to make a man in My image."

For the rabbis, it is the gendered understanding of "*adam*" in Genesis 1:27 that leads to difficulties in dealing with the pronouns in the verse. Partly to address this pronoun inconsistency, the sages resort to a fanciful midrash to explain this verse. The midrash states that this *adam*, this one creature was created with double eyes, limbs, heads and sexes; and then split into individual males and females. By means of this fantastical and often-cited midrash, *he* became *them*.[59]

It is interesting to note that a similar "midrash" is described by Plato. In the *Symposium*, Plato has Aristophanes depict a double creature, resembling the one in the midrash, to explain the origin of love. This creature challenges the gods. He then is punished by being divided. Love, for Aristophanes, involves the search for one's literal "other half." Aristophanes concludes, "The desire and the pursuit of the whole is called love."[60] It is possible that both Plato and the ancient rabbis drew on a similar popular myth when traveling to their distinct interpretive destinations.

The biblical affirmation that male and female were both created by the Creator, at the same time, with no spiritual distinction, is particularly radical when one considers the male-female social and historical context within which this text was originally chanted and written. This male-dominated and female-subordinated context is even reflected in the language of the verse. "...Male [*zachar* in Hebrew] and female [*n'kayvah* in Hebrew] did He create them." According to the two most cited biblical dictionaries, Male, that is, *zachar* refers to one who is remembered. Female, that is, *n'kayvah*, refers to one who is penetrated, pierced or blasphemed.[61] Yet, Genesis 1:27, remarkably, transcends its own language to assert unambiguously the spiritual equality of man and woman.

Rabbi Leo Baeck (1873-1956), the foremost voice of Progressive Judaism of his generation, writes, "Above all demarcations of races and nations, castes and classes, oppressors and servants, givers and recipients, above all delineations even of gifts and talents stands one certainty: *adam*. Whoever bears this image [that is, God's image] is created and called to be a revelation of human dignity."[62]

The first creation narrative is a literary masterwork of philosophy, theology and psychology. It is this poem that is at the spiritual foundation of ethical monotheism. It is this sacred textual platform on which the Hebrew, Christian and Muslim scriptures and religions are built.

As we have seen, this first narrative includes a God who gloriously stands separate from and above His creation. At a distance, this God considers what He has done and declares it "*tov maod*, very good!" This first narrative also includes the creation of man and woman, the crowning achievement of God's creativity. In this account, humanity is creation's culmination. These human creatures are even mistaken by the angels for the Divine. We see in this biblical text a first man and woman much closer to the angels than to their fellow creatures. We see a man and woman who were created by God—but, most significant, never touch Him, or each other.

In the next chapter, we examine the second creation narrative, the Eden experience. In Eden, relationship replaces distance and strife overshadows peace. It is in Eden that God, man and woman are in direct contact, get to know each other, conflict, struggle, disappoint and, in the final verses, come to terms. At the end of the next chapter, we discover a more complete portrait of who we are by integrating the two creation narratives—by drawing from *both* of these beautiful, elaborate, profound and separate poems of beginnings.

3

Innocence, Intimacy and Insight in the Garden

Man was created a little lower than the angels, and has been getting a little lower ever since.

—Mark Twain

In Bereshit, the first Genesis creation narrative, the principle character is also the only actor. It is God, *Elohim*, alone, who speaks and separates, names and makes, creates and blesses, sees and considers, arranges and rests. In Eden, the second Genesis creation narrative, the focus of our chapter, our cast has grown to four. There is the Lord God (*YHWH-Elohim*), the man, the woman and the serpent—unlike in the previous creation account, now an ensemble cast with each actor taking a turn in assuming the leading role, each of them acting on and acted upon by the others. The new lush set, this garden, has become complex and peopled, conflictual and precarious—and rife with meaning.

But what is the meaning of the Eden narrative? In contemporary America, this second creation account is the most "well-known" text in the Hebrew Bible. People who know no other part of the torah can often describe Eve being formed from Adam's rib, Adam's and Eve's tasting the prohibited fruit with the encouragement of the serpent, the couple's recognition that they are naked and their exile from the garden.

However, for most Christians and Jews, it is difficult to describe the Eden text without "interpretive blinders." The Harvard University professor, James Kugel,[63] drawing on his scholarly examination of extra-biblical texts that date from 300 years before and 100 years after the Common Era, points out that this is not a new phenomenon. Interpretation of the sacred text began in the earliest decades following the canonization of the Bible, and perhaps even before.[64] By the time of the early talmudic rabbis and the beginnings of Christianity, the most critical of the formative periods for both religions, texts were understood in characteristic and proscribed ways. Christianity and Judaism may have taken different interpretive paths, but neither of these religions took its unique path devoid of interpretation.

The interpretative blinders are graphically demonstrated when one asks a group of contemporary secularly-educated adult Americans to describe the second creation narrative, that is, to describe what is the actual plot of the biblical Eden story. In public lectures and classes that I have given throughout the United States, with Jews, Christians, Muslims, agnostics, atheists and others in the audience, I learn that the second Genesis creation account is a story about the fall of mankind from Divine grace and the introduction of sin into a pristine world. I learn that the Garden of Eden is the after-life, a paradise, the "*olam ha'bah*," a heaven, a foretaste of the Messiah and Shabbat. I learn that the serpent is Satan, that nakedness is sexual innocence, that the sin of eating the fruit involves carnal knowledge, that Eve is a temptress who is driven by her erotic wishes, that Adam is a dupe of Eve. Interestingly, none of what I learn from this process is explicitly stated in the Genesis text. And yet, and even more interesting, for each of these contemporary interpretations, there is a long interpretive history.

It is the interpretation of the Eden text, more than any other text in the Book of Genesis, that differentiates Christian from Jewish understanding. References to Eden, Eve and Adam are plentiful and theologically-weighty in the Christian Bible and the Apocrypha. This is not the case, however, when one examines the Hebrew Scripture. Astonishing to many, these key names from our second creation narrative, Eden, Eve and even Adam, are virtually absent in the twenty-four books of the Tanakh, that is, the entire Hebrew Bible that includes, for example, the books of Genesis, Deuteronomy, the prophets, the kings, psalms, chronicles, Ruth, Job, proverbs and Ecclesiastes.

The last reference in the Book of Genesis to Eden is found in the aftermath of the murder of Abel by his brother, Cain. Genesis 4:15-16 reads, "And the Lord put a mark on Cain, lest anyone who met him should kill him. Cain left the presence of the Lord and settled in the land of Nod, east of *Eden*." Following this Genesis reference, there are two ways in which Eden is referred to in the rest of the Hebrew Bible. Eden is a name of a specific person(son of Joah, a Levite),[65] and Eden is used as a poetic parallel by the prophets, to mean the opposite of "wilderness." Isaiah states, "For the Lord shall comfort Zion: He will comfort all her waste places; and He will make her wilderness like *Eden*, and her desert like the garden of the Lord."[66] Or Ezekiel, who prophesizes to the Israelites, exiled by the Babylonians, about their future return to Jerusalem, "Thus says the Lord

GOD; In the day that I shall have cleansed you from all your iniquities I will also cause you to dwell in the cities,...And they shall say, This land that was desolate is become like the garden of *Eden*; and the waste and desolate and ruined cities are become fenced, and are inhabited. Then the heathen that are left round about you shall know that I the Lord build the ruined places...I the Lord have spoken it, and I will do it."[67] It is interesting to note that, in the entire Tanakh, Eden is not mentioned as a location where the first couple sinned.

The final reference to the name, Eve, in the twenty-four books of the Hebrew Bible is found in Genesis 4:1. The text reads, "And Adam knew *Eve* his wife; and she conceived, and bare Cain, and said, I have gotten a man from the Lord. And she again bare his brother Abel." The Hebrew Bible never again mentions Eve, nor her disobedience.

Following a description of Adam's life span of nine hundred and thirty years in Genesis 5:5, Adam is referred to in the Hebrew Bible only four times, although three of these are challenged by scholars.[68] As we saw in Chapter Two, the Hebrew word, "*adam*," can mean the person, Adam, man or humanity. The only biblical verse, after Genesis 5:5, that scholars agree upon refers directly to Adam, the Eden figure, is found in the repetition of the Genesis genealogical table, that is, Adam begot Seth who begot Enosh, etc.[69]

The other verses from the Hebrew Bible in which Adam *may be* referred to follow:

> Remember the days of old, consider the years of many generations: ask your father, and He will show you; your elders, and they will tell you. When the most High divided for the nations their inheritance, when He separated the sons of *Adam* [or mankind], He set the bounds of the people according to the number of the children of Israel. For the Lord's portion is His people; Jacob is the lot of His inheritance.[70]

> If I covered my transgressions as *Adam* [or men], by hiding my iniquity in my bosom: Did I fear a great multitude, or did the contempt of families terrify me, that I kept silence, and went not out of the door [to aid the stranger]? Oh that one would hear me! behold, my desire is, that the Almighty would answer me, and that mine adversary had written a book [describing the ways in which I have sinned].[71]

> For I [the Lord God] desire goodness, and not sacrifice; and the knowledge of God more than burnt-offerings. But they like *Adam* [or men[72]] have transgressed the covenant: there have they dealt treacherously against Me.[73]

The paltry and trivial references to the second creation narrative and to its major players, in the post-Genesis remainder of the Hebrew Bible are striking. In the twenty-four books canonized by the Jewish community, there is no reference to the fall of mankind, to how sin was introduced into a world that was previously unmarred, to how the first couple's transgression was transferred to future generations, to how Adam's and Eve's erotic longings and curiosity were the cause of their disobedience and exile, or to how humanity was better off in the Garden. For scriptural discussion and expansion of the Eden experience, one must turn to the Apocrypha and the Christian Bible.

The Apocrypha is a collection of historical and ethical books, for example, the Book of Judith, the Wisdom of Solomon, Tobit, the Maccabees, Baruch, Esdras, written in Hebrew (except for 2 Esdras which was written in Latin), that date from 300 BCE to 100 CE. They are included as part of the Bibles of the Roman Catholic and Orthodox Churches, but not included in the Hebrew Bible or most Protestant Scriptures. The importance of the literature of the Apocrypha is that these books serve as a theological bridge between the ideas of Tanakh Judaism and the beliefs that find their way into the Christian New Testament.

In the books of the Apocrypha, the sin of Adam plays a significant theological role. A few examples follow:

> For the first Adam bearing a wicked heart transgressed, and was overcome; and so be all they that are born of him.[74]

> For God created man to be immortal, and made him to be an image of His own eternity. Nevertheless through envy of the devil came death into the world: and they that do hold of his side do find it.[75]

> O thou Adam, what has thou done? for though it was thou that sinned, thou art not fallen alone, but we all that come of thee.[76]

This focus on, and concern about the sin of the Garden, seen in the Apocrypha but not in the Hebrew Bible, is greatly expanded in the New Testament. Some examples follow:

> We also joy in God through our Lord Jesus Christ, by whom we have now received the atonement. Wherefore, as by one man [Adam] sin entered into the world, and death by sin; and so death passed upon all men, for that all have sinned:…Nevertheless death reigned from Adam to Moses, even over them that had not sinned.[77]

> For since by man [Adam] came death, by man [Jesus Christ] came also the resurrection of the dead. For as in Adam all die, so also in Christ shall all be made alive.[78]

> So also it is written, The first man Adam became a living soul. The last Adam [Jesus Christ] became a life-giving spirit.[79]

As we can see from these verses from the Christian Bible, it is the sin of the first man in the Garden that, for Paul, and later Augustine, Calvin, Milton and Wesley, requires a Jesus to atone. Whereas, for Judaism, Adam's and Eve's experiences, for the most part, signify the beginning of human history, and therefore is essentially unmentioned in the Tanakh, for Christianity, Adam and Eve are the foundation stones of its theology. For, if there is no Adam, then there is no fall. If there is no fall, there is no atonement. If there is no atonement, then there is no need for Jesus. If there is no Jesus, then there is no Christianity, humanity's single hope for salvation.

It is this Christian theological equation, rooted as it is in the assertion of a factual Adam and a accurate account of his transgression, that impels a large number of Christians to read the second creation narrative as history—not as allegorical homily. In a 1997 survey of American religious attitudes, Gallup-ABC News found that forty-four percent of all Americans believed that each word of the Bible should be read literally, and that the Genesis creation accounts were historically accurate.[80]

The unfortunate aspect of this fundamentalist attitude toward the bible generally, and the two Genesis creation narratives specifically is that a literal reading takes these transcendent biblical masterpieces of poetry, psychology, theology, philosophy and folklore, and reduces them to an ancient newspaper article. This literal reading trivializes a work of the summit of human creativity and imagination, inspired by the Divine, and makes it merely good reporting. Ironically, it is the literal reading of Genesis that takes the words of these sacred texts in vain.

A Selective Biblical Exegesis

> And the Lord God (*YHWH Elohim*) formed man from the dust of the earth. He blew into man's nostrils the breath of life. And man became a living being.[81]

YHWH Elohim: **The Lord God.** Just as the Genesis text shifts abruptly from first to second creation narratives, significantly, the name of God suddenly changes as well. The entire action of the first creation account centers around *Elohim* exclusively. As we saw in the last chapter, *Elohim* is an omnipotent God of nature who stands over and apart from the earth and all of its fullness, creating and considering, proclaiming and blessing, but never touching His creatures, nor walking with or among them.

The Divine actor of the second creation narrative is YHWH Elohim, the Lord God, who, from the beginning of this second narrative to its conclusion with the painful exile of His first-born son and daughter from the garden, is a God of involvement.[82] First, we see *YHWH Elohim,* the Lord God, blowing into man's nostrils to give him life. Then the Lord God plants for man a garden in Eden and takes man and puts him in the garden. We see Him concerned about man's loneliness and offering him animals as helpmates. Then, that failing we see the Lord God casting man into a deep sleep and creating woman.

Even after man and woman taste the prohibited fruit, the Lord God stays involved with his children, although He is now angry and disappointed. After being heard walking in the garden at the breezy time of day, the Lord God asks man a chilling question—it is the first question asked in the Bible—"Where are you?" and then has the first dialogue with His creatures (Lord God to man, Lord God to woman and Lord God to serpent). The second creation narrative concludes with a poignant image—*YHWH Elohim,* the Lord God, making garments of skins so that His disappointing children, His Adam and His Eve, His firstborns will not venture out into the harsh cold world unclothed and unprotected.

Formed man from the dust of the earth. Not only is the nature of God different in the two Genesis creation accounts, but so is the character of man. As we saw in Chapter Two of this book, God declares His intent to create humanity and then creates male and female in His image. In Creation Narrative One, there is no mention of the dust of the earth. Humanity is in the image of God, with no recipe.

In Creation Narrative Two, man is a composite creation with ingredients specified. Adam is made from blending the dust of the earth with the breath of God. This human is as much earth as he is heaven. As much animal as he is angel. As much worldly creature as he is enlivened by the Divine. As much a frightened and fragile vessel as he is a manifestation of the Lord God on earth.

So, with these more earthy characters introduced—YHWH Elohim, a hands-on God, as close to man as his next breath; and the first man, dust-God, animal-angel—the scene is set for the action that is the second biblical creation narrative.

The Lord God said, "It is not good for man to be alone; I will make a fitting helper (*ayzer k'negdo*) for him." And the Lord God formed out of the earth all the wild beasts and all the birds of the sky, and brought them to the man to see what he would call them; …but for Adam no fitting helper was found. So the Lord God cast a deep sleep upon the man; and, while he slept, He took one of his ribs and closed up the flesh at that spot. And the Lord God fashioned the rib that He had taken from the man into a woman; and He brought her to the man. Then the man said,

"This one at last
Is bone of my bones
And flesh of my flesh.
This one shall be called Woman,
For from man was she taken."

Hence a man leaves his father and mother and clings to his wife, so that they become one flesh.[83]

Man with Woman. As we saw in Chapter Two, the crowning achievement of God's creativity was the simultaneous creation of male and female, each in God's image. In this first biblical text, man and woman are clear spiritual colleagues and equals. Elizabeth Cady Stanton, the suffragist and reformer, in the *Woman's Bible* she edited in 1892, appreciated the equality of the sexes in the first creation narrative. However, she expressed deep suspicions concerning the motives of the author of the second story. She saw in this second account that the woman, Eve, was a creative after-thought and the first sinner. For Stanton, this narrative was written to support and justify the woman's subordination to her husband's wishes. Stanton wrote, My own opinion is the second story was manipulated by some Jew, in an endeavor to give 'heavenly authority' for requiring a woman to obey the man she married."[84]

In the second creation narrative, we see God feeling Adam's loneliness, his vulnerability and his profound yearning for a fitting helper. No animal will do. So God takes the matter into His own able surgical hands.

The Genesis text, usually sparing in its details and lacking repetition, asserts twice in the same verse that Adam is asleep during the creation of woman. Our text states, "So the Lord God cast a deep sleep upon the man; and while he slept…" Why is the text so insistent that Adam was asleep during the surgery? The ancient rabbis offer many midrashim to answer this question[85] Some of these are misogynist in content and tone.[86] Some of these associate this deep sleep with an event mysterious and awe-inspiring about to happen.[87] Some of these suggest the need for general anesthesia during such a delicate operation.[88]

Two of Freud's students, Otto Rank and Theodor Reik, also wrote "midrashim" to uncover the meaning of Adam's deep sleep. Otto Rank understands this rib scene as a reversal involving childbirth. Instead of Eve, the earth goddess Adamah, giving birth to the hero Adam, characteristic of a wide variety of pagan myths,[89] the Genesis Adam gives birth to Eve. Consistent with Freud's oedipal theory, Adam enjoys his mother's (Eve's) fruit and has sexual relations with her. God, the father, then punishes the couple for their incestuous sin by exiling them from Eden forever.[90]

Theodor Reik disagrees with his friend Otto Rank. Reik argues instead that the Adam rib story is a disguised tale involving male initiation rites. Mostly drawing on the cultural research of Mircea Eliade, Reik sees in the "birth" of Eve the same stages Eliade observed in male puberty rituals in pre-literate cultures. According to Reik, first, the initiate is separated from his mother and society (Adam's deep sleep). Then, a physical sign of his new status is required, for example, circumcision or decorative cuttings (the removal of Adam's rib, a symbolic circumcision). Last, the initiated returns to society with license to be a fully sexual adult (Adam's marriage to Eve).

My rabbinic and psychoanalytic forefathers' explanations for Adam's deep sleep are interesting, creative and elegant. However, for me, the answer to the question of why the Torah states twice that Adam is asleep when Eve is brought forth from him is so that no one may misunderstand and think that man had any active part in creating woman. In the Hebrew Bible, woman, like man, although using a piece of man in her fashioning, was created by God alone.[91]

And who is this woman to man? What is the importance of this "fitting helper," this *ayzer k'negdo*, to her Adam? The Hebrew word, "*k'neged*," usually translated as "fitting" or "comparable" in our passage is controversial. For some, including the greatly-influential medieval commentators, Rashi and the Ramban, this word has more of a connotation of "contrary" than "fitting." The Hebrew root, "*nagad*," means to stand boldly opposite. It is this connotation of "*ayzer k'negdo*" that inspired Rashi to write, in his comment on these Torah verses, "If the man is worthy, then the woman will be a helpmate. If the man is not, then the woman will be opposite to him, and fight him."[92]

Our Genesis excerpt concludes with man enthusiastically and poetically welcoming his helpmate, "This one at last is bone of my bone and flesh of my flesh." And, in what perhaps is the most romantic verse in the Torah, Genesis comments on the nature of the male-female relationship, and how it derives from our vulnerability, "Hence a man leaves his father and mother and clings to his wife, so that they become one flesh."

The man and the woman of our second creation narrative are in intimate relation. They are sometimes helpmates, sometimes opposites, but always "bone of my bone and flesh of my flesh." The man and woman of the garden are passionately connected by history, biology and need. It is this relationship, this primal connection, that inexorably leads our Adam and our Eve into the crisis of Eden.

> Now the serpent was the shrewdest of all the wild beasts that the Lord God had made. He said to the woman, "Did God really say: You shall not eat of any tree of the garden?" The woman replied to the serpent, "We may eat of the fruit of the other trees of the garden. It is only about fruit of the tree in the middle of the garden that God said: 'You shall not eat of it or touch it, lest you die.'" And the serpent said to the woman, "You are not going to die, but God knows that as soon as you eat of it your eyes will be opened and you will be like Divine beings who know good and bad [everything]." When the woman saw that the tree was good for eating and a delight to the eyes, and that the tree was desirable as a source of wisdom, she took of its fruit and ate. She also gave some to her husband, and he ate. Then the eyes of both of them were opened and they perceived that they were naked; and they sewed together fig leaves and made themselves loincloths.[93]

The serpent. Serpents have a extensive history in the language and texts of the ancient Near East. They are connected with guile and duplicity in both the Hurrian and Ugaritic languages, and the term, "serpent" is considered a derogatory term in Hitite documents that have been deciphered.[94]

The character of the serpent in our second creation narrative has provoked great controversy between religions concerning its meaning. In its understanding of this figure, Judaism generally stays close to the plain sense of the biblical text. The serpent is considered an animal, not unlike other animals, although possessing some special characteristics and abilities, that is, cunning and speech to be explained later. In our text, the serpent is described as a wild beast who, like other beasts, is made by the Lord God. There is no reference in the Hebrew Bible generally, or in the Genesis text specifically to this animal as being an angel, fallen or otherwise.

In the version of the garden story found in the *Koran*, the serpent has been fully replaced by a mutinous angel, variously referred to as Iblis or Satan. The Muslim sacred text reads:

> When We [the Divine "We"] said to the angels, "Prostrate yourselves to Adam", they prostrated themselves, but not Iblis [Satan]: he refused. Then We said: "O Adam! verily, this is an enemy to thee and thy wife: so let him

not get you both out of the Garden, so that thou art landed in misery…But Satan whispered evil to him: he said, "O Adam! shall I lead thee to the Tree of Eternity and to a kingdom that never decays?" In the result, they both ate of the tree, and so their nakedness appeared to them: they began to sew together, for their covering, leaves from the Garden: thus did Adam disobey his Lord, and allow himself to be seduced. But his Lord chose him (for His Grace): He turned to him, and gave him Guidance. He said: "Get ye down, both of you,—all together, from the Garden, with enmity one to another: but if, as is sure, there comes to you Guidance from Me, whosoever follows My Guidance, will not lose his way, nor fall into misery.[95]

There are interesting differences between the Genesis and Koran creation narratives. The serpent, a wild beast in Genesis, has been replaced by an angel who refuses to bow down to Adam. This is a theme, predating Muhammad, discovered in many classical Jewish midrashim involving the jealousy of humanity by angels.[96] In the Koran, it is Adam, not his wife, who has direct communication with The evil figure, Iblis/Satan. Finally, when compared with Genesis, the punishment of exile from the garden is a less harsh prison sentence. God gently reassures His disobedient and wandering children that He will be there to guide them in their painful Diaspora when they turn to Him.

In Christian texts, from Revelation through the present, the serpent-Satan-devil association is made explicit. Examples from the apocalyptic visions in the New Testament Book of Revelation follow:

And the great dragon was cast out, that old serpent, called the Devil, and Satan, which deceives the whole world: he was cast out into the earth, and his angels were cast out with him. And I heard a loud voice saying in heaven, Now is come salvation, and strength, and the kingdom of our God, and the power of his Christ: for the accuser of our brethren is cast down, which accused them before our God day and night.[97]

And I saw an angel come down from heaven, having the key of the bottomless pit and a great chain in his hand. And he laid hold on the dragon, that old serpent, which is the Devil, and Satan, and bound him a thousand years, and cast him into the bottomless pit, and shut him up, and set a seal upon him, that he should deceive the nations no more, till the thousand years should be fulfilled: and after that he must be loosed a little season.[98]

By the sixteenth century, this serpent-Satan-devil association is firmly established in Christianity. John Calvin (1509-1564), the Protestant reformer and prolific biblical exegetes, in his commentary on our passage,[99] wrestling with the

Torah text that fails to mention Satan, writes, "The innate subtlety of the serpent did not prevent Satan from making use of the animal for the purpose of effecting the destruction of man. For since he required an instrument, he chose from among animals that which he saw would be most suitable for him." And to the question of why Moses, for Calvin the author of Genesis and the other books of the Pentateuch, chose to keep the relationship between Satan and the serpent secret, Calvin asserts that Moses had to speak in a language simple enough for the people of that day. "We have elsewhere said, that Moses, by a homely and uncultivated style, accommodates what he delivers to the capacity of the people; and for the best reason; for not only had he to instruct an untaught race of men, but the existing age of the Church [the Hebrew religion] was so puerile, that it was unable to receive any higher instruction."

A century later, this literary image of serpent-Satan-devil is artfully and poetically expanded in John Milton's "midrash" on the second creation narrative, *Paradise Lost*.[100] Milton writes:

> Who first seduced them to that foul revolt?
> That infernal Serpent; he it was whose guile,
> Stirred up with envy and revenge, deceived
> The mother of mankind, what time his pride
> Had cast him out from Heaven, with all his host
> Of rebel Angels, by whose aid, aspiring
> To set himself in glory above his peers,
> He trusted to have equaled the Most High,
> If he opposed, and with ambitious aim
> Against the throne and monarchy of God.

For the rabbis, any dualism, for example, flesh-spirit, good-evil, God-devil, violated the basic principles of monotheism.[101] Within this theological context, Abraham ibn Ezra (1089-1164), a highly-influential and progressive biblical commentator, deeply distressed by the teaching that the serpent in Eden was actually the devil, wrote a disputation of this interpretation.[102] Ibn Ezra first asks why these interpreters do not look at the end of the narrative. How could Satan be condemned to crawl on his belly or to eat the dust of the earth; and further, what sense is there in the idea that the descendents of Eve can bruise Satan's head? Anticipating the arguments of Calvin and Milton to arise centuries later, Ibn Ezra argues that, if Satan only temporarily exploits the serpent's body as an instrument of his devilish plot, then why does God punish the serpent? Either God is unjust and punishes a creature who is not at fault, or God is less wise than Satan who is able, by these devilish devices, to trick him. Both of these conclusions were untenable to this commentator.

Abraham ibn Ezra therefore concludes that the serpent in the second creation narrative is not Satan or the devil—but a serpent. But what kind of serpent is this that walks and speaks and plots? Umberto Cassuto (1883-1951), the Jewish historian, biblical and Semitic scholar, offers an answer, uncharacteristically psychoanalytic, to this question. For Cassuto,[103] and I wholeheartedly agree, the conversation that we read in the second creation narrative between Eve and the serpent is actually a dialogue that is taking place in the woman's mind, "between her wiliness and her innocence, clothed in the garb of a parable…Interpreting the text in this way, we can understand why the serpent is said to think and speak; in reality it is not he who thinks and speaks but the woman who does so in her heart."

Why they ate the fruit. Three questions involving our hero's and heroine's motives arise when examining the cause of the crisis in the garden. Why does Eve eat the fruit? Why does Eve then choose to offer it to her husband? And why does Adam then take his bite? The Torah offers no information concerning the second and third of these questions. For the first—why does Eve eat the fruit—the Torah gives us some detail, although conflictual and meager. We learn from the text that Eve found the fruit appealing to the senses, "that the tree was good for eating and a delight to the eyes." In addition, the text offers a contradictory motive for Eve, that she knew this action would increase her understanding, "and that the tree was desirable as a source of wisdom." So was Eve a creature ruled by her sensuality or by her curiosity, a hedonist or a scholar—or by some other motive?

It is interesting to note that the Torah text never describes how Eve learns of God's command not to eat of the prohibited trees in the garden. It is in Genesis 2:16-17, *before* Eve was created a full five verses later, that God commands Adam concerning the fruit trees. The torah states, "And the Lord God commanded the *man,* saying, 'Of every tree of the garden you are free to eat; but as for the tree of knowledge of good and bad you must not eat of it…'" How is it that this command was communicated to Eve? Did God do this Himself in a scenario not included in the Torah? Or was the command communicated to Eve by Adam? And, if so, why does Eve augment the command so that when she is speaking to the serpent, she says that not only can we not eat the fruit, but we should not even touch it? Was this emendation her own, Adam's or God's?

The midrashic literature weaves an elaborate story that places Eve's expansion of the "touching" restriction, and the resulting doubt it provoked, in the center of her downfall. The serpent, hearing Eve's emendation, touched the tree and then asked Eve, "Did I die?" Then, he pushed her toward the tree to have her touch it as well. Then, the serpent ate a piece of fruit and asked Eve the question again, "Did I die?" The serpent then invited Eve to taste. It was at this point, that Eve began to doubt the words of her husband and of God. Eve said to the serpent, "All the things that I was told are lies." It was only then, now replete with doubt, that Eve took the fateful bite.[104]

Or was eve's defiance of the command motivated by positive impulses? If one views the second creation narrative—not as fall, but as a "painful but necessary 'graduation'"[105] from a pre-human and childhood existence to the conflictual world of living as a morally-responsible adult—then Eve is this graduation's valedictorian. "A modern reader can easily see Eve as the heroine of the story, bravely crossing the boundary from animal to human and willingly sharing her new found wisdom with her mate."[106]

But then, why does Adam eat the fruit that Eve offers him? To emphasize the gravity of Adam's action, the Torah is even more terse and devoid of detail than usual. Genesis 3:6 reads, "She also gave some to her husband, and he ate." There is no information in the text as to motive.

Was Adam a dupe of Eve, that is, was Adam even aware that he was eating the forbidden fruit when he did so? Or was he knowingly, but passively complying with his wife's wishes? Or was he in collusion with Eve's fatal ambition or her wish to transcend the ignorant animal experience that was Eden? Or did Adam, as John Milton suggests, taste his wife's fruit out of love?

In *Paradise Lost*, written in 1667, Milton offers a romantic midrash to explain Adam's motivation. Adam chose to eat the fruit offered him, knowing that it was the prohibited fruit, and also knowing that Eve had already tasted it and would die, because Adam could not tolerate the idea of living a life, even in Paradise, without Eve.

Describing Adam's words the moment before he *chose to taste* the forbidden fruit, Milton writes,

> How can I live without thee! how forego
> Thy sweet converse, and love so dearly joined,
> To live again in these wild woods forlorn!
> Should God create another Eve, and I
> Another rib afford, yet loss of thee
> Would never from my heart: no, no! I feel

The link of Nature draw me: flesh of flesh,

Bone of my bone thou art, and from thy state

Mine never shall be parted, bliss or woe...

If death Consort with thee, death is to me as life;

So forcible within my heart I feel

The bond of Nature draw me to my own;

My own in thee, for what thou art is mine;

Our state cannot be severed; we are one,

One flesh; to lose thee were to lose myself.

So, according to Milton, Adam in eating Eve's fruit *chose* to die, rather than to live an eternity in Eden without her. Along these same romantic interpretive lines, Mark Twain, in his midrash on selective biblical stories,[107] describes Adam's eulogy for the wife he had lived with for centuries following the exile, and just buried. Adam says, through his tears, "Wherever Eve was, that place was Eden."

All that remains of the second creation narrative for this couple, recently transformed by the fruit and guilt they share, living in Eden, joined tightly together by their history, biology, and fears for the future, is that they learn of the consequences of their action.

They heard the sound of the Lord God moving about in the garden at the breezy time of day; and the man and his wife hid from the Lord God among the trees of the garden. The Lord God called out to the man and said to him, "Where are you?" He replied, "I heard the sound of You in the garden, and I was afraid because I was naked, so I hid." Then He asked, "Who told you that you were naked? Did you eat of the tree from which I had forbidden you to eat?" The man said, "The woman You put at my side—she gave me of the tree, and I ate." And the Lord God said to the woman, "What is this you have done!" The woman replied, "The serpent duped me, and I ate." Then the Lord God said to the serpent,
  "Because you did this,
  More cursed shall you be
  Than all cattle
  And all the wild beasts:
  On your belly shall you crawl
  And dirt shall you eat
  All the days of your life.
  I will put enmity
  Between you and the woman,

And between your offspring and hers;
They shall strike at your head,
And you shall strike at their heel."
And to the woman He said,
"I will make most severe
Your pangs in childbearing;
In pain shall you bear children.
Yet your urge shall be for your husband,
And he shall rule over you."
To Adam He said, "Because you did as your wife said and ate of the tree
about which I commanded you, 'You shall not eat of it,'
Cursed be the ground because of you;
By toil shall you eat of it
All the days of your life:
Thorns and thistles shall it sprout for you.
But your food shall be the grasses of the field;
By the sweat of your brow
Shall you get bread to eat,
Until you return to the ground—
For from it you were taken.
For dust you are,
And to dust you shall return."
The man named his wife Eve, because she was the mother of all the living.
And the Lord God made garments of skins for Adam and his wife, and
clothed them.[108]

O humanity, where are you? *YHWH Elohim*, the Lord God, involved with
His children, in the garden with them, sees them, and is not pleased. These second creation creatures were formed by Him, not to be mere images, in His likeness, clones, but rather, because they are part heaven and part earth, to be His
partners in completing creation, His representatives on earth, His children and
His friends, His comfort and His company.

The Lord God can certainly appreciate why His daughter, and then son chose
to defy His command and eat the fruit. He knows that challenging authority is
part of growing up, part of what is necessary for them to become His full partners. But why the hiding? Why the lies? Why the blaming everyone else but
themselves? Why the renunciation of responsibility for their actions?

The Lord God has seen His children, knows them, loves them, worries about
them, and is deeply disillusioned.

Interestingly, our text begins not with God moving about in the garden, but,
more precisely, with Him being *heard* "moving about in the Garden at the breezy

time of day." Adam and Eve, guilty, vigilant to every sound that may be God, the possibility of being seen, of being found out, like the frightened person who evaluates every creak in an old house as intruder, hear God at a time when sounds would be difficult to interpret.

Vulnerable, ashamed, and terrified, Adam and Eve do what people do, and hide. First they hide their nakedness, and then themselves.

Like the image of the serpent, what is meant by "naked" has been controversial. For Christianity, sexual innocence has been associated with life in the garden before the fall and sexuality with the knowledge obtained from eating the fruit of the prohibited tree. The first couple's shame of their nakedness is sexual shame. A consequence of this is that all people after Adam are born soiled by the garden, stained by original sin. This sin involves two parts. Both of these are a result of tasting the fruit. They are the curse of mortality and the reality that birth requires carnal union; and is hereditary. Saint Augustine (354-430), the most influential Christian theologian after Saint Paul and credited with developing the concept of original sin, asserts that neither mortality nor sexual desire was natural, but a result of the sin of the garden.[109] Tertullian, an early and important Church Father (160-230), in a letter to "his sisters in Christ," wrote, "Dear Sisters, You are the devil's gateway…You are she who persuaded Adam whom the devil did not dare attack. Do you know that every one of you is an Eve? The sentence of God on your sex lives on in this age; the guilt, of necessity lives on and visits today's and tomorrow's men and women alike."[110]

The traditional Jewish sources have been less focused on sex as the sin of the garden. The *Genesis Rabbah* and Rashi both assert, in fact, that the first couple was sexual in the garden *before* eating the fruit, that their sexuality, therefore, is not associated with their sin. In Genesis Rabbah, the classical midrashic text, Abba Halfon ben Koriah asks where Adam was when Eve was having her conversation with the serpent. The answer Rabbi Halfon provides is that he was napping happily and heavily after having made love with his wife.[111] Rashi maintains that the serpent's motive in wishing to destroy the first couple's happiness derives from seeing them enjoying sexual relations and his resulting envy. Rashi comments on Genesis 3:1, "The verse comes to teach you the cause of the serpent's assailing the first man and woman. He saw them unclothed, indulging in marital relations unashamedly and he coveted the woman."[112]

If the couple's shame about their nakedness is not sexual shame, then what does it symbolize? Within classical Jewish sources, Adam and Eve's "sin" is understood as their nakedness of gratitude toward God and all that He has provided them, and nakedness of *mitzvot*, that is, that they are devoid of a moral center.[113]

This deficit of a moral center is most graphically illustrated by Adam and Eve's devastating responses to God's garden interrogation.

To Adam, God asks, "Did you eat of the tree from which I had forbidden you to eat?" Then, in what may be the most cowardly single sentence in Western literature, Adam not only blames Eve for his behavior, but also God. Adam replies, "The woman *You* put at my side—she gave me of the tree, and I ate."

Eve at least does not explicitly blame God in her response, but also, like her lover, Eve takes no responsibility for her actions. God asks Eve, "What is this that you have done?" Eve's reply: "The serpent duped me and I ate."

YHWH Elohim, The Lord God, heartsick, and discouraged by His "crowning achievement of creation," the utter lack of moral center in His only daughter and His only son, frustrated in His creative ambitions and aspirations, felt hopeless and alone. He considered His children—and then His options.

The Punishment: Nature in conflict. God's sentence was unique for each of the lawbreakers. The serpent, from this time forward, will crawl on his belly, eating dirt and engage in mortal battle with the woman and her descendents. The woman, and all women to come, will have harrowing labor pains, inescapable because she is also cursed with sexual desire. No longer an equal of her husband, Eve and all women will be ruled by men. Lastly, man is given a life sentenced to work the unyielding fields for his food, and then to die.

One of the purposes for this harsh conclusion of the second Genesis creation account is also shared by most creation myths of other cultures. Creation accounts attempt to explain bio-social realities that are inexplicable by other means.[114] Why are serpents and people enemies? Why do women have erotic longings and brutal labor pains? Why in the cultures in which this story evolved are there strict hierarchical distinctions between the sexes? Why is life so hard for men who work the fields? Why do people die?

Beyond the individual sentence for each of the three guilty parties, there is a theme underlying the punishment meted out by the Lord God, that is, a theme underlying what will characterize post-Eden human experience. Before the Eden exile, humanity and animals and nature all lived in a non-conflictual state of harmony. After the exile, as is implied in the curses, nature, including human nature, becomes conflictual. For the first time, woman is now at odds with the serpent. Man is now at odds with the soil and the field. Woman and man are now at odds with each other, and within themselves. Our creation narrative indicates that the prehistoric and natural human experience is characterized by peace and balance and harmony, while post-Eden human experience proper is hardship, struggle and conflict.

Within Jewish tradition, the return to a quasi-Eden conflictless state will only come with the arrival of the Messiah. This is made most explicit in the teachings of the classical prophet, Isaiah, and then essentially repeated by Micah,[115] and again two centuries later with the Book of Zechariah.[116]

The Prophet Isaiah taught:

> And it shall come to pass in the end of days [the age of the Messiah], that the mountain of The Lord's house shall be established as the top of the mountains, and shall be exalted above the hills; and all nations shall flow unto it. And the peoples shall go and say: 'Come ye, and let us go up to the mountain of The Lord, to the house of the God of Jacob; and He will teach us of His ways, and we will walk in His paths.'...And they shall beat their swords into plowshares, and their spears into pruning hooks; nation shall not lift up sword against nation, neither shall they learn war any more. O house of Jacob, come ye, and let us walk in the light of The Lord.[117]

> And there shall come forth a shoot out of the stock of Jesse [the Messiah], and a twig shall grow forth out of his roots. And the spirit of The Lord shall rest upon him, the spirit of wisdom and understanding, the spirit of counsel and might, the spirit of knowledge and of the fear of The Lord...And righteousness shall be the girdle of his loins, and faithfulness the girdle of his reins. And the wolf shall dwell with the lamb, and the leopard shall lie down with the kid; and the calf and the young lion and the fatling together; and a little child shall lead them. And the cow and the bear feed; their young ones shall lie down together; and the lion shall eat straw like the ox. And the sucking child shall play on the hole of the asp, and the weaned child shall put his hand on the basilisk's den. They shall not hurt nor destroy in all My holy mountain; for the earth shall be full of the knowledge of The Lord, as the waters cover the sea.[118]

The prophetic vision of the messianic era is, like the pre-exile Eden experience of the second creation narrative, of a world and person without conflict. All peoples of the world are in harmony worshipping one God. All peoples have conquered their impulse for contention and war. All peoples have transformed their implements of destruction into tools for farming. Even nature has a new order, with the wolf lying down with the lamb and the lion eating straw.[119]

But Eden differs, in one crucial way from the days of the messianic. The first man was placed, without participation, awareness or volition, in the garden by the Lord God. For humanity to achieve the messianic, men and women must actively work at it. In Jewish thought, the messianic days of harmony "can be obtained only if man develops fully,...if he knows the truth and does justice, if he develops his power of reason to a point which frees him from the bondage of man and from the bondage of irrational passion."[120] Humanity can only attain the messianic if he does "not make the things that matter most be at the mercy of the things that matter least."[121] He can only discover this new Eden if he "does justice, loves mercy and walks humbly with his God."[122] This heaven on earth will come if he becomes, as a community and species, the Divine image.[123]

The Jewish Sabbath, for many modern commentators, is a time when one both re-experiences Eden and anticipates the messianic. Erich Fromm,[124] (1900-1980), the biblical and talmudic scholar and psychoanalyst, profoundly influenced by the philosophical insights of Hermann Cohen,[125] developed a theory of the Sabbath different from the legalistic one proposed in the Mishnah.[126] Fromm concludes from his analysis of Jewish texts and Shabbat practices that anything that interferes with the physical world is prohibited "work" on Shabbat. Shabbat rest is a state of peace between humanity and nature, reminiscent of Eden prior to the exile.

Therefore, the second Genesis creation account, with its lush description of a primordial time of peace and harmony among humans and between men, women and nature, lays the foundation for the Shabbat and the messianic. In addition, the Eden experience defines our unfinished task—to re-establish a world of peace and harmony, where men, women, animals and plants can live together without conflict. The task is to work for the day when one can complete creation[127] and build a new Eden. This Eden, however, should be populated by a new-and-improved Adam and Eve. This garden, to *be Eden*, should be home for an individual, this time, with a more highly-developed moral center.

Integrating Creation: God, Humanity and relationship

As we have seen in this, and the previous chapter of this book, Genesis includes two elaborate, beautiful, profound and separate visions of creation. In these two narratives, we have seen two distinct descriptions of God with two distinct "personalities" and names. We have seen two distinct images of humanity with two distinct accounts of origin and essence. We have seen two distinct images of male-female relationship with two distinct descriptions of the "tie that binds."

How can one reconcile these two very different creation poems? The traditional Jewish perspective is that the second creation narrative is a sort of "close-up" on the first, that what one sees in Creation II is a more specific version of what is described more generally in the twilight hours of the final day in the first narrative. Rashi, reflecting this traditional perspective on the relationship between the two narratives, writes, "G-d formed man, etc. and caused the Garden of Eden to sprout for his benefit and placed him in the Garden of Eden and put him into a deep sleep. The one who hears this may think that this is a different story, but, in reality, it is the details of the first…This all happened on the sixth day…It is important to remember that when the Torah speaks on a subject in general terms and follows that by specific actions, what follows is not a new subject but rather a clarification."[128]

It is interesting to note that this traditional condensation of the first and second creation narratives is also implied in Michelangelo's "midrash" on creation that he painted on the ceiling of the Vatican's Sistine Chapel begun in 1508. In one of the series of ceiling frescos, the six days of creation are elaborately depicted. The panels, in which there is no human included, are directly drawn from the first creation account, for example, God's creation of the heavenly bodies, separation of light and darkness. The depiction of the creation of man and woman, however, confuses the first and second creation narratives, with one panel depicting a bearded, virile, older Divine Creator reaching out and almost touching a youthful and relaxed just-formed Adam, and then, another panel in which God stands over Eve who has just emerged from Adam, still fast asleep.[129]

One of the most significant difficulties with the traditional view, that Creation II is merely a more specific version of Creation I, is the number of alterations and contradictions when comparing the two texts.[130] Some examples follow:

1. In Creation I, all manner of plants and vegetation were created on the third day. "And God said, 'Let the earth sprout vegetation:…' The earth brought forth vegetation: seed-bearing plants of every kind, and trees of every kind bearing fruit with the seed in it. And God saw that this was good. And there was evening and there was morning, a third day."[131]

In Creation II, however, the creation of man precedes the creation of vegetation. "When no shrub of the field was yet on earth and no grasses of the field had yet sprouted,…the Lord God formed man from the dust of the earth."[132]

2. In Creation I, the birds and land animals were created on the fifth and sixth days, both before the creation of man. "God said, 'Let the waters bring forth swarms of living creatures, and birds that fly above the earth across the expanse of the sky.'…God said, 'Let the earth bring forth every kind of living creature: cattle, creeping things, and wild beasts of every kind.' And it was so. God made wild beasts of every kind and cattle of every kind, and all kinds of creeping things of the earth. And God saw that this was good. And God said, 'Let us make man in our image, after our likeness…'"[133]

In Creation II, on the contrary, the birds and land animals are created after man, to be a fitting helper to him. "The Lord God said, 'It is not good for man to be alone; I will make a fitting helper for him.' And the Lord God formed out of the earth all the wild beasts and all the birds of the sky, and brought them to the man to see what he would call them."[134]

3. In Creation I, the male and the female were created simultaneously. "God created humanity in His image, in the image of God did He create it, male and female did He create them."[135]

In Creation II, however, the woman is formed fifteen verses after the man. "And the Lord God fashioned the rib He had taken from the man into a woman; and He brought her to the man."[136]

4. In Creation I, God is referred to as "*Elohim*" exclusively. The term, "*YHWH*," usually translated into English as the Lord, is not used.

In Creation II, on the other hand, "*Elohim*" is never written by itself, but always paired with "*YHWH*, the Lord God. Interestingly, the only exception to this is found in the dialogue between Eve and the serpent. "Now the serpent was the shrewdest of all the wild beasts that the *Lord God* [*YHWH Elohim*] had made. The serpent said to the woman, 'Did *God* [*Elohim* not *YHWH*] really say: You shall not eat of any tree of the garden?' The woman replied to the serpent, 'We may eat of the fruit of the other trees of the garden. It is only about fruit of the tree in the middle of the garden that *God* [*Elohim* not *YHWH*] said: You shall not eat of it or touch it, lest you die.' And the serpent said to the woman, "You are not going to die, but *God* [*Elohim* not *YHWH*] knows that as soon as you eat of it your eyes will be opened and you will be like Divine beings [also *Elohim*] who know good and bad [everything]."[137] The name, "YHWH," is never uttered by the serpent, nor the woman in their conversation that results in the transgression of Eden.

Examining these and other textual inconsistencies, and paying special attention to the names of the Divinity used in each of the two creation narratives, the documentary hypothesis theorized that the first and second creation accounts were composed by distinct communities within Israel at different historical periods. This hypothesis, whose origins can be traced to earlier Jewish and Christian biblical commentators, for example, Abraham ibn Ezra, Maimonides, Hugo Grotius and Baruch Spinoza, rapidly developed and gained influence when the study of the Bible shifted from the church and synagogue to the university in the eighteenth and nineteenth centuries. It was Julius Wellhausen (1844-1918), the leading German biblical scholar of his generation, who was the most influential of the proponents and developers of the documentary hypothesis in regard to the Pentateuch.[138]

Wellhausen's thesis was that Judaism evolved monotheism over an extended historical period, beginning with the animism of the patriarchs (Abraham, Isaac and Jacob, circa 1800 BCE) and culminating with the development of ethical monotheism with the teachings of the prophets one thousand years later. Wellhausen hypothesized that the Torah text was comprised of four historically-separate sources or documents. The purist and oldest of these, according to Wellhausen, is the J or Yawist document from the ninth century BCE which uses the *YHWH* name for God. The other three documents reflect a "deterioration toward formality and institutionalism." They are (a) The E or Elohist source which uses the *Elohim* name for God (eighth century BCE), (b) the D or Deuteronomist source associated with King Josiah (late seventh century BCE) and (c) the P or Priestly document, originating at the time of, or following, the destruction of the First temple (586 BCE). Wellhausen concluded that the Torah was given its final form with the redaction and editing of the Priestly circles at the time of Ezra (circa 450 BCE). Although contemporary biblical scholars argue about some of the details of Wellhausen's conclusions, for example, the dating of specific sources, the biblical verses reflecting specific documents, the further division of the sources into subdocuments, biblical scholars today generally accept the basic tenets.

The first creation narrative, because of its abstract and philosophical themes and the absence of *YHWH* from the text, is generally understood as a P document. The Eden account, because of its use of *YHWH Elohim* for Divinity, is understood as being from the J source. But what about the redaction of these two narratives? Why were there two separate biblical accounts, sometimes contradictory in theme and content, placed side-by-side in the final Torah? Proponents of the documentary hypothesis would answer these questions by conjecturing that the final editor of the Pentateuch copied the original verbatim texts, which reflected different historical periods and philosophical viewpoints, and joined them together, paying limited attention to the variations in style, language, character, name of God, underlying theology or other factors. And so, Creation I and Creation II, according to this theory, are different from each other and include textual discrepancies for one of three reasons, (a) the final editor's hesitancy to offend any particular long-standing literary tradition or group within Israel, (b) a less constricted attitude than our own concerning textual inconsistencies, or (c) carelessness in the editing process.[139]

For me as a biblical psychoanalyst, both of these theories, the traditional and the documentary, are unsatisfactory in explaining the existence of the two different creation narratives. The traditional view, in its advocacy of condensing the two stories into one, leads to a loss of specificity required of the serious student of the torah when doing a careful exegesis of the two narratives[140]. If one views the Eden story as merely a more focused camera angle on the Bereshit account, then one will tend to minimize or ignore, for example, how *Elohim* and *YHWH Elohim*, or Divine-image-Adam and dust-breath-Adam are considerably different "characters" in our two opening acts. The traditional view collapses the two narratives into one, and, by virtue of this process, loses precious data.

The documentary hypothesis, with its emphasis on the discrete origins of certain passages in the sacred text, is also unsatisfactory. Both the psychoanalytic and the rabbinic perspectives lead one to conclude, when scrutinizing a text or clinical material, that there is no such thing as nonsense. If this assertion is true for specific verses of text, is it not also true for the way in which the texts are woven together in relation to each other? In addition to the understanding of the specific creation narrative, is the juxtaposition of the two narratives not meaningful in its own right?

My view, in contrast with both the traditional and documentary theories, is that the final editor of the Genesis creation accounts chose to have both of these narratives included and contiguous because each of them, by itself, only conveys half the story—about the nature of God, humanity and relationship. It is my view that it is only by taking the two narratives together, and understanding them as a single, multifaceted and meaningfully-redacted text, that one can appreciate the whole truth about who we are and who God is.

Who is He? As we have seen, in our exegesis of *Elohim* and *YHWH Elohim*, the "hero," God, in each of the two creation narratives is different from each other. In Creation I, in Bereshit, *Elohim* is a distant and all-powerful "leading man" who stands above His creation and His creatures, considers them, blesses them, declares them as good—but never walks among them, speaks with them or touches them. In Creation II, our divine hero, no longer the only leading man, is *YHWH Elohim*. This "character" breathes into His creation, speaks with him, performs surgery on him, walks among his creatures, takes an interest in them, becomes disappointed with them and, after sewing clothing for their journey, punishes them by banishing them from His garden.

The rabbis of the Talmud interpreted the distinction between these two names of God as reflecting different attributes. For them, *Elohim* was associated with God's attribute of judgement, while *YHWH* represented mercy. For example, in the midrashic discussion of a verse that comes between the first and second creation narratives, "Such is the story of heaven and earth when they were created, when the Lord God made earth and heaven,"[141] the rabbis taught:

> "The Lord [YHWH] God [Elohim] made earth and heaven…" What can this be compared with? This may be compared to a king who had some empty glasses. Said the king: 'If I pour hot water into them, they will burst; if cold, they will contract [and snap].' What then did the king do? He mixed hot and cold water and poured it into them, and so they remained [unbroken]. Even so, said the Holy One, blessed be He: 'If I create the world on the basis of mercy alone, its sins will be great; on the basis of judgment alone, the world cannot exist. Hence I will create it on the basis of judgment [Elohim] and of mercy [YHWH], and may it then stand!' Hence the expression,' the Lord God [YHWH Elohim].[142]

Umberto Cassuto, in his comprehensive and scholarly commentary on Genesis 1-3, critiques the way in which *Elohim* and *YHWH* has been interpreted in the creation accounts by both the rabbis and the proponents of the documentary hypothesis.[143] When applying the rabbinic judgement-mercy dichotomy to the content of the creation narratives, as well as other Torah texts, one comes upon conceptual contradictions. Does not Elohim in the first creation narrative demonstrate mercy for His creatures by creating for them a world that is "very good?" How is Elohim in this narrative demonstrating judgement? In addition, YHWH, in the second creation narrative, not only demonstrates compassion for His first children, but also judgement on them.

The documentary theory, with its assertion that *Elohim* and *YHWH* as primarily reflective of diverse literary and historical traditions, minimizes the appreciation for the specific *meanings* of these terms for the Deity. I agree with Cassuto who, concluded from his lifelong study of biblical texts, that each of the two names of God has a specific meaning and "tone." For Cassuto, citing the history of *Elohim* as a generic god in the ancient Near East before He became the God of monotheism, *Elohim* denotes a more abstract and philosophical creator God. *Elohim* is a God of the material world, transcending and ruling nature and the source of life. On the contrary, and complementing *Elohim*, *YHWH*, whose history was always as a God of Israel, corresponds with the Deity with whom one has a direct and personal relationship. In addition, *YHWH* is used in Genesis when there is an ethical aspect to the text. Cassuto concludes, "…the name *Elohim* had necessarily to be used in the story of creation [the first creation account], for there God appears as the Creator of the *material* universe, and as the Master of the world who has dominion over everything and forms everything by His word alone, without there being any direct relationship between Himself and nature...In the narrative of the garden of Eden, on the other hand, God appears as the Ruler of the *moral* world, for He enjoins a given precept on man, and demands an account of his actions; that apart, stress is laid here on His personal aspect, manifested in His direct relationship with man and the other creatures."[144]

Only by taking the two creation narratives together does one gain a complete concept of God, as transcendent ruler of the universe and as close to us as our next breath. It is the development and unification of this God of Nature and of Involvement that was Judaism's monotheistic gift to the world.

The most graphic example of how Judaism combines the *Elohim* of Creation I with the *YHWH* of Creation II is found in the synagogue liturgy. Twice a day, the worshipper recites the Shema, the affirmation of God's oneness, with its blessings. As proscribed by the rabbis in the Mishnah two thousand years ago, the Shema is always preceded by two benedictions.

In the first benediction antecedent to the Shema, God's creation of the *natural* world is praised and blessed. "Blessed are You, *YHWH*, our God, King of the Universe, Who forms light and creates darkness, makes peace and creates all. He Who illuminates the earth and those who dwell upon it, with compassion; and in His goodness renews daily, perpetually, the work of creation. How great are Your works, *YHWH*, You make them all with wisdom, the world is full of Your possessions...May You be blessed, *YHWH*, our God, beyond the praises of Your handiwork and beyond the bright luminaries that You have made—may they glorify You—selah."[145]

In the second benediction recited by the worshipper immediately prior to the Shema, God's personal *relationship* with Israel is gratefully acknowledged and praised. "With abundant love have You loved us, *YHWH*, our God; with exceedingly great pity have You pitied us. Our Father, our king, for the sake of our forefathers who trusted in You and whom You taught the decrees of life, may You be equally gracious to us and teach us. Our Father, the merciful Father, Who acts mercifully, have mercy upon us, instill in our hearts to understand and elucidate, to listen, learn, teach, safeguard, perform, and fulfill all the words of Your Torah's teaching with love...Blessed are You, *YHWH*, who chooses His people Israel with love.[146]

And then, in a wonderful example of how the medium is the message, the Shema prayer is intoned. The Shema explicitly declares God's oneness, "Hear O Israel, the Lord, our God, the Lord is one." Examining the Hebrew, we find both *Elohim* and *YHWH*, nature and involvement, unified. Hear O Israel, the Lord (*YHWH*, the God with whom you and Israel have a personal and direct relationship, the God of the second pre-Shema benediction, the God from the garden of Eden), our God (*Elohim*, the God who created the material world from afar, the God of the first benediction and creation account). The Lord (*YHWH repeated*) is one. And so, twice a day, when the worshipper recites the Shema, Bereshit and Eden, *Elohim* and *YHWH*, transcendent creator and caring parent, God of Nature and God of Involvement are declared "one and the same."

Who are we? As we saw in our exegeses of the Adams in the two creation narratives, two aspects of the human soul are revealed. Adam I is created in God's image, two creatures, one male and one female, created simultaneously and is never alone. Adam II is a more earthy figure. Created from the complex mixture of soil and Divine breath, This Eden Adam is an involved and vulnerable hero, alone and lonely, who searches for a soulmate. This second Adam clings to his wife. Then, Eden man and woman hide from themselves and their God. Unable to own their personal responsibility for what they have done, Eden man and Eden woman are banished from their paradise.

The Bereshit Adam, only made in God's image, is our goal and ideal.[147] The Eden Adam is our reality. It was the prophets who harangued Adam II to become Adam I, to struggle to shift from the empty ritual to the ethical, from the tribal to the universal.[148] It was Mordecai Kaplan who understood the whole aim of Judaism as integrating Adam II with Adam I, that is, that the aim of Judaism is to impel Jews to become a "people in the image of God."[149]

Each of us is both Adam I and Adam II. Each of us struggles with the world, with involvement and relationship, and with ourselves. Each of us wrestles with our desires, defects, vulnerability, fears, and with the ethical. *Each of us is a human who struggles to be human.* Perhaps it is precisely this human struggle with oneself that *is* in the Divine image.

The Chasidic master, Rabbi Simha Bunam of Pzhysha, in the early nineteenth century, taught that each of us is born with two pockets. In one, a slip of paper reads, "You are but dust and ashes." In the other, the paper reads, "The world was created for your sake." When one is feeling conceited, he should reach into the first pocket. When one is feeling disheartened, he should reach into the second.[150] Irrespective of how we are feeling at any given time, we always carry *both* of those slips of paper.

The two creation narratives, each a masterpiece of poetry, philosophy, theology, psychology and folklore, taken together, offer a complete picture of the human that neither of them alone provides. We are both Adam I and Adam II, the crowning act of God's creativity and merely dust and ashes. We are both the human who struggles with his humanity, and the human who struggles to *be* human, to be an image of God.

In Part Two of this book, we examine how we change by studying this Adam I-Adam II struggle in more detail. In Chapter Four, we address the question of how Abraham, and all of us, can transcend paganism and become true monotheists—worshipping God over idols and thereby, prizing people over things, and ethical values over material possessions. In chapter Five, we explore our journey from self-absorption to maturity by examining the biblical Jacob's life. In our examination, we see this patriarch travel from a *Jacob* who is the narcissistic trickster, passive in relation to his mother's schemes, deceiving himself, his brother and father, to an *Israel*, wrestling with himself, leader of his people and progenitor of Joseph, the Book of Genesis' apogee and hero.

It is the duel creation—Bereshit and Eden, *Elohim* and *YHWH-Elohim*, Adam I and Adam II—with its mixed imagery concerning God, humanity and relationship, that lays the foundation for the remainder of the biblical text, and of our inquiry into it.

PART II
How We Change

All great literature is literature of transformation. From Homer's Odysseus, to Sophocles' Oedipus, to Virgil's Aeneas, to Shakespeare's Hamlet, to Miller's John Proctor, the narrative that lasts is propelled by character and circumstance from who the hero was, to who the hero becomes.

The Book of Genesis, as well, is rich with accounts of transformation. We see Abraham walking up the mountain, eager to follow his God's command to sacrifice his beloved Isaac. With slaughtering knife in hand, Abraham suddenly hears a new divine voice, and Isaac's life is spared. That day is the day that Abraham becomes a monotheist.

Jacob, terrified that the morning will bring death to him and his entire family, wrestles with beings, divine and human, throughout the night, and ultimately prevails. As the sun rises, we see a Jacob who is blessed, limping and changed.

We see Judah, a central figure in the sale of his brother Joseph into slavery many years before, willing to sacrifice his own life and freedom to save Benjamin. Confronted by the same temptation, to rid himself of his father's favorite son, Judah makes a new choice. The now-repentant and transformed Judah begs for his youngest brother's life.

We see a Joseph, a spoiled self-absorbed adolescent, become the spiritual hero of the Book of Genesis. It is the adult Joseph, forever changed by his bitter years in Egyptian slavery and dungeons, that not only forgives his brothers, but also discerns that his suffering by their jealous and hateful hands as part of a divine plan.

For the psychologist, biblical scholar and cleric, how we change is the beating heart of the inquiry.

4

Paganism in Everyday Life: Abraham, Isaac and the Altar

What has once come to life clings tenaciously to its existence. One feels inclined to doubt sometimes whether the dragons of primeval days are really extinct.

—*Sigmund Freud, "Analysis Terminable or Interminable"*

No single narrative in Western literature has provoked the eruption of argument, controversy, creativity, interpretation and angst as Genesis 22:1-19. In this biblical text, referred to by Jews as the *"Akedah"* (Hebrew for the binding), less than three hundred and fifty Hebrew words in all, the near-sacrifice of Isaac by his father is described. Sculptors, painters, poets, musicians, philosophers, theologians and commentators, in our and ancient times, have struggled with the implications of God's ordering this murder. They have wondered and worried about what it was that happened when the aged Abraham, early that morning, rose, traveled for three days, took his beloved son to the mountain, bound him to the altar there, prepared him for the slaughter; and then, abruptly interrupted by a voice from heaven, substituted for his son a ram caught in the thicket.

Although there are some ancient examples of artistic depictions of the Akedah created by Jews, found in the synagogues of Dura-Europos in Syria (third century CE) and Beth-Alpha in the Galilee (three hundred years later),[151] and some drawings found in a number of medieval Passover Haggadahs, prayer books and Bibles, the vast majority of artistic representations of the Akedah are found within the Christian context. The Princeton University's index of Christian art lists over one thousand four hundred-fifty separate works that take as subject the sacrifice of Isaac. Judaism, which like Islam, has prohibitions concerning representations of the human form, developed the art of midrash. Jewish biblical commentary, therefore, is textual. Christianity, which generally did not have widespread prohibitions concerning representations of the human, and because of its lower rates of literacy, developed to a high art its biblical commentary in the form of sculpture, painting and frescos. For Christians, art is pictorial midrash.

The Akedah was a central motif for the early Christians. They saw in the story of Abraham (the father willing to sacrifice his son) and Isaac (carrying his own wood to his death) a prefiguration of the crucifixion. According to early Christian understanding, Jesus is the ram of the Akedah, caught in the thicket by his horns. It is Jesus' crucifixion which completes what was interrupted by the angel of God on the mountain. Whereas the Hebrew Bible's Isaac's life was saved by the angel of the Lord, God, the Father, in the Christian Bible, is described as, "He who spared not His own son."[152] This early Christian association of Akedah with crucifixion is demonstrated by the number of burial sites adorned with depictions of the Akedah. For example, in the catacombs of Rome, dating from before a time when the crucifixion was artistically represented, there are over twenty-two frescos and ninety reliefs and mosaics on sarcophagi in which the Akedah is the subject.[153]

In the Renaissance, Brunaleschi, Donatelo, Ghiberti and Titian, among many others, depicted the Akedah. Caravaggio (1573-1610) painted a terrified Isaac whose throat is about to be slashed by an ancient Abraham. Caravaggio paints this Abraham as irritated by the angel's interruption. midrashically interpreting and revising the Genesis text, Caravaggio has the angel, not speaking to Abraham from afar in heaven, but next to him at the altar, the angel holding Abraham's arm back from murdering the child with his right hand and indicating the ram to be substituted with his left.[154] In 1635, Rembrandt offers a similar biblical interpretation in his painting of the sacrifice text. In this work, the angel, again not trusting the words spoken from heaven to save the child, with one angelic hand, forcefully restrains Abraham's arm which has just, that moment, dropped the knife. The scene is a particularly uncomfortable one, with Abraham powerfully arching Isaac's face back to expose his neck.[155]

Many poets, for example, Mark Van Doren, Itzik Manger, Emily Dickinson, drew on the Akedah text as inspiration. Wilfred Owens' interpretation and use of the biblical text is particularly interesting and provocative.

Wilfred Owen (1893-1918) wrote his poem, "The Parable of the Old Man and the Young," in a trench in World War I. The young poet was killed in France one week before the Armistice. Twenty of his poems, including this one, were published posthumously.[156] Owens' poetry was the text that Benjamin Britten used in his "war Requiem." His Akedah poem reads:

So Abram rose, and clave the wood, and went,
And took the fire with him, and a knife.
And as they sojourned both of them together,
Isaac the first-born spoke and said, My Father,
Behold the preparations, fire and iron,
But where the lamb for this burnt-offering?
Then Abram bound the youth with belts and straps,
And builded parapets and trenches there,
And stretched forth the knife to slay his son.
When lo! an angel called him out of heaven,
Saying, Lay not thy hand upon the lad,
Neither do anything to him.
Behold, A ram, caught in a thicket by its horns;
Offer the ram of Pride instead of him.

But the old man would not so, but slew his son,
And half the seed of Europe, one by one.

Artistically developing a similar midrashic interpretation in which the Akedah is viewed as a clash between generations about war, the sculptor George Segal, fifty years after Owens' poem, carved "Abraham and Isaac." Segal's statue was created in memory of the four Kent State University students who were shot and killed by the Ohio National Guard during anti-Vietnam demonstrations, May 4, 1970. The statue, offered to and rejected by Kent State now stands between the library and chapel at Princeton.

Segal's "Abraham and Isaac," a bronze, eighty-one inches tall, shows two human figures, alone on a irregularly-shaped rock-like platform. The older man stands, knife in hand, squarely in front of a kneeling young man, bound only by his arms, seemingly-begging for his life. Eerily stark, there is no altar, no ram to take the young man's place, and alas, no angel to interrupt the slaughter.[157]

In modern philosophy, the Akedah has been a significant focus of attention and controversy, with the two major distinct philosophical schools of interpreting Abraham in the Akedah established by Immanuel Kant and Soren Kierkegaard. Immanuel Kant (1724-1804), the father of the Enlightenment, was deeply disturbed by the Genesis 22 text. Kant argues, celebrating individual conscience over obedience, that any voice of God that commands an action that is in violation of the moral law cannot be, "no matter how majestic the apparition may be, and no matter how it may seem to surpass the whole of nature" *not* God. Turning his attention specifically to the Akedah, Kant writes, "Abraham should have replied to this supposedly divine voice [commanding that he kill his son], 'That I ought not to kill my good son is quite certain. But that you, this apparition, is God—of that I am not certain, and never can be, not even if your voice resounds from the heaven.'"[158] For Kant, the Abraham and God of the Akedah were no heroes.

For Soren Kierkegaard (1813-1855), the Danish philosopher who had far-reaching influence on Protestant theology and existentialism, Abraham, as is understood in *Fear and Trembling*,[159] was a great champion, "a knight of faith. As God's knight, Abraham struggles alone and agonizingly with a single question. Should Abraham, like other people, conform to the universal laws of morality? Or, because of his unique relationship with and obligation to God is he bound by a different divine imperative? Kierkegaard questions whether an Abraham is obliged, because he is an Abraham, to take a leap of faith, to transcend universal morality and place his sonhood to God above his fatherhood to Isaac, and his individual faith over the ethical. Kierkegaard refers to this as the "teleological suspension of the ethical." It is because the Abraham of the Akedah struggles alone with these transcendent issues of faith that Kierkegaard concludes, "I cannot understand Abraham. I can only admire him."[160]

In the religious sphere, the Akedah is a central narrative for all three Western religions. Although not mentioned in the remainder of the Tanakh, reference to Genesis 22 is abundant and central in the Talmud, midrash and the Jewish liturgy. The Akedah is one of the biblical texts read and discussed each year on Rosh Hashanah, the beginning of the most somber penitential period of the Jewish calendar.[161] According to the Talmud, it is because of the Akedah that Jews blow the ram's horn on this day in order to temper God's judgement. "Rabbi Abbahu asked, 'Why do we blow a ram's horn on the New Year?' The Holy One, blessed be He replied, 'So that I may remember on your behalf the binding of Isaac, the son of Abraham, and account it to you as if you had each bound yourself before Me.'"[162] This strong liturgical association of the binding of Isaac and God's forgiveness for the present-day Jew is repeated every morning in the synagogue. After reading the Akedah, included in the daily Orthodox prayer book, the worshipper prays, "Master of the world, may it be Your will that you remember the covenant You made with our fathers. Even as Abraham, our father, held back his compassion from his only son and desired to slay him in order to do Your will, so may Your mercy hold back Your anger from us...Master of all worlds, it is not on account of our righteousness that we offer our supplications before You, but on account of Your great compassion. What are we? What is our life?…We are Your people…the children of Abraham, Your friend, to whom You made a promise on Mount Moriah [the setting for the Akedah]; we are the descendents of his only son, Isaac, who was bound on the altar."[163]

As we already discussed in our brief examination of Christian art and the Akedah, the crucifixion symbolism draws heavily on the Genesis text. Isaac and Jesus each carries his own altar wood to his slaughter. The ram substitute (stuck in the thicket by his horns) and Jesus each "wears" a crown of thorns. Mount Moriah, where Abraham brings his beloved son to sacrifice, and the Temple Mount in Jerusalem, where God brings his beloved son to be sacrificed, is, by biblical tradition, the same place.[164]

In the Koran, there is also an Akedah text. It reads:[165]

> Father Abraham said, "My Lord, grant me righteous children."
> God gave him good news of a good child.
> When Abraham grew enough to work with him, he said, "My son, I see in a dream that I am sacrificing you. What do you think?" His son said, "O my father, do what you are commanded to do. You will find me, GOD willing, patient."
> The Most Merciful never advocates evil
> They both submitted, and Abraham put his son's forehead down to sacrifice him.
> God called him: "O Abraham.
> "You have believed the dream." God thus reward the righteous.
> That was an exacting test indeed.
> God ransomed his son by substituting an animal sacrifice.
> And God preserved his history for subsequent generations.
> Peace be upon Abraham.
> God thus reward the righteous.
> He is one of our believing servants.

It is interesting to note that in the Koran text, Abraham's son is consulted and is a willing sacrifice. This is not the case in the Genesis narrative, although one finds a voluntary and informed Isaac in many midrashim[166], in the biblical interpretations of Josephus[167] and in the Book of Jubilees found in the Dead Sea Scrolls.[168] In these sources, Isaac, having been informed by his father what is to happen, asks his father to bind his hands tightly. Some of these texts were probably known to Muhammad. It is also important to consider that in the Arabic text of this story, the son's name is not specified. Some scholars wonder whether the son described in the Koran is Isaac or Ishmael.[169] By Muslim tradition, contrary to Genesis Chapter 21, Abraham does not banish Hagar (Sarah's handmaiden) and Ishmael (Abraham's oldest son) into the wilderness. Instead, Abraham travels with Hagar and Ishmael to Mecca to complete the sacrifice.

The Genesis account of Abraham's binding of Isaac, more than any other single biblical narrative, has inspired our spiritual, theological, liturgical, intellectual and aesthetic creativity—and has, at the same time, deeply disturbed our sleep.

Infanticide (attempted or completed, ritual or motivated by other purposes, performed by fathers or their surrogates, practiced on both daughters and sons, on infants and older children) is a central motif found in much of the literature and mythology of the ancient and classical Near East. In the Bible, the god to whom children were most frequently sacrificed by refractory Israelites and gentiles alike was Moloch, a Canaanite god of fire who originates from the third millennium BCE.

Next to the place dedicated to the gentler gods had been erected a platform of movable stones under which a huge fire already raged. On the platform stood a stone god of unusual construction. It had two extended arms raised so that from the stone fingertips to the body they formed a wide inclined plane, but above the spot where they joined the torso there was a huge gaping mouth, so that whatever was placed upon the arms was free to roll swiftly downward and plunge into the fire. This was the god Moloch.

Slaves heaped fresh timber under the statue, and when the flames leaped from the god's mouth, two priests grabbed one of the eight boys, and raised him high in the air. Muttering incantations they approached Moloch's outstretched arms, dashed the child upon them and gave the boy a dreadful shove downward, so that he scraped along the stony arms and plunged into the fire. As Moloch accepted him with a belch of fire there was a faint cry, and then an anguished scream as the child's mother protested. The priests had noticed this breach of religious solemnity and were angry.[170]

Child sacrifice to this Canaanite god is explicitly referred to and vehemently denounced in the Hebrew Bible. In Leviticus, God commands Moses, "You shall say to the children of Israel,…or to the strangers that sojourn in Israel, that give of his seed to Moloch; he shall surely be put to death: the people of the land shall stone him…And if the people of the land hide their eyes from that man, when he gives of his seed to Moloch, and put him not to death; then I will set My face against that man, and against his family."[171] In 2 Kings, the text states, "And he defiled Topheth, which is in the valley of the children of Hinnom [the site for

Moloch worship], that no man might make his son or his daughter to pass through the fire to Moloch."[172]

Twelve hundred years after Abraham, Isaac and the altar, the prophets are still horrified and appalled by the Israelites who are sacrificing their children in Moloch's valley. Jeremiah states, "For the children of Judah have done evil in my sight, saith the Lord: they have set their abominations in the house which is called by my name, to pollute it. And they have built the high places of Tophet, which is in the valley of the son of Hinnom, to burn their sons and their daughters in the fire; which I commanded them not, neither came it into my heart."[173] The prophets, Ezekiel and Second Isaiah[174] further confirm Jeremiah's contention that feeding the children to the fiery Moloch was still practiced by Israelites up until the Babylonian exile and captivity.

Greek mythology, and the Athenian plays that draw on its heroes and themes as subjects, are also replete with child sacrifice. Two examples of this are Iphigenia and Oedipus.

Child sacrifice to assure a favorable military outcome or fertile growing season, or to appease a god who has been offended was not uncommon in the ancient Near East. Plutarch, the Greek essayist and biographer, reported that ritual child sacrifice in the Roman Empire was still being practiced in his own time, as late as 115 CE.[175]

When unfavorable winds detained the Greek army at Aulis for days, prohibiting the ships from sailing into battle with the Trojans, the oracle Calchas told Agamemnon that he must sacrifice his daughter to appease the god Artemis, who Agamemnon had offended and who was the cause of the poor sailing weather. Misleading his daughter and wife Clytemnestra that Iphigenia was to be married to Achilles, the child sacrifice-bride was brought to Aulis. In one version of the myth, Agamemnon actually sacrificed her to Artemis. Interestingly, and reminiscent of the Akedah, in other versions of the same myth, in the final moment before Iphigenia was slaughtered by her father, the god Artemis took pity on her and substituted a deer on the altar. In this second version, Artemis then carried the young woman in a cloud to Tauris where she became the god's high priestess.

Euripides (485-406 BCE) drew on both versions of the myth in his two plays, "Iphigenia in Aulis" and "Iphigenia in Tauris."[176] In the latter work, Iphigenia describes her experience of *being* the sacrifice:

> Greek hands lifted me at Aulis
> And led me like a beast where, at the altar,
> My father held the sacrificial knife.

I live it all again. My fingers, groping,
Go out to him like this and clutch his beard
And cling about his knees. I cry to him:
"It is you yourself, yourself, who brought me here,
You who deceived my maidens and my mother!
They sing my marriage song at home, they fill
The house with happiness, while all the time
Here I am dying at my father's hands!
You led me in your chariot to take
Achilles for my lord, but here is death
And the taste of blood, not kisses, on my lips!"

In addition to propitiating the gods to obtain a particular favorable outcome, child sacrifice in the literature of the ancient Near East was often motivated by intergenerational conflict and competition for power. We have already seen this theme in the Cronus-Zeus clash in Hesiod's "Theogony," in which Cronus sequentially eats each of his children so that he or she will not usurp his heavenly power (see Chapter Two). One also sees this theme in the stories concerning the births of Abraham, Moses, Jesus and Oedipus.[177]

Oedipus, more than any other hero of Greek mythology, is well known today, mostly because of Sigmund Freud's use of this figure as the organizing metaphor for his psychoanalytic insights. In Sophocles' tragedy, "Oedipus Rex,"[178] first performed in 431 BCE, we enter the narrative in the middle. A famine is ravishing the land of Thebes, killing the children, crops and animals. The King of Thebes, Oedipus, desperately wishes to understand why the gods have sent this famine, and to take all steps necessary to make it end. Reluctantly, the blind seer Tiresias tells the King that the gods are angry with Thebes because the murder of the previous king, Laius, was never avenged. Oedipus conducts a relentless inquiry into the matter himself.

The play reads like a contemporary well-constructed murder mystery. With each clue that Oedipus obtains gradually tightening the noose of guilt around Oedipus' own neck—the audience only a few steps ahead of the characters on the stage.

What we and Oedipus discover is that when Laius and Jocasta, the King and Queen of Thebes, first learn that they are to be parents, they consult the oracle at Delphi. The oracle tells the young couple that the son that is in Jocasta's womb would row up and kill his father, Laius, and have sexual relations with his own mother. When Oedipus is born, to prevent the prophesy from coming true, the couple give the infant to a servant to take him to the distant Mount Citaeron in Corinth, to pierce and shackle his ankles there. The name "Oedipus" is Greek for "Swollen feet." The servant is to leave him to starve and die in that isolated spot. Years later, during the inquiry, an ancient shepherd tells King Oedipus that he took pity on the infant and, unbeknownst to Laius and Jocasta, carried the infant to be raised by the childless King and Queen of Corinth.

There the boy grows to be a young man, ignorant of his history and of his adoption, until when sixteen years old, Oedipus overhears a conversation that changes his life course. During a drunken banquet in the palace, the prince hears a comment that makes him suspect that he was adopted by, not born to the royal couple.

In a deluge of emotion, Oedipus travels to Delphi to inquire of the oracle as to the identity of his biological parents. When the prince arrives, the oracle does not answer Oedipus' question, but instead, repeats the prophesy told to his parents sixteen years before—that Oedipus will kill his father and have sexual relations with his mother. The oracle says, "You are fated to couple with your mother, you will bring a breed of children into the light no man can bear to see—you will kill your father, the one who gave you life."

> Oedipus, terrified and overwhelmed by the prophesy, forgetting that he came to the oracle uncertain of who his parents were, rides impetuously away from Corinth and his adopted parents, attempting to prevent the prediction from coming true. On the road from Delphi, King Laius and his retinue approach and refuse to yield. Oedipus, in a rage, kills the entire royal party.

Later, on that same journey in which Oedipus desperately flees from Corinth and his past, Delphi and his future, and himself and his present, our hero solves the riddle of the Sphinx. As a result of this, Oedipus is rewarded with King Laius' Theban throne and wife.

Once the murder mystery is solved, Jocasta, Oedipus' mother and wife, hangs herself. Oedipus, in a torrent of self-accusation and guilt, gouges out his eyes and is exiled to Mount Citaeron in Corinth yet again. Movingly, the play ends with the just-blind Oedipus being slowly led off the stage by his young daughter Antigone.

It is interesting to note that Sigmund Freud's understanding of the hero in the Sophocles' play involved a significant creative misreading, a sort of midrash, somewhat distant from the original text. Unlike the hero of Freud's Oedipal complex, Sophocles' Oedipus' murder of his father and sexual contact with his mother did not reflect Oedipus' "oedipal" wishes, but rather his fate. Also, whereas Freud's Oedipus is motivated by a profound and primal longing for his mother, Sophocles' Oedipus obtained his mother as wife as part of a prize package, for solving the riddle of the Sphinx.[179]

Most significant, Freud's Oedipus is rife with competitive and murderous wishes toward his father. It is these wishes of the son, for Freud, that create in the child's mind a fear of the father and of the potential for castration, what the child imagines will be the mode of retaliation by his father. Therefore, for Freud, the oedipal wishes of the child precede the fantasy of aggressive retaliation by the father.

For Sophocles' Oedipus, the situation is just the opposite. Before Oedipus longs for his mother and wishes to kill his father, he is sentenced by his parents to a brutal death on an isolated and distant mountain. For the Greek playwright, the "Laius Complex," the father's murderous wishes toward the son in order to prevent his future usurpation of the father's power, precedes the oedipal. That is, for Sophocles, but not for Freud, infanticidal wishes precede the patricidal.[180]

The clash of generations over power and the resulting demand for infanticide is also a central theme in the legend concerning Abraham's birth. In the Torah, we do not meet Abraham until he is already seventy years old when he is called by God to leave his land, his kindred and his father's house.[181] For information concerning Abraham's birth, we need to turn to the midrashic literature.[182]

Nimrod, the mightiest king of his day, an astrologer, the grandson of Noah, saw in the stars that there was a man to be born who would rise up against him and overturn his gods. He consulted his advisers. The court unanimously agreed that a large building should be constructed in which all pregnant women in the realm will reside throughout their confinements. If the child is a boy, he will be killed by the midwife. If the child is a girl, then all manner of gifts and honors will be given to the mother. Then, mother and daughter will be released from the building. The building was constructed, the proclamations were issued and the officers were designated to execute Nimrod's wishes. More than seventy thousand infant boys were killed during these evil days.

It was about this time that Terach married the mother of Abraham. When she learned of her pregnancy, she hid this from her husband and all others. When her day had come to give birth, Abraham's mother was terrified. She walked for a long distance, alone, into the wilderness and gave birth to her son in a remote cave.

Abraham's mother, knowing that her son was the one Nimrod feared, abandoned the infant in the cave. Before leaving him, she said, "Alas that I bore you when Nimrod is king…Better that you perish here in this cave than I see you dead at my breast."

God then took pity on the infant Abraham, weeping in the cave, and sent His angels to nurse the child. Miraculously, it was on the tenth day that Abraham walked out of the cave as the sun was just setting. Abraham, awed by the beauty of the stars, worshipped them. Then, in the morning, the stars were gone from the sky. Abraham, disheartened, realized that they were no gods. Later that day, the sun rose full in the sky. Abraham, dazzled by its light, worshipped the sun. And then, alas, it set, leaving Abraham yet again sad and godless. That very evening, Abraham marveled at the moon's glow, until a cloud obscured his newest god, deserting him again without the Divine.

Abraham then cried out in joy and understanding, "The stars and the sun and the moon are no gods, but there is One who sets them all in motion. It is He, and only He, who I will worship."

The motif we see in the Abraham story, massive infanticide commanded by a father-surrogate whose power is challenged by the birth of a religious hero, is also seen in the well-known biblical stories of the births of Moses and Jesus. Both of these paramount figures were born, like Abraham, during evil days. Moses' birth is preceded by the command by Pharaoh that all Hebrew boys be killed. Moses is only saved because of the intervention of a righteous Gentile, the unnamed daughter of Pharaoh. Aware of what she is doing, Pharaoh's daughter bravely defies her father's orders and has the infant Hebrew Moses, floating in his ark down the Nile, retrieved and redeemed. "And the daughter of Pharaoh came down to wash herself at the river; and her maidens walked along by the river's side; and when she saw the ark among the flags, she sent her maid to fetch it. And when she had opened it, she saw the child: and, behold, the babe wept. And she had compassion on him, and said, This is one of the Hebrews' children. Then said Miriam, Moses' sister, to Pharaoh's daughter, Shall I go and call for you a nurse of the Hebrew women, that she may nurse the child for you? And Pharaoh's daughter said to her, Go."[183]

It is thirteen hundred years after the birth of Moses, forty-two generations following the birth of Abraham that Herod, King of Israel, is informed by the three wise men from the East that they are seeking the infant who is the "King of the Jews."[184] Herod, distraught by this infant "King," summons the priests and scribes of Israel to discern what Scripture reveals as to the location of the birth of the Messiah. Herod is informed that the place will be Bethlehem. The King, deceiving the wise men about his motives—lying to them that he would also like to worship the infant—asks them to return to Jerusalem on their way back to the East and inform Herod where they find this child. The wise men, after finding Jesus in the manger, having been warned by God in a dream not to return by Jerusalem, travel back to their home avoiding Herod.

Then, Joseph also has a dream. In this one, an angel tells Joseph to take his wife, Mary, and the infant Jesus and flee to Egypt until Herod is dead. There, the infant Messiah is safe, but not the children of Bethlehem and its environs.

Herod orders the "murder of the innocents." The Book of Matthew states, "Then Herod, when he saw that he was mocked by the wise men, was enraged, and sent forth, and killed all the children that were in Bethlehem, and in all the coasts thereof, from two years old and under, according to the time which he had diligently enquired of the wise men. Then, that which was spoken by Jeremiah the prophet was fulfilled, In Rama was there a voice heard, lamentation, and weeping, and great mourning, Rachel weeping for her children, and would not be comforted, because they are all dead."[185]

The biblical text of the Akedah is set within a long-standing, tenacious and voluminous classical literature and history of child sacrifice. From Canaan's Moloch to Hadrian's Rome; from Cronus to Agamemnon to Laius to Nimrod to Pharaoh to Herod; both pagans and Israelites even in the days of the prophets Jeremiah and Ezekiel; motivated by religious fervor or a wish to propitiate irascible and unpredictable gods or to perpetuate one's own power; the sacrifice of the child persists as a ubiquitous and stubborn classical theme and practice in the ancient Near East. It is within this literary and historical context that our biblical Akedah text was first written, redacted and chanted.

Isaac, before the Akedah, is the consummate precious child. Abraham is one hundred and Sarah ninety years old when Isaac is born. Only after years of trying to have children and suffering with their childlessness, only after Abraham confronting God about Sarah's infertility and how it calls into question all that God has promised him and his seed, the couple learn from messengers of God that their prayers are finally answered. Astonished by this news, the couple laughs (*tzachak* in Hebrew) and thus, Isaac (*Yitzhak*) is born.

But Isaac before the Akedah is not only a precious child to this tiny and aged nuclear family, Isaac is *the* precious child to monotheism. It is important to keep in mind that Isaac is not Abraham's only or even oldest son. When Sarah failed to conceive, she offered Abraham her handmaiden Hagar, an Egyptian, so that Sarah could have a child with Abraham by means of this substitution. This was a custom widely practiced in the ancient Near east. The Torah states, "Now Sarai Abram's wife bare him no children: and she had an handmaid, an Egyptian, whose name was Hagar. And Sarai said unto Abram, Behold now, the Lord has restrained me from bearing: I pray you, go into my maid; so that it may be that I may obtain children by her."[186] It was from this Abraham-Hagar union that the first son Ishmael was born.

Yet, like other genesis narratives, for example, Jacob vs. Esau, Joseph vs. his ten older brothers, the covenant that God makes with Abraham and with the Jewish people is not through Abraham's oldest son Ishmael, it is with the younger, the genetic son of Abraham and Sarah.[187] According to the Bible, God's covenant is through precious Isaac. This is made explicit in the Torah text. "And God said, Sarah thy wife shall bear you a son indeed; and you shall call his name Isaac: and I will establish my covenant with him for an everlasting covenant, and with his seed after him. And as for Ishmael, I have heard you: Behold, I have blessed him, and will make him fruitful, and will multiply him exceedingly; twelve princes shall he beget, and I will make him a great nation. But my covenant will I establish with Isaac."[188]

In the biblical chapter immediately preceding the Akedah text, the position of one son over the other is secured when Abraham, requested by Sarah and supported by God, banishes Hagar and Ishmael into the wilderness. "And Abraham rose up early in the morning, and took bread, and a bottle of water, and gave it unto Hagar, putting it on her shoulder, and the child, and sent her away: and she departed, and wandered in the wilderness of Beer Sheva."[189]

Therefore, when Abraham, knife in hand, is standing over his bound son Isaac on Mount Moriah, the ancient patriarch is not only about to kill the long-awaited beloved child of his and his wife's old age, but also, Abraham is about to slaughter his future. All of Abraham's hopes for the world, the aspirations that he worked toward since being called, all of God's promises to him, lie on the altar bound. At that moment, it is monotheism itself that hangs by the thinnest thread.

The personality of Abraham before the Akedah is well-developed and consistent in the Torah text. Abraham, a prince of faith who leaves all he knows behind when God commands him to do so, is also a figure who negotiates. He negotiates with family in Genesis Chapter 13, with allies in 14, with neighboring princes in 20, and even with God in 18.

When God tells Abraham that He will be destroying the people of the sinful towns of Sodom and Gomorrah, Abraham argues:

> Abraham came forward and said, "Will You sweep away the innocent along with the guilty? What if there should be fifty innocent within the city; will You then wipe out the place and not forgive it for the sake of the innocent fifty who are in it? Far be it from You to do such a thing, to bring death upon the innocent as well as the guilty, so that innocent and guilty fare alike. Far be it from You! Shall not the Judge of all the earth deal justly?" And the Lord

answered, "If I find within the city of Sodom fifty innocent ones, I will forgive the whole place for their sake." Abraham spoke up, saying, "Here I venture to speak to my Lord, I who am but dust and ashes: What if the fifty innocent should lack five? Will You destroy the whole city for want of the five?" And the Lord answered, "I will not destroy if I find forty-five there." But Abraham spoke to Him again, and said, "What if forty should be found there?" And the Lord answered, "I will not do it, for the sake of the forty." And Abraham said, "Let not my Lord be angry if I go on: What if thirty should be found there?" And the Lord answered, "I will not do it if I find thirty there." And Abraham said, "I venture again to speak to my Lord: What if twenty should be found there?" And the Lord answered, "I will not destroy, for the sake of the twenty." And Abraham said, "Let not my Lord be angry if I speak but this last time: What if ten should be found there?" And the Lord answered, "I will not destroy, for the sake of the ten."[190]

What is extraordinary about this narrative, unique in Western literature, is its depiction of God, humanity and our relationship. In this text, God is not a distant despot, but rather a *constitutional* monarch.[191] In this passage, much-cited in Jewish sources, God is governed by the same rules as His creatures, obligated to live up to high ethical standards. The man demands of his God, "Shall not the Judge of all the earth act justly?" In these verses, Abraham not only approaches God, but also, like Job much later in the same Tanakh, challenges Him, makes Him think, demands a dialogue, requires an answer, and ultimately changes His mind. It is precisely this negotiating Abraham who is so prized by Jewish tradition.

In rabbinic discussions comparing the righteousness of Noah with Abraham, it is Abraham's readiness to argue, even with his God, that is highly valued.[192]

The Zohar, the thirteenth century Jewish mystical commentary on the Torah, states:

> When Noah came out of the ark
> he opened his eyes and saw the whole world [and all humanity] completely destroyed.
> He began to weep for the world [and complain to God]...
> Noah scolded, "Master of the world, You are called Compassionate!
> You should have shown compassion for Your creatures [and not sent a flood to destroy your glorious creation]!"
> The Blessed Holy One answered him, "Foolish shepherd!
> So now you say this, but not when I spoke to you tenderly, saying
> 'Make yourself an ark of gopher wood...As for Me, I am about to bring the Flood...to destroy all flesh...[Go into the ark, you and all your household] for you alone have I found righteous before Me in this generation'

I [God] lingered with you and spoke to you at length
so that you would ask for mercy for the world!
But as soon as you [Noah] heard that you would be safe in the ark,
the evil of the world did not touch your heart.
You built the ark and saved only yourself and your family.
It is only now that the world has been destroyed that you bother to open
your mouth to utter questions and complaints'"
Rabbi Yohanan said "Come and see the difference between Noah and the
righteous heroes of Israel!
Noah did not shelter his generation
and did not pray for them like Abraham.
For as soon as the Blessed Holy One said to Abraham
'The outcry of Sodom and Gomorrah is so great,'
immediately, 'Abraham came forward and asked,
"Will You sweep away the innocent along with the guilty?"
Abraham countered the Blessed Holy One with more and more words
until finally Abraham implored the Blessed Holy One to forgive the entire
generation, if just ten innocent people could be found…
And Noah, the Blessed Holy One lingered with him and spoke many
words to him [over many hours];
The Blessed Holy One said to Himself, 'Perhaps, *now*, Noah would ask for
mercy for his generation.'
But Noah [unlike Abraham] did not care and did not ask for mercy.
He just built the ark for himself, and alas, the whole world was destroyed
as a result.[193]

And yet, the Abraham of the Akedah is uncharacteristically wordless, more
like the Zohar's Noah than himself, when God commands him to sacrifice his
own son. This Abraham, negotiator par excellence of the torah, is suddenly, surprisingly and utterly mute. Everett Fox comments on Abraham's seeming eagerness to sacrifice Isaac. "We are told of no sleepless night, nor does he ever say a
word to God. Instead, he is described with a series of [active] verbs: hurrying,
saddling, taking, splitting, arising, going."[194]

It is Abraham's atypical silence and unambivalent eagerness to do the sacrifice
that cries out for explanation.

The Akedah: A Selective biblical Exegesis

After these things God (***Elohim***) tested Abraham, and said to him, "Abraham!"
And he said, "Here am I." God said, "Pray take your son, your only son, whom
you love, Isaac, and go-you-forth to the land of Moriah, and offer him up there as
a burnt offering upon one of the mountains of which I shall tell you." So Abraham

rose early in the morning, saddled his ass, and took two of his lads with him, and his son Isaac; and he cut the wood for the burnt offering, and arose and went to the place of which God had told him. On the third day Abraham lifted up his eyes and saw the place afar off. Then Abraham said to his lads, "Stay here with the ass; I and the lad will go yonder and worship, and come again to you." And Abraham took the wood of the burnt offering, and laid it on Isaac his son; and he took in his hand the fire and the knife. So they went both of them together. And Isaac said to his father Abraham, "My father!" And Abraham said, "Here am I, my son." Isaac said, "Behold, the fire and the wood; but where is a lamb for the burnt offering?" Abraham said, "My son, God Himself will provide the lamb for the burnt offering." So they went both of them together. When they came to the place of which God (**Elohim**) had told him, Abraham built a slaughter-site [an altar] there, and laid the wood in order, and bound Isaac his son, and laid him on the altar, upon the wood. Then Abraham put forth his hand, and took the knife to slay his son. But the angel of the Lord (***YHWH***) called to him from heaven, and said, "Abraham, Abraham!" And he said, "Here am I." He said, "Do not lay your hand on the lad or do anything to him; for now I know that you fear God, seeing you have not withheld your son, your only son, from me." And Abraham lifted up his eyes and looked, and behold, behind him was a ram, caught in a thicket by his horns; and Abraham went and took the ram, and offered it up as a burnt offering in the place of his son. So Abraham called the name of that place The Lord will provide; as it is said to this day, "On the mount of the Lord it shall be provided." And the angel of the Lord called to Abraham a second time from heaven, and said, "By myself I have sworn, says the Lord, because you have done this, and have not withheld your son, your only son, I will indeed bless you, and I will multiply your descendants as the stars of heaven and as the sand which is on the seashore. And your descendants shall possess the gate of their enemies, and by your descendants shall all the nations of the earth bless themselves, because you have obeyed my voice." So Abraham returned to his lads, and they arose and went together to Beer-Sheva; and Abraham dwelt at Beer-Sheva.[195]

After these things. Many, ancient and contemporary commentators, have conjectured about the meaning of this phrase that introduces the Akedah text. Protestant biblical exegetes, for example, John Wesley, Matthew Henry, John Calvin, understand the phrase to be a reference to the myriad trials that Abraham was subjected to prior to the Akedah, each of these preparing him for this ultimate test of faith.

John Calvin, the sixteenth century Protestant reformer, writes:

Abraham had passed an unsettled life in continued exile up to his eightieth year; having been harassed with many contumelies and injuries, he had endured with difficulty a miserable and anxious existence, in continual trepidation; famine had driven him out of the land whither he had gone, by the command and under the auspices of God, into Egypt. Twice his wife had been torn from his bosom; he had been separated from his nephew; he had delivered this nephew, when captured in war, at the peril of his own life. He had lived childless with his wife, when yet all his hopes were suspended upon his having offspring. Having at length obtained a son, he was compelled to disinherit him, and to drive him far from home. Isaac alone remained, his special but only consolation; "after these things," Abraham was enjoying peace at home, but now God suddenly thundered out of heaven, denouncing the sentence of death upon this son.[196]

The traditional Jewish sources explain "after these things" in two separate principle ways. In these midrashim, there is symmetry. In the first of these stories, it is heaven that is having impact on the world, whereas in the second, it is a conversation on earth that has impact on heaven.

Rabbi Johanan, in the Talmud, states that "after these things" refers to an incident that happened in the Heavenly Court, reminiscent of a similar scenario that introduces the Book of Job.[197] Satan, the Accuser, approached God and challenged Abraham's faithfulness. When Isaac was weaned, Abraham had given a great feast for all who lived in his land. "Satan said to the Almighty; Sovereign of the Universe! To this old man Thou didst graciously bestow the fruit of the womb at the age of a hundred, yet of all that banquet which Abraham prepared, he did not have even one turtle-dove or pigeon to sacrifice before You!...Replied the Holy One, blessed be He, Yet were I to say to Abraham, Sacrifice thy son before Me, he would do so without hesitation. So, immediately, God did test Abraham."[198]

The second story, the very earthly one, involves the two half brothers Ishmael and Isaac. Ishmael bragged that his circumcision at thirteen years old was more meaningful than Isaac's because Isaac was only an infant, eight days old, and therefore was not able to make choices or fully conscious when Abraham cut his foreskin. Isaac, defending himself to his brother, said, "If God desired of me that I be slaughtered, I would not refuse." The midrash continues, "Said the Holy One, blessed be He, [who was eavesdropping], This is My moment! Immediately, God did test Abraham."[199]

God (*Elohim*) tested Abraham. A stunning and remarkable aspect of the Akedah text is that it is the divine name, *Elohim*, who orders Abraham to sacrifice his son, while it is the messenger-angel of a different divine name, *YHWH, who* abruptly stops the action.

In Part One of this book, we saw how it was *Elohim* alone who was the "leading man" in the first creation narrative. In that text, *Elohim* is the creator of the material world. It is *Elohim* who stands gloriously above and apart, at a creative distance, from all His human, non-human and inanimate creatures. On the contrary, it is *YHWH*, in the second creation account, who walks and speaks with His human creatures. *YHWH* feels their loneliness, expects great things from them, is disappointed with them, makes clothes for them and then exiles them from the Garden. In the two creation texts, *Elohim* is an impersonal God of nature, while *YHWH* is a very personal God of involvement.

In addition, in Chapter Three, we saw that the rabbis understood *Elohim* to signify the judging aspect of God. It was *YHWH*, for the sages, that was associated with divine mercy and compassion. While this talmudic conception of the two divine names added little to our exploration of the creation texts, this rabbinic distinction holds more promise in explaining the shift from *Elohim*, the commander, to *YHWH*, the redeemer, in the Akedah.

A story from the Talmud illustrates this rabbinic dichotomy between God's judgement and compassion.

> Rabbi Yohanan says: How do we know that the Holy One, blessed be He, prays? Because it says, [in Isaiah[200]] "I will bring them to My sacred mountain, and let them rejoice in *My* house of prayer." It does not say "in *their* house of prayer," but "*My* of prayer." From here you see that the Holy One, blessed be He, must pray. The rabbis of the Gemara ask: What could God pray? Rabbi Zutra said: May it be My will that My mercy should suppress My anger, and that My attribute of mercy should dominate My attribute of judgement and all My other attributes, so that I may conduct Myself with My children with mercy, and that I should not deal with them, like a harsh judge, according to the strict letter of the law.[201]

As was also previously discussed, *Elohim* has much older roots in Semitic pagan culture and history than does *YHWH*. *El and its variations are* names of God or the gods that were shared by both the Canaanites speaking Ugaritic and the Israelites speaking Hebrew. *Elohim*, the major biblical name for God, found more than two thousand times in the Tanakh, has a plural ending. It is interesting to note that, even within the Hebrew Bible itself, Elohim signifies both the one God of Israel and the many gods or even goddesses of Israel's neighbors. One example will serve to demonstrate this point that was already made in more detail in Chapter Two. In the Ten Commandments, the Torah text states, "Thou shalt have no other *gods (elohim)* before Me."[202]

When *Elohim* tests Abraham, then, who is it that is Abraham's divine examiner? Who is this *Elohim* at the beginning of the Akedah? Is *Elohim* a remote God of nature, a God of the cosmos, impersonally claiming Isaac's life? Or is *Elohim* a God, in that initial phase of the narrative, whose harsh demand on His Abraham has overtaken His compassion for His chosen one and people? Or is *Elohim* a pernicious pagan deity, a "sacred executioner,"[203] and like other pagan deities in the ancient Near East thirstily requiring only the most precious and beloved of blood to prove to itself that the worshipper is devoted?

Pray take your son, your only son, the one you love, Isaac. Jewish and Christian biblical commentators alike take note of the unusual style of this phrase. Why does God not simply say, "Take Isaac?" Although they disagree concerning what Abraham says and what motivates God, both religious schools of exegesis agree that the Torah here is reporting only one side of a dialogue, having omitted Abraham's part of the conversation.

According to Rashi, God said, "Take your son." Abraham replied, "Which son? I have two." Then God said, "Your only son." Abraham responded, "Each of my sons are the only son to his mother." Then God said, "The one you love." Abraham then replied, "I love them both." It was only then, according to Rashi and the midrashic literature he summarizes, that God made His command to Abraham perfectly manifest—"Isaac."[204]

Rashi asks why God was not more direct concerning His command. The great medieval Jewish commentator, sensitive to the beloved Abraham's advanced age, fragility and state of mind, suggests, "So that God not confuse Abraham suddenly, and cause Abraham to become bewildered and deranged."

Within the Christian tradition, Matthew Henry, in his early eighteenth century verse-by-verse commentary to the Old and New Testaments, also imagines a dialogue between God and Abraham. God said, "Take your son." Abraham said, "How about all my bullocks instead?" God replied, "No. It must be your son." Abraham then asked God, "How about my servants or my steward?" God replied, "No. It must be your son." Abraham then asked, "My adopted son, Ishmael?" God said, "No. It must be your only son by Sarah." Abraham then objected, "But since Ishmael was sent away, I have only Isaac left. Does it have to be Isaac?" God said, "Yes! It must be Isaac, your joy and laughter. Do not send for Ishmael. It must be Isaac!" Abraham complained, "But Isaac is the one I love, my very soul." God said, "I know, Abraham. But it must be your *beloved* son to matter."[205]

Rather than attributing God's motive in lengthening the command to God's compassionate concern for the aged and troubled Abraham as Rashi did, the

Protestant commentators assert that God, by prolonging the command, was sharpening the blade of the Akedah.

John Wesley, the eighteenth century founder of the Methodist Church, comments:

> God appeared to Abraham as He had formerly done, called him by name Abraham, that name which had been given him in ratification of the promise that he would be a father of a multitude: Abraham, like a good servant, readily answered, Here am I; what saith my Lord unto his servant? Probably Abraham expected some renewed promise of the greatness and number of his descendents, but to Abraham's great amazement that which God hath to say to him is in short, Abraham, go kill thy son; and this command is given Abraham in such aggravating language as to make the test abundantly more grievous. When God speaks, Abraham, no doubt, takes notice of each word, and listens attentively to it: and each word here is a *sword in his bones*; the trial is steel'd with trying phrases. Is it any pleasure to the Almighty that He should afflict? No, it is not; yet when Abraham's faith is to be tried, God seems to take pleasure in the aggravation of the trial.[206]

And go-you-forth (*lech-lecha*) to the land of Moriah. The Hebrew phrase that God uses to order Abraham to go forth to sacrifice his Isaac, "*lech-lecha*," is only found in one other place in the entire Tanakh—at the beginning of Abraham's story in the Bible. After ten generations of God's absolute silence, by tradition more than nine hundred years after God spoke to Noah, like a sudden thunderclap from the heavens, God calls to Abraham. What God says to the seventy-year-old soon-to-be Patriarch not only changes Abraham's life, but also radically alters the world. "The Lord said to Abram, '*Lech-lecha*, Go-you-forth from your country, from your kindred and from your father's house to the land which I will show you.'"[207] In response to this command, Abraham follows God into a new land, and invents monotheism.

Ten biblical chapters and at least forty years later, Abraham is now closer to the end of his spiritual journey than to the beginning. Again, the voice, like a unexpected thunderclap rings out from heaven, "*Lech-lecha*, Go-you-forth." And again, Abraham follows God to a place which God will show him. This time, however, that place is Moriah, a three day journey, and the purpose is human sacrifice.

Interestingly, the first time "*lech-lecha*" is commanded by God, when Abraham leaves where he lives and all he knows, is also the first time in the Bible that God ever communicates with Abraham. The Akedah, which is introduced by the same phrase, is the last time in the sacred text that God speaks directly to the aged patriarch. To Abraham, after the Akedah, God is stone silent.

When *"lech-lecha"* is spoken by God for the first time, Abraham is asked to renounce his past. In our Akedah text, when God again utters those same words, it is then that Abraham is commanded to slaughter his future.

Offer him up there as a burnt offering (*olah*). Abraham is given his explicit instructions. Take Isaac and offer him up as a burnt offering, in Hebrew an *"olah."* The root, *"alah,"* of this word involves ascent. that is, the smoke ascending to the heavens after a sacrifice is wholly consumed by fire. The word, *"olah,"* is used six times in the Akedah text.

Throughout the Tanakh, *"olah"* consistently means a burnt offering. Three examples follow:

And Noah built an altar unto the Lord; and took of every clean beast, and of
every clean fowl, and offered burnt offerings (*olah*) on the altar.[208]

An altar of earth you shall make unto Me, and shall sacrifice thereon your burnt
offerings (*olah*), and your peace offerings.[209]

Though you offer Me burnt offerings (*olah*) and your meat offerings, I will not
accept them.[210]

The ancient rabbis were deeply distressed by a number of aspects of the Akedah text. How could God make His promise of an eternal covenant through Isaac in one chapter; then order his slaughter in another; and then, change His mind again a few verses later? The rabbis developed midrashim that maintained that Abraham fundamentally misunderstood God's sacrificial command. midrashically altering the meaning of the word and playing with the ascent aspect of *"olah,"* God, in the midrash, after Abraham is interrupted in his mission by the angel, says to Abraham, "Did I tell you to slaughter your son? No. I told you to take him up. You have taken him up. Now take him down."[211]

It is poignant to note that when the Jewish scribes-sages of the third century BCE translated the Akedah into Greek for inclusion in the Septuagint, they translated *"olah"*, as *"holokautoma,"* Greek for a completely consumed sacrifice. Six hundred years later, when Jerome translated the Bible into Latin, *"olah"* became *"holocaustum."* It is for this reason, and for others, that many are displeased with referring to the murder of one-third of the Jews in the world in the 1940's as the "Holocaust," with its biblical associations to the Akedah and to the ritual sacrifice to honor God.

So Abraham rose early in the morning. Immediately following God telling Abraham the what (offer Isaac up as a burnt offering) and the where (at a mountain which I shall show you), we read that Abraham rises early to prepare for the journey and the sacrifice. The space between these two verses is the loudest silence in the Bible. In this textual fissure, we read of no negotiation with God, no argument with Sarah, no guilty or comforting words to Isaac, no description of Abraham's troublesome dreams or sleep. Instead, the impression of the Torah text is that Abraham eagerly awakes the next morning, anxious to embark on his religious mission.

In the previous biblical chapter, the night before expelling Hagar and Ishmael into the wilderness, Abraham also, using almost identical language, wakes early to do the task. "And Abraham rose up early in the morning, and took bread, and a bottle of water, and gave it unto Hagar, putting it on her shoulder, and the child, and sent her away: and she departed, and wandered in the wilderness of Beer Sheva."[212] However, in this first "sacrifice" of a son, of Ishmael, unlike in the Akedah, Abraham's troubled mind is made explicit. "And the thing [the banishment of Hagar and Ishmael] was very grievous in Abraham's sight because of his son."[213]

For the vast majority of traditional Christian and Jewish commentators, Abraham's willingness and eagerness to do what God tells him to do is highly praised. For example, in the context of a discussion of when a boy should be circumcised during the eighth day, the rabbis of the Talmud taught, "The whole day is valid for circumcision, but that the zealous are early to perform their religious duties, for it is said [in the Akedah], 'And Abraham rose early in the morning!'"[214] This zeal of Abraham to carry out the child sacrifice to God is also explicitly prized by all of the most influential medieval rabbinic commentators, for example, Rashi, the Ramban, Abraham ibn Ezra and Maimonides.

Among the Christian biblical commentators, John Calvin argues the heroism of Abraham's eagerness to sacrifice his son most explicitly and articulately. He writes:

> This promptitude [to do God's will in Genesis 22] shows the greatness of Abraham's faith. Innumerable thoughts might come into the mind of the holy man; each of which would have overwhelmed his spirit, unless he had fortified it by faith. And there is no doubt that Satan, during the darkness of the previous night, would heap upon Abraham a vast mass of cares. Gradually to overcome them, by contending with them, was the part of heroical courage. But when they were overcome, then immediately to gird himself to the fulfillment of the command of God, and even to rise early in the morning to do it, was a remarkable effort. Other men, prostrated by a message so dire and terrible, would have fainted, and have lain torpid, as if deprived of life; but the first dawn of morning was scarcely early enough for Abraham's haste.[215]

The enthusiastic and unambivalent praise for Abraham's obedience to God's command to sacrifice his son and his evident eagerness to do the act, rising *early in the morning*, saddling his ass…, is challenged by many Akedah interpreters since the early nineteenth century.[216] As we already discussed earlier in this chapter, Immanuel Kant, writing in 1798, was one of the first to propose, within his larger vision of a pure moral religion based on reason, an ethical critique of the Akedah. He questions the divinity of any God who would order such a grotesquely unethical act. Kant proposes that Abraham, instead of rising early in the morning to sacrifice his son, should have said to God the night before, "That I ought not to kill my good son is quite certain. But that you, this apparition, is God—of that I am not certain, and never can be, not even if your voice resounds from the heaven."[217]

Martin Buber (1878-1965), the Jewish existential philosopher and biblical translator and scholar, was also troubled by Abraham's mute eagerness to follow what he thought was God's voice ordering the sacrifice. Buber, like Kant, asserts that if one's moral conscience experiences a "divine" voice ordering some act of cruelty, then the voice must be totally rejected. Since Moloch, according to Buber, sometimes can appear to be God, one must only listen to God's voice when it commands you (quoting Micah[218]) "to act justly, love mercy and to walk humbly with your God."[219]

The intensity of the critical rhetoric concerning Abraham's seemingly blind and passive obedience to God's authority in Genesis 22, his silent rising early in the morning, is particularly marked in the commentaries on the Akedah written by contemporary scholars who are from the post-Nazi genocide and post-Vietnam War generation. Michael Lerner (born in 1943), rabbi and Editor of *Tikkun Magazine*, drawing on midrashic traditions concerning Abraham's father's and Nimrod's attempt to murder Abraham in a furnace, wonders whether the voice Abraham hears ordering him to sacrifice his son is merely a psychopathological repetitive voice from his own past, a voice that perpetuates the child abuse he experienced, rather than the voice of God. Lerner writes, "Like so many of those in the land that he left, Abraham hears the voices of the gods of his past, now in the voice of God, telling him to do to his own son what was done to him. As he was thrown into the fire, so he will pass on the pain to his beloved."[220]

Burton Visotzky, born soon after World War II, a rabbi on the faculty of the Jewish Theological Seminary, describes Abraham as a depressive who is prone to physical violence and lives his last years alienated from his entire family. Visotzky writes, "Abraham dwells in Beer Sheva, far from Isaac, far from Sarah who is in Hebron, far from Ishmael and Hagar in Egypt. In the end, Abraham is close only to

God." Later, commenting on the Torah text that describes Isaac and Ishmael joining together to bury their father Abraham, Visotzky wonders, "Did each shovel the dirt with a barely concealed glee, inwardly satisfied to be burying their abuser?"[221]

And then there is the question whether Abraham rises early in the morning and, although a man of considerable wealth, saddles his own ass in order that the household, and especially Sarah, not be awoken. Sarah is, after all, wholly absent from the Akedah text. Did she know that Abraham was planning to sacrifice their long-hoped-for and long-awaited child? If she knew, could she have approved?[222]

In the biblical chapter that immediately follows the Akedah, we learn that Sarah dies at the age of one hundred twenty-seven. The rabbis almost universally conclude from this that it was the Akedah—either the fact of the near-slaughter of her beloved son by her own husband, or because of inaccurate information she received that Isaac was, in actuality, murdered—that killed her.[223] This leads one to determine that, when Abraham rose early in the morning to walk with his God to the mountain and sacrifice his and Sarah's son, Sarah was unaware of the nature of her husband's journey. Abraham was, by his own choice, excruciatingly alone.[224]

On the third day. Abraham's sacrificial venture was not the impulsive passionate act of a mad zealot, swept away by his love for God and the command he heard.[225] The Torah is explicit that Abraham had three full days to consider. For both John Wesley and Rashi, Abraham's sacrifice of his Isaac was a deliberate, conscious and rational plan.[226]

The three day walk to Moriah, the excruciating lonely journey of Abraham, his son, the donkey and two servants, is imagined to be a silent, isolated and tormented pilgrimage for the Patriarch. Given the total lack of detail in the Torah about what transpired during those three portentous days, many midrashim, classical and contemporary, have been created to fill in this textual gap. Abraham is pictured as staring straight ahead, narrow and single-minded in his resolve, never discussing with any of the travelling party what is on his mind or in his plans.

Some midrashim describe additional trials that challenge Abraham's determination on the road from Beer Sheva to Moriah during these three days.[227] In one of these, that I find particularly provocative and unsettling, the donkey travelling with the group turns to his master Abraham and asks, "My master, are you *sure* that the voice you heard was God's voice?"

> **Where is a lamb for the burnt offering?** Throughout the Akedah text, we see Abraham rising, saddling, taking, cutting, speaking, but it is not until almost halfway through the narrative that we hear for the first and last time from Isaac.

The father and son had just left the donkey and the two lads behind. Now, Abraham carrying the fire and the knife, and Isaac, carrying the wood for the altar, are alone together for the first time and walking toward their shared and separate destination. It is at this point that Isaac seems to suspect and question what is about to happen. Isaac says to his father that he sees the fire and the knife for the ritual sacrifice, "but where is a lamb for the burnt offering?" Abraham, paradoxically, lies to his son and accurately predicts the future. Abraham replies, "My son, God Himself will provide the lamb."

The rabbis of the Talmud and midrash, for arithmetic and emotional reasons, assert that Isaac is thirty-seven years old at the time of the Akedah.[228] If one assumes, as the midrash does, that Sarah at the age of one hundred twenty-seven dies soon after hearing of Abraham's attempted slaughter of her beloved son,[229] then Isaac must have been thirty-seven on Mount Moriah. Sarah, after all, according to the Torah text, was ninety years old when she gave birth to Isaac.[230]

Isaac's manhood is also maintained because of the troubling nature of the Akedah narrative and the heroic figures who are its principle characters. To understand the story as an ancient Abraham leading his young unaware and passive lad/lamb to his slaughter is much more emotionally distressing than understanding Isaac as an autonomous grown man. And yet, what is indicated by the Hebrew of the actual Torah text is that Isaac was a boy, probably a young adolescent, old enough to carry his own wood but innocent and docile in his relationship with his father.[231]

The Genesis 22 biblical text uses the term, "na'ar," five times. Three of these are in reference to the two assistants who accompany Abraham and Isaac to Moriah. Two times "na'ar" is a reference to Isaac himself. "On the third day Abraham lifted up his eyes and saw the place afar off. Then Abraham said to his lads (*na'ar*), 'Stay here with the ass; I and the lad (*na'ar*) will go yonder and worship, and come again to you.'" "Then Abraham put forth his hand, and took the knife to slay his son. But the angel of the Lord called to him from heaven, and said,…'Do not lay your hand on the lad (*na'ar*) or do anything to him.'"

"*Na'ar*" in Tanakh Hebrew means a boy, from infancy to adolescence.[232] In order to harmonize the ages in the Sarah texts and to make the Akedah more emotionally tolerable to the rabbis, the young boy Isaac in Genesis 22 is transformed in the rabbinic imagination into a thirty-seven-year-old man with choice and volition.

So in our Akedah text, the young boy Isaac asks his father, "Where is a lamb for the burnt offering?" not yet consciously aware that he *is* the lamb and the offering. Reviewing the rest of the Torah, after this Akedah question, we discover that Isaac never again speaks to his father.

And bound Isaac his son. The Torah text offers us no details about what Abraham or Isaac are feeling, whether they walk close together or at a distance from each other, or whether they are speaking with each other as they approach the place where Abraham will construct the slaughter-site. For these details, one must turn to the midrashic imagination.

The most moving of these midrashim that takes as subject these final moments immediately preceding Abraham's binding of Isaac on the altar was written by a person who was neither Jewish, nor a cleric, nor aware of the vast midrashic library on the Akedah. The Danish philosopher, Soren Kierkegaard in *Fear and Trembling* (1843), wrote four separate and creative versions of this same moment.

In one of Kierkegaard's four scenarios, Abraham tries desperately to explain to Isaac why he needs to sacrifice him. The young Isaac cannot understand. So Abraham, heroically, decides to sacrifice his own social face and fatherhood. To his son, Abraham pretends that he has suddenly become an insane and blood-thirsty idolater so that Isaac will maintain his faith in God, at the expense of losing his faith in Abraham.

Kierkegaard writes,

> Abraham left the lads behind and went on alone up the mountain with Isaac beside him. But Abraham said to himself: "I won't conceal from Isaac where this way is leading him." He stood still, laid his hand on Isaac's head to give him his blessing, and Isaac bent down to receive it. And Abraham's expression was fatherly, his gaze gentle, his speech encouraging. But Isaac could not understand him [Abraham's plan to sacrifice Isaac], Isaac's soul could not be uplifted; he clung to Abraham's knees, pleaded at his feet, begged for his young life, for his fair promise; he called to mind the joy in Abraham's house, reminded of the sorrow and the loneliness. Then Abraham lifted the boy up and walked with him, taking him by the hand, and his words were full of comfort and exhortation. But Isaac did not understand him. Abraham climbed the mountain in Moriah, but Isaac did not understand him. Then Abraham turned away from Isaac for a moment, but when Isaac saw his father's face a second time it was changed, Abraham's gaze was wild, his mien was one of horror. He caught Isaac by the chest, threw him to the ground and said: "Foolish boy, do you believe I am your father? I'm an idolater. Do you believe this is God's command? No, it is my own desire." Then Isaac trembled and in his anguish cried: "God in heaven have mercy on me, God of Abraham have mercy on me; if I have no father on earth, then be Thou my father!" Below his breath Abraham said to himself: "Lord in heaven I thank You; it is after all better that my son believe that I am a monster than that he lose faith in You."[233]

The denouement of the Akedah has now been reached. The rabbis paint a midrashic picture of the scene with great emotional intensity. Isaac begs his father to bind him tightly so that he not move and negate the sacrifice. Isaac, bound and gagged on the altar, his father, cheeks wet with tears, standing over him with knife poised and ready, awaits the fatal blow. The angels in heaven weep. Their tears fall on Isaac and Abraham and the altar. They plead with God to change His mind.[234]

And then, loudly, suddenly, urgently, without warning, the angel of the Lord (*YHWH*) calls to Abraham two times, "Abraham, Abraham!" And the knife falls. The rabbis of the Zohar ask why the angel calls twice. The Zohar answers because the second time Abraham hears his name called, only then has he been awoken and transformed, only then is he an "other," a man with a changed set of ears so that he can hear different words from his God.[235]

So Abraham returned to his lads. Throughout its nineteen verses, while sketchy in some of its details concerning dialogue, behavior and state of mind, the Akedah text is unusually explicit and precise concerning who did what to and with whom. We know whom Abraham took with him on his sacrificial pilgrimage. We know, when he embarked up the mountain, with whom he traveled and who they were that were left behind. We read twice in the text, referring to Abraham and Isaac, and leaving no room for ambiguity, that "So they went both of them together."

Given this context, the final verse of our text in which Abraham returns (*vayashav*, the Hebrew verb is singular) to his lads from the top of Mount Moriah is perplexing and troubling. Where is Isaac?

There are three answers from the traditional midrashic sources, all quite fanciful, to explain why Isaac is not with Abraham at the end of the text. The first conjectures that Isaac traveled immediately following the Akedah to an academy where he studied Torah.[236] The second states that, since Isaac robbed death at the last moment, that Abraham worried about retaliation for this from the Evil Eye. In order to avoid discovery by this vindictive force, Abraham sent Isaac home at night.[237] The third imagines an Isaac who needed to recover from the traumatic experience he had just suffered through. The angels, who had wept over his altar and begged God to save his life, now carry Isaac to paradise where he convalesces for a period of three years.[238] Menahem Mendel of Kotzk, the nineteenth century Chasidic master, also commenting on our verse, taught that although it was painful for Abraham to bind Isaac on the altar, it was even more difficult to release him. For Abraham realized that Isaac, as long as Isaac lived, would never forget that his own father almost took his young life from him.

A fourth explanation, far from fanciful, as to where Isaac is at the end of the Akedah offers a poignant glimpse into the hearts and minds of the Jews who lived during the most tragic and bloody period of European history before the twentieth century. In the eleventh, twelfth and thirteenth centuries, Christian Europe organized a series of Crusades to "save" the sacred sites of Christendom in the Holy Land from the Muslims who defiled them. Quickly, the focus of the Crusader's rage and violence expanded from the Muslim living in the Holy Land to the Jew living in Christian Europe. On their way to defeat the children of Muhammad, in a frenzy of religious fervor and demonic aggression, the Crusaders decided to punish the "Christ killers." It was rumored that Godfrey of Bouillon, the leader of the First Crusade, had pledged that he would not lead his army to the Holy Land until the crucifixion of the Lord Jesus was satisfactorily avenged by spilling every drop of Jewish blood in Europe.

In the three Crusades, spanning more than three hundred years, one Jewish community after another was given the choice of conversion or death. In most cases, in Cologne, Worms, Mainz, Norwich, Lynn, York and countless other towns and villages, Jews chose death over conversion. Mass suicides of entire towns in a single day was not uncommon.

For all Jewish communities in Christian Europe, living with the imminent possibility that each Jewish parent will be required to kill his children before killing himself, the Akedah took on new and terrifying significance. On May 27, 1096, at the beginning of the First Crusade, the entire Jewish community of Mainz, well over one thousand people, was slaughtered or slaughtered themselves. The following early twelfth century Hebrew liturgical poem describes the martyrdom of Mainz and the way in which these Jews understood their experience in the context of the Akedah:

> Oh, how the children cried aloud!
> Trembling, they see their brothers slaughtered;
> The mother binding her son,
> Lest he profane the sacrifice by shuddering;
> The father making the ritual blessing to sanctify the slaughter.
>
> Compassionate women strangle their own children;
> Pure virgins shriek bitterly;
> Brides kiss their bridegrooms farewell;
> And all rush eagerly to be slaughtered.

Almighty Lord, dwelling on high,

In days of old the angels cried out to You to put a halt to *one* sacrifice.

And now so many are bound and slaughtered;

Why do the angels not clamour over *my* infants?[239]

We now return to the question of where is Isaac at the end of the Akedah. Shalom Spiegel (1899-1984), Professor of Medieval Hebrew Literature at the Jewish Theological Seminary, in his scholarly volume in which he cites Hebrew poetry, midrashim and homilies that survive from this period, asserts that the Jews living during the Crusades found comfort in interpreting the final verse of the Akedah, "So Abraham returned to his lads [without Isaac], as confirming that Abraham did in actuality sacrifice Isaac at Mount Moriah.[240] After all, people taught, reasoned and believed, how could God expect more from us, that is, completed child sacrifices, than He did from Abraham, His chosen one. "Many medieval Jewish communities suffering persecution saw themselves as re-enacting the drama of the Akedah without the redemptive ending."[241]

It is interesting to note in the context of the Spiegel assertion, that the prophetic reading—the Haftarah, in most cases, chosen as a subtle elaboration and interpretation of the specific weekly Torah portion—paired with the chanting of the Akedah text in the yearly Torah cycle in the synagogue is 2 Kings 4:1-37. In this text, Elisha, a prophet of God, revives the dead child of the righteous Shunnamite woman. "Elisha came into the house, and there was the boy, laid out dead on his couch…Elisha put his mouth on the dead boy's mouth, Elisha's eyes on the dead boy's eyes, and Elisha's hands on the dead boy's hands. As Elisha bent over the corpse, the child's body became warm,…and the boy opened his eyes."[242]

Wherever Isaac was at the end of the Akedah, it is clear that Abraham travels down the mountain and back to Beer Sheva a different man than when he left only three days before. But what was it that changed on that isolated mountaintop, long ago, when Abraham bound his son and took the knife to slay him? What is it that happened in the Akedah that still resonates within our psyche and our soul?

What Happened on Mount Moriah

God, Abraham and the Akedah can be viewed through three discrete conceptual prisms. These are the traditional, the socio-historical and the psychological.

The traditional view, irrespective of its origins in Judaism, Christianity or Islam, holds that not only is the text perfect and sacred, but also, for the most part, are the principle characters of God and Abraham. The many gaps and ambiguities in the Akedah narrative are filled in by developing a running commentary that interprets God and Abraham "upward," that is, that provides the most positive "spin" on their behavior and motivations. For example, for the traditionalist, God only tests those He knows will pass. Or God, at the beginning of the story, knows how it will end. Or God really did not mean to have Abraham sacrifice his son at all, but rather He meant to have Abraham merely *prepare* his son for a sacrifice. It was Abraham who misunderstood the command.

Turning from God to Abraham: Abraham does not question God's command to kill Isaac, nor delays his embarking on the sacrificial mission because Abraham is a faithful God-fearing servant anxious to fulfill all of God's wishes. Or Abraham answers Isaac's question about the lamb with a lie, "God Himself will provide the lamb," because of compassion for his vulnerable Isaac. Or Abraham, out of concern for Isaac's safety, returns alone to Beer Sheva, only after taking steps to guard against the retaliation of the Evil Eye.

The rabbinic understanding of Isaac as a thirty-seven-year-old man, contradictory to the actual Hebrew text, also is an example of the traditionalist's tendency to interpret upward. If Isaac is an aware and cooperating mature sacrifice then the emotional and theological sting of God and Abraham conspiring to kill the young innocent is lessened.

The second view conceptualizes God and Abraham within a specific social and historical context. From this perspective, God is not timeless nor is Abraham necessarily a model to emulate. Both of these characters and the Akedah itself, function within a circumscribed milieu. This socio-cultural milieu is inhabited and dominated by gods who demand human blood to prove obedience, where the most righteous of the devotees readily and willingly sacrifice to their gods that which is most beloved to them, and where children are seen as property and merely a means to an end.

Within this socio-historical position, the Akedah represents both the old and the new. The Akedah narrative is firmly embedded in a pagan sacrificial worldview, while stretching culture toward a shift in paradigm. The new paradigm is characterized by a worldview where human life is considered sacred, where ethics take precedence over obedience and where God no longer demands human blood for His worship.

The psychological viewpoint constructs the Akedah narrative as a story about "Every Man." Whereas the traditional position assumes that Abraham represents the heroic ideal, and the socio-historical perspective assumes that Abraham represents a prototype who lived within a specific time and place, the psychological perspective assumes that the struggles that Abraham grapples with in the Akedah are *our* struggles.

In the Akedah, Abraham and we are forced to confront ourselves. We are forced to confront our ambivalence about the younger generation, the helpless, innocent and the vulnerable. We are forced to confront our impulse to sacrifice our children to our own agenda. We are forced to confront our eagerness to betray our future, hope, aspirations, ideals and goals.

We, like Abraham in the Akedah, struggle with our paganism each day. Paganism is not just the worship of statues or the Earth goddess, that is, the reverence for the concrete over the abstract Deity. Paganism is placing things and ideologies above people, and possessions and ego above ethical values.[243] Paganism, whether it is the paganism of Abraham in the Akedah text or our form of paganism in the early twenty-first century, is placing the things that matter most at the mercy of the things that matter least.[244]

Firmly within this psychological perspective, W. Gunther Plaut, a rabbi and biblical commentator, writing about the Akedah, contends, "The story may thus be read as a paradigm for the father and son relationship. In a way, every parent seeks to dominate his child and is in danger of seeking to sacrifice him to his parental plans or hopes. In the biblical story [of the Akedah], God is present and can therefore stay the father's hand. In all too many repetitions of the scene, God is absent and the knife falls."[245]

It is this psychological perspective that is the conceptual backdrop within which we now explore what took place on Mount Moriah.

Abraham, rather than a knight of faith, is a hero of transformation. When he rises early in the morning, saddles his ass and takes his son, his donkey and his two lads for the three-day journey to Moriah, Abraham is listening to one type of divine voice. This voice is a much more ancient and generic God of nature. He is a God like the gods with whom he grew up and that he shares with his Semitic neighbors. At the beginning of the Akedah, Abraham is listening to *Elohim* who requires, at this point in human history, like Moloch, what *El* and his divine relatives have always required—the blood of the beloved.

When Abraham arrives at the top of Moriah, with only his son as human witness, Abraham hears a new voice, a new God. This God is a God of personal relationship and involvement, compassion and ethics. *YHWH*, and His messengers, do not require human blood as sacrifice. On the contrary, *YHWH* and His court thoroughly detest the practice.

When the angel calls to Abraham from heaven the first time, Abraham still hears the voice of the primordial God with the old command. By the time the angel calls the second time from heaven, Abraham has changed. As the Zohar says Abraham has become an "other" with new ears. Abraham is now, for the first time, able to hear a brand new divine message. What Abraham hears with his new ears is that human life is sacred above all things.

What made it possible for Abraham to hear the new and different voice on Mount Moriah? How did Abraham become a monotheist that day? What was it that led to Abraham's transformation?

The answer is two-fold. First, Abraham became exquisitely aware of himself. The three days of silent torment, his slow and excruciating pilgrimage to Moriah, was Abraham's transformative experience, his "self analysis." Many cultures from different epochs describe how self awareness is essential to an individual choosing a new choice. For the Delphi Oracle, it was, "Know thyself."[246] For John in the Christian Gospel, it was, "the truth shall make you free."[247] For Maimonides, it was self awareness as the basis of *teshuvah*, true repentance.[248] For Freud, it was making the unconscious conscious.[249]

Second, on Moriah, when Abraham bound his son on the altar, perhaps for the first time in Isaac's life, Abraham *saw* Isaac. Before this, Abraham may have viewed Isaac as an instrument of his own hopes and plans, or as a confirmation of God fulfilling a promise He had made to Abraham, or as a precious fruit of Sarah's and his aged marriage. Moriah and the altar forced Abraham to look directly into Isaac's eyes and face, and as a result, to see God.

We know that it is much more difficult to hurt the other when we see the other as a self, when we truly apprehend the other's personhood. The existential philosophers refer to this as recognizing the other as subject.[250] The cognitive psychologists, who have researched the maturational development of this capacity in children, describe this phenomenon as, "every 'you' is an 'I' to the 'you.'"[251] It is this same human capacity that Carl Rogers[252] and Heinz Kohut[253] refer to as, "empathy," the psychotherapist's most important agent of therapeutic change. For the rabbis of the Talmud and Muhammad in the Koran, it is the teaching that whoever destroys a single life destroys the world; and whoever saves a single life saves the entire world.[254]

In addition, the recognition of the other as self is the essential teaching of the single most radical statement of universal and ethical monotheism in any sacred text—that each of us, without exception or qualification, is created in God's image.[255]

So, in the Akedah, when Abraham is at the verge of sacrificing his son, bound and terrified on the altar, who is this Isaac to Abraham? What does this Isaac symbolize for us in this shared cultural dream?

First, Isaac represents all those who depend upon us for their very survival, dignity and contentment. Isaac represents all those who follow us, sometimes unaware, where we are leading them, for example, our children, our spouses, our parents, our colleagues, employees and employers, our friends. Isaac represents all those in our lives who are positively and negatively impacted by our choices and behavior.

Second, Isaac represents the most profound and hidden psychological level of each of us. We each carry within us a terrified and helpless Isaac, bound to our altars, from whom we distance ourselves, and often disavow.

Last, Isaac, for us as well as for Abraham, represents our dreams, our aspirations, our meaning, our life's purpose. For Abraham, standing over his son in that barren and isolated mountain, knife in hand, Isaac was his and God's single link to the future. It was this bound and about-to-be-slaughtered Isaac who was Abraham's and God's only hope for monotheism.

Abraham Joshua Heschel wrote, "Man must strive for the summit to survive on the ground."[256] And yet, too often, do we, like Abraham in the Akedah, try to level and destroy our own mountaintops.

Abraham's struggle with himself on Mount Moriah is *our* struggle. We need to grapple with our own paganism that sees ourselves and others as means to an end. We, like Abraham on Moriah, need to become true monotheists who have a profound reverence for human life—our own and others'.

What these sparse, troubling, complex and multi-layered nineteen verses of the Torah teach us is that human transformation *is* possible, only when we find that God within each of us that forcefully restrains our arm when we, like Abraham, are all too ready to slaughter our Isaacs.

5

From Jacob to Israel: Transformation in a Larger Context

Midway on our life's journey, I found myself in dark woods, the right road lost. To tell about those woods is hard, so tangled and rough and savage, that thinking of it now I can feel the old fears stirring. Death is hardly more bitter.

—*Dante Alighieri "The Divine Comedy"*

For no individual in the Bible is there such a comprehensive and continuous biography as there is for the Jacob of the Book of Genesis. For Abraham, Jacob's grandfather, the text and God are silent until Abraham is fully seventy years old. It is only then that we discover an already-aged Abraham, following God's abruptly-audible voice commanding him to leave his father's house and land. The biography of Isaac, Jacob's father, only slightly more complete than Abraham's has a number of large and significant gaps—between Isaac's birth and the Akedah, between the Akedah and his marriage to Rebecca, between his failing health and eyesight at age one hundred and Isaac's death eighty years later.

The biographer of Jacob has a much happier time with his subject. First of all, he has interesting and meaningful information concerning at least one set of grandparents. In addition, he has access to critically-significant data concerning both of his subject's parents. For example, he knows about a traumatic experience that his subject's father suffered when he traveled with his father to Mount Moriah many years before Jacob's conception. He knows how Jacob's parents met and about their early marriage. He also knows something about the long and suffering years of infertility that preceded Jacob's birth and how the couple dealt with this, and the subject's mother's prenatal and childbirth experience. In addition, Jacob's biographer has invaluable and voluminous information concerning the relationship between Jacob and his twin brother. This includes some word-for-word dialogues between the two boys. The biographer knows which parent allied with which son. He even knows something about what motivated these momentous and hurtful alliances.

Jacob's biographer has an almost-linear and -continuous history of his subject's length of days from before Jacob was born to his death at age one hundred forty-seven. As primary source, this biographer has the Book of Genesis, twenty-six of its fifty chapters, devoted to Jacob's birth, life, death and children.

For the psychoanalytically-informed biographer, the Genesis account of Jacob's experiences reads like modern case history. We first learn about who Jacob and his family are. We see the nature and quality of his parents' relationship with each other and with their children. We sense the psychic conflict with his twin brother. We discover the parental context within which the sibling struggles are positioned. We perceive the nature and intensity of Jacob's ambivalent relationship with each of his parents. We recognize the power differential between Jacob's mother and father. We observe the ways in which each of the parents declares *one* of the sons as the *one* the parent supports and loves. For the psychoanalytic biographer, Jacob's character is lucidly and articulately revealed in the biblical narrative which spans Jacob's first forty years of life, all of which are spent within the parental home.

Then the psychoanalytic case history in the Book of Genesis describes the middle phase of Jacob's "treatment." It is in this phase that one sees the "analysand's" response to his new life circumstances, with new difficulties. We see Jacob surviving in the wilderness, a refugee from his brother's rage. We see him reacting to God's abundant blessing with less than a mature response. We see our "patient" find his way toward becoming his own person in relation to his crude and conniving uncle/father-in-law. We see Jacob deal with a household filled with conflictual and competitive wives, concubines and children.

It is during this phase of Jacob's "treatment" that he develops the insight and strength to do what he was unable heretofore to do. At this point in the narrative, Jacob leaves his father-in-law's home at the head of his large and complex family, and returns to his parental homeland. At the end of this phase of his "treatment," Jacob faces his brother and himself.

For the psychoanalytic case historian, the single critical "session" of Jacob's "treatment" is the night that Jacob wrestles with the angel and emerges from the experience limping, renamed "Israel," and transformed.

The astute and objective psychoanalytic biographer, scrutinizing the clinical record neatly laid out for him in the Book of Genesis, discovers that Jacob's transformation is neither complete nor consistent. Although Jacob is a more cohesive figure than he was before he wrestled the angel, the analysand sometimes reverts to old patterns and habits. He still, sometimes, refuses to recognize his responsibility for his suffering. He still, sometimes, shows a tendency toward deception. He still, sometimes, demonstrates an insensitivity to the feelings of those he does not favor.

Enveloped by the vast wealth of clinical data in Jacob's case history that comprises the last half of the Book of Genesis, the psychoanalytic case historian conjectures that important features of the case of Jacob are representative of all human cases, both ancient and contemporary. The psychoanalytic case historian sees in the biblical clinical narrative evidence that Jacob does in fact change, although this transformation is limited. In his quieter, more contemplative and less defended moments, the psychoanalyst wonders whether Jacob's limitation in becoming fully transformed is actually a limitation of the contemporary psychoanalytic perspective. Perhaps, psychoanalysts expect too much from their patients—expecting that radical characterological transformation should occur in a single generation. Considering both his ancient and contemporary analysands, Jacob's psychoanalyst speculates that what this biblical case history demonstrates is that Jacob's becoming *partly* Israel is necessary for his son Joseph to become *fully* Joseph.

Before There Was a Jacob

When attempting to understand the character of Jacob's father Isaac, it is significant to note that there are no stories in the Torah involving Isaac as an *active* agent. In the Book of Genesis, we read about Isaac's birth, his circumcision eight days later, his weaning and then, his being led to the slaughter-site on Mount Moriah by his father. In each of these biblical narratives, Isaac is passive and almost completely silent. Isaac's only reported utterance before age forty in the Book of Genesis is a question he poses to his father, innocent and docile in its tenor, "Behold, the fire and the wood; but where is a lamb for the burnt offering?"[257]

Then, surprisingly, Isaac is absent from the text in which Sarah, his mother, is buried.[258] In addition, unlike all of the other major male figures in the Genesis narrative, for example, Ishmael, Esau, Jacob and every one of Jacob's twelve sons, the Torah makes explicit that it is Isaac's father, through his servant Eliezer, who finds a wife for Isaac. The text reads:

Abraham was now old, advanced in years, and the Lord had blessed Abraham in all things. And Abraham said to the senior servant of his household, who had charge of all that he owned, "Put your hand under my thigh and I will make you swear by the Lord, the God of heaven and the God of the earth, that you will not take a wife for my son from the daughters of the Canaanites among whom I dwell, but will go to the land of my birth and get a wife for my son Isaac." And the servant said to him, "What if the woman does not consent to follow me to this land, shall I then take your son back to the land from which you came?" Abraham answered him, "On no account must you take my son back there![259]

In this and other Torah texts, there is no evidence that the forty-year-old Isaac is either involved in his father's plan to marry him to one of his cousins, or, for that matter, even aware of it.

Eliezer, Abraham's chief servant, travels to Abraham's brother's land. There, Eliezer meets an energetic and gracious young girl who takes care of him and his animals. Later, Eliezer discovers that this girl is Abraham's brother's granddaughter, Rebecca. The text describes this encounter that has far-reaching consequences:

Rebecca…came out with her jar on her shoulder. The maiden was very beautiful, a virgin whom no man had known. She went down to the spring, filled her jar, and came up. Eliezer [testing her] ran toward her and said, "Please, let me sip a little water from your jar." "Drink, my lord," she said, and she quickly lowered her jar upon her hand and let him drink. When she had let him drink his fill, she said, "I will also draw for your camels, until they finish drinking." Quickly emptying her jar into the trough, she ran back to the well to draw, and she drew for all his camels.[260]

Rebecca easily passes the test. She is young, a virgin, beautiful, compassionate and, most important and unlike the description of Isaac thus far, active. Rebecca *quickly* lowers the jar to allow Eliezer to drink. She then *quickly* empties the jar to allow her to water the stranger's camels. Then, Rebecca *runs* to tend to the animals. It is Rebecca's character—her vigorous and humane treatment of the stranger—that marks her as the one chosen to marry Isaac.

Isaac, three years after his mother's death, meditating in the field at the end of the day, sees the caravan of Eliezer and Rebecca approach. In a highly romantic and telling verse of the biblical text, Isaac finds comfort for Sarah's death in Rebecca. The text is generally translated as, "Isaac brought Rebecca into the tent of his mother, Sarah. He married Rebecca, and she became his wife, and Isaac loved her. Isaac was then consoled for the loss of his mother."[261] The literal translation of the Hebrew is different. It reads, "And Isaac brought her into the tent and she *was* Sarah, his mother..."[262] Rashi, commenting on this verse, and drawing on its more precise Hebrew meaning, writes, "Isaac brought her to the tent and, behold, she is his mother Sarah. That is, she became the image of his mother Sarah. For, as long as Sarah was alive, [she followed the Jewish law, the halakhot, and made the home a pleasant place, that is,] a candle burned from Friday to Friday, a blessing was constantly in the dough, and a cloud [of the Divine Presence] hung over the tent. When Isaac's mother died [these things] ceased and when Rebecca arrived, they returned."[263]

Within the Protestant Christian tradition, John Calvin also comments on this Torah verse. Noting the profundity and duration of Isaac's mourning for his mother, Calvin writes:

> Since Isaac's grief for the death of his mother was only now [three years later] first assuaged, we infer how great had been its vehemence; for a period sufficiently long had already elapsed. We may also hence infer, that the affection of Isaac was tender and gentle: and that his love for his mother was of no common kind, seeing he had so long lamented her death. And the knowledge of this fact is useful to prevent us from imagining that the holy patriarchs were men of savage manners and of iron hardness of heart, and from becoming like those who conceive fortitude to consist in brutality.[264]

The first twenty years of Isaac's and Rebecca's marriage is without children. Infertility in the Genesis matriarchs, Sarah, Rebecca and later, Rachel, is a consistent motif of the biblical narrative. In each case, the chosen son is not born by natural events, but rather, involves a special divine act. First, Isaac is born to a mother, ninety years old and significantly beyond her years of childbearing. Her pregnancy is commanded by God and announced by His angels to the astonished elderly couple. Jacob is born to a much-younger mother. However, although probably sixty years her mother-in-law's junior, Rebecca also needs a special act of God to become pregnant, "Isaac pleaded with the Lord on behalf of his wife, because she was barren; and the Lord heard Isaac's plea and Isaac's wife, Rebecca, conceived."[265] This narrative is essentially repeated with Jacob's Rachel, "And God remembered Rachel, and God attended to her, and opened her womb."[266] The result of this latter divine edict is the birth of Joseph.

This literary motif—that the chosen one in a given generation is not born by natural circumstances, but requires direct and miraculous intervention on the part of God—is one of the roots for the similar, but more concrete version of this narrative one finds in Christian theology. Jesus is also not born by natural circumstances, but requires the impregnation of Mary by the Holy Spirit.

While the three Hebrew matriarchs suffer their infertility in a somewhat similar way, the patriarchs have divergent reactions to their wives' unhappy childless state. Abraham is amused and laughs when God informs him that God will, in fact, fulfill His promises and grant the old couple a child. Isaac turns to God on Rebecca's behalf. Jacob shows anger at Rachel for her demand for a child. Unlike his father and grandfather, there is no biblical text describing Jacob entreating God to give Rachel a child.

Isaac's marriage is unlike his father's or his son's. Both Abraham and Jacob marry more than one woman and have additional concubines. When their wives are found to be infertile, both Abraham and Jacob conceived children by their concubines as substitutes. Interestingly, this ancient Near Eastern solution to the problem of a woman's infertility is not even mentioned in the Isaac-Rebecca Genesis narrative. So Isaac remains in a monogamous relationship with Rebecca, and, for twenty years, prays that she conceive.

A perusal of the Genesis stories, in which Isaac is depicted operating outside of the family dramas between father and sons, reveals that Isaac forges no new paths. We read that Isaac, like his father, chose to lie about Rebecca's relationship to him to protect his life. We see Isaac traveling the same geographical turf that Abraham traveled. The Torah makes this aspect of Isaac and his narrative explicit when it says, "Isaac dug anew the wells that were dug in the days of his father, Abraham…And Isaac gave them the same names that his father had given them."[267]

As we have seen, an examination of the biblical text, before Jacob and Esau are born, eloquently describes the character of Isaac and Rebecca. Isaac is a passive, vulnerable, sensitive, tender and inward man. He forms deeply emotional, exclusive and dependent relationships with his mother and his wife. Isaac transmits his father's insights and values, but he does not have any of his own. He is a stabilizer, rather than a builder. He is a link in a chain of tradition, rather than a pioneer. Isaac is more a son, father, heir and husband than he is an independent voice. And then, Isaac quickly fades out of the Torah text with Jacob's move to Rebecca's brother's home and land.[268]

On the contrary, Rebecca is an active and single-minded heroine. It is Rebecca's understanding of her husband, her sons and of God's wishes that animates the drama that preoccupies the protagonists in the remaining chapters of the Book of Genesis.

Who is Jacob: The Early Years

The struggle between the twin brothers, Jacob and Esau, begins in utero. The text describes this conflict in graphic aggressive language. The text reads, "And the children *ratsats* (in biblical Hebrew), that is, cracked in pieces, bruised or crushed each other within Rebecca."[269]

The attribution of character, the sharp distinction between Jacob and Esau, also begins even before the twins are born. Although, as we will see in this section, the Genesis text itself views both Jacob's and Esau's characters in their early years with significant ambivalence, with Jacob described in the Torah text more negatively than Esau, this is not the case when reading how the post-biblical rabbis of the midrash understood each of the twins. For the midrashic sages, Jacob's motives and behavior were interpreted in the most positive light possible. Esau's were generally understood hypercritically. For example, the midrash, commenting on the prenatal difficulties that Rebecca had with her pregnancy, anachronistically taught that when Rebecca walked by a place where Torah was being studied, a synagogue or academy, then Jacob would try to emerge from her womb. When she walked by a shop where idols were being made, it was Esau that would struggle to be born.[270] According to the midrashic imagination and reflecting its attribution of Jacob's and Esau's differential temperaments, it was these fetal excitements and predilections that led to Rebecca's maternal distress.

The harsh talmudic and midrashic interpretation of Esau derives more from the association of Esau with Edom and Rome than any of his specific characteristics reported in the actual biblical text. In the Torah, we are told that Esau is Edom[271], the ancestor of Amalek (Israel's eternal enemy) and Haman (the first figure in history to order the slaughter of all Jews and the villain of the Jewish holiday of Purim). Later, for the rabbis of the second century CE, the tortured generation of sages during the reign of Emperor Hadrian, and for succeeding generations of Jewish biblical commentators, Edom and Esau were understood as the progenitors of the despised Romans.[272]

Reflecting this attitude toward Esau, in the Talmud, when God comes to judge the Jewish people, it will not be Abraham nor Jacob who will plea for God's forgiveness, but Isaac because Isaac, like God, had a wicked child (Esau). Since Isaac loved his Esau, the Talmud asks, cannot God love His Jewish children who do evil?[273]

Another example of this post-biblical interpretive degrading of Esau involves the rabbinic understanding of the misspelling of the word, "twins (*ta-omiym* in Hebrew), in the Torah verse, "When Rebecca's time to give birth was at hand, there were *twins* in her womb."[274] *Ta-omiym* is spelled here without the Hebrew letter, "yod." Rashi comments, "Here the yod is missing, whereas when Tamar's pregnancy involving her twins is mentioned,[275] the yod is present. This is because in Tamar's case, both twins were righteous. In Rebecca's case, however, only one was righteous and the other one, [Esau], was evil [and therefore the letter Yod that signifies the Lord is missing]."[276]

An example of how this post-biblical negative spin on Esau's character is transmitted by the rabbis from generation to generation is found in the schedule of synagogue scriptural readings. Each Shabbat, in the synagogue, a reading from the Five Books of Moses is paired with a reading from the prophetic literature, the "Haftarah." These pairings were established two thousand years ago by the sages of the Talmud. Interestingly, it is when all synagogues read the portion entitled, "*Toledot*,"[277]—the section of the Torah in which Jacob is in the most unfavorable of lights, that is, Jacob manipulating Esau out of his birthright, Jacob, in league with his mother, deceiving his blind father to steal Isaac's blessing from Esau—that the Haftarah is most disdainful. The prophetic reading for this week expresses divine contempt, not toward Jacob, but toward Esau and his people. The Prophet Malachi states, "I have loved you, says the Lord. Yet you say, How have You loved us? Was not Esau Jacob's brother? says the Lord: *yet I loved Jacob, and I hated Esau*, and laid Esau's mountains and his heritage waste for the dragons of the wilderness. Whereas Edom says, We are impoverished, but we will return and build the desolate places; thus says the Lord of hosts, Edom shall build, but *I will throw down*; and Edom shall be known as the border of wickedness, and, The people toward whom *the LORD has rage forever*."[278]

Just as Esau's character is interpreted downward by the talmudic, midrashic and later rabbinic commentators on the Bible, Jacob's character is interpreted upward by these same post-biblical sources. A careful examination of the Genesis text itself reveals something different. In the Torah, we see an Esau who is limited and impulse-driven, but nonetheless a sympathetic figure. Jacob's character, however, as depicted in the Bible itself, is dominated by moral flaws. In each of the principle dramas of Jacob's first forty years of life, the theft of Esau's birthright and blessing, and even Jacob's reaction to the first communication from God, the Genesis text unmistakably depicts Jacob as manipulative, deceptive, and self-absorbed. It is to these principle dramas of Jacob's first forty years that we now turn to discover *who Jacob is* at the beginning of his story.

The Genesis text describes a Rebecca, suffering greatly with her pregnancy. She "inquires of the Lord," who informs her that there are two nations in her womb, and that the "older [of the twins] will serve the younger."[279] And yet, there is no evidence that this "election of Jacob over Esau,"[280] this prophesy, is ever shared with Rebecca's husband, Isaac, Jacob or Esau. On the contrary, the distressing family drama of parent vs. parent, son vs. son and parent vs. son is played out in the text without any explicit sign of God's hand at work.

Instead, what is most explicit is the clash of four idiosyncratic personalities. Isaac is a sixty year old man when the twins are born. His life, to that point, has been dominated by his passivity to his larger-than-life father and over-dependency on his mother and wife. Rebecca, strong-willed and single-minded, is unambiguous about her likes and dislikes. She is resourceful and tireless in getting her agenda realized. Esau, a skillful hunter, is a man of action and a slave of impulse. And then there is Jacob. He is so ruled by his intense ambition and malignant envy of his twin brother that he emerges from Rebecca's birth canal holding onto his brother's heel. The Genesis text emphasizes the significance of this sign of Jacob's character by connecting this experience of birth with Jacob's name. Jacob, "Ya-akov" in Hebrew, refers directly to the heel, "akev."[281] The name also alludes to "akav," one who supplants by trickery,[282] that is, trips up the rival's heel.[283]

In this Genesis family, it is opposites who ally and attract—the passive father with the active Esau, the active mother with the passive Jacob. Genesis reads, "When the boys grew up, Esau became a cunning hunter, a man of the fields, but Jacob was a mild man who stayed in camp. Isaac loved Esau because Isaac had a taste for game; but Rebecca loved Jacob."[284]

Because Esau was the firstborn son, by custom and law generally accepted by the peoples of the ancient Near East as well as the Israelites,[285] he would receive on his father's death two portions of the inheritance. Jacob would be entitled to only one. It is this right of property, the birthright of the primogeniture, that Jacob first extorts from his brother.

> Once when Jacob was cooking up a stew, Esau came in from the fields, weary. And Esau said to Jacob, "Give me some of that red (adom) stuff to gulp down, please, for I am faint"—which is why he was named Edom. Jacob said, "First sell me your birthright." And Esau said, "I am at the point of death, so of what use is my birthright to me?" But Jacob said, "Swear to me first." So he swore to him, and sold his birthright to Jacob. Jacob then gave Esau bread and lentil stew; Esau ate and drank, and he rose and went away. Thus did Esau scorn his birthright.[286]

The characters of the two youths is well elucidated in this brief biblical passage. We see a weary Esau, dominated by his impulses, who *needs food* immediately, willing to sell his double portion of his future inheritance for today's bowl of soup. The Genesis text further conveys Esau's impulsivity by using in one verse four verbs to express his intense drive toward action, "Esau ate and drank, and rose and went away."

We see a Jacob, by himself, unlike in the next scenario in which the action is meticulously directed by his mother, cooking up a stew and a scheme. How long has Jacob studied Esau's character to know his rival's vulnerabilities? How long has Jacob tried to have Esau exactly where he has him today? How long has Jacob waited to take advantage of his brother's characteristic need for immediate gratification? How long has Jacob been plotting to reverse what Esau was entitled to by the "accident of birth?"

Interestingly, at the end of the passage, in a different literary voice, the biblical author harshly comments on Esau's behavior, "Thus did Esau scorn his birthright," but does not judge, or even refer to Jacob's.

The centerpiece of an inquiry into the four principle personalities of our Genesis family is the blessing narrative. More clearly than in any other story in the Bible, the complexity and interaction of character is elucidated, preserved and exposed in this text.

> When Isaac was old and his eyes were too dim to see, he called his older son Esau and said to him, "My son." He answered, "Here I am." And he said, "I am old now, and I do not know the day of my death. Take your weapons, I pray you, your quiver and bow, and go out into the fields and trap some deer for me. Then prepare a dish for me such as I love, and bring it to me to eat, so that my soul can bless you before I die." Rebecca had heard what Isaac had said to Esau, his son…Rebecca said to Jacob, her son, "I heard your father speaking to Esau, your brother…Now, my son, listen to my voice, to what I command. Go to the flock and fetch me two choice kids, and I will make of them a dish for your father, such as he loves. Then take it to your father to eat, so that he may bless you before he dies." Jacob answered Rebecca, his mother, "But Esau, my brother, is a hairy man and I am a smooth man. If my father touches me, I shall appear to him as a deceiver and bring upon myself a curse, not a blessing." His mother said to Jacob, "Upon me shall be your curse, my son! Just do as I say and go fetch the kids for me." Jacob got them and brought them to his mother, and his mother prepared a dish such as his father loved. Rebecca then took the best clothing of Esau, her older son, which was in the house, and had Jacob, her younger son, put them on; and she covered his hands and the smooth of his neck with the skins of the kids. Then she put in the hands of Jacob, her son, the meat and the bread that she had prepared. Jacob went to his father and said, "Father." And Isaac said, "Here I am, my son, who are you?" Jacob said to his father, "I am Esau, your firstborn; I have

done as you told me. Pray sit up and eat of my venison, that your soul may bless me." Isaac said to his son, "How did you find it so quickly, my son?" And he said, "Because the Lord your God brought it to me." Isaac said to Jacob, "Pray, come near that I may feel you, my son—whether you are really my son Esau or not." So Jacob approached his father Isaac, who felt him and said, "The voice is the voice of Jacob, yet the hands are the hands of Esau." Isaac did not recognize Jacob, because his hands were hairy like Esau's, his brother; and so Isaac blessed him. Isaac asked, "Are you my very son Esau?" And when Jacob said, "I am,"...then his father Isaac said to him, "Come close and kiss me, my son"; and Jacob went up and kissed Isaac. And Isaac smelled his son's clothing and Isaac blessed Jacob, saying, "See, the smell of my son is like the smell of the fields that the Lord has blessed. "May God give you of the dew of heaven and the fat of the earth, Abundance of new grain and wine. Let peoples serve you, And nations bow to you; Be master over your brothers, And let your mother's sons bow to you. Cursed be all who curse you, Blessed be all who bless you." And then, as soon as Isaac finished blessing Jacob, and Jacob had just left Isaac, Esau, his brother, came in from his hunting...And Esau said to his father, "Pray sit up and eat of my venison, that your soul may bless me." Isaac, his father, said to Esau, "Who are you?" And Esau said, "I am Esau, your son, your firstborn!" Isaac greatly trembled. And Isaac asked, "Who? Where is he who hunted game and brought it to me, and I ate of it before you came, and I blessed him? now he shall be blessed!" When Esau heard the words of his father, he wept exceedingly. Esau said to his father, "Bless me too, my Father!" But Isaac answered, "Your brother came with deception and took away your blessing." Esau said, "Is not he then rightly named Jacob (*Ya-akov*) for he supplants (*akav*) me these two times? First he took away my birthright and now he has taken away my blessing!"[287]

Isaac's blindness, an important literary device in this narrative, has been the center of rabbinic discourse in the Talmud and midrash. Louis Ginzberg,[288] in his five-volume anthology of Jewish legends, offers three separate explanations, two of which also serve the purpose of criticizing Esau. In the first, Isaac becomes blind as a result of the smoke from incense that emanates from the worshipping of idols, practiced by Esau's two Canaanite wives within Isaac's own home. A second explanation views Isaac's lack of vision as representing Isaac's chronic blindness to the faults of his older son. Overly-influenced by the pleasures of his stomach and the taste of the meat Esau obtains for him, Isaac cannot see Esau, the hunter, clearly. A third explanation for Isaac's blindness conjectures that it is a delayed effect of Isaac's experience during the Akedah (see Chapter Four), when his father bound the young Isaac on the altar to sacrifice him to God. As Abraham lifted his knife to slaughter the innocent Isaac, the angels wept large and sad tears. Each of these angelic tears fell into Isaac's eyes and ultimately, years later, weakened them.[289]

Although Isaac is blind in the Genesis blessing narrative, a careful reading of the text causes one to seriously question whether Isaac does not "see" the plot in which he is the alleged dupe. Evidence for this position arises from the number of times in the text itself that Isaac concerns himself with the identity of the son he is addressing, as well as from the content of the blessing he offers Jacob in Esau's garb. At least four separate times in the ten verses describing the Isaac-Jacob encounter, Isaac questions whether this is Jacob or Esau. When Jacob first enters, Isaac asks him, "Who are you?" After wondering how Esau could return so quickly with his meal of venison, killed, dressed and cooked, Isaac asks to touch his son to determine whether he is Esau or not. Then, a moment later, after observing that this Esau has the voice of Jacob, Isaac asks again, "Are you really my son, Esau?" Finally, only after smelling Esau's clothing that Jacob dons, does Isaac bless him. Isaac's suspicions concerning the deception directly clash with the "omniscient" voice of the text that asserts, ignoring Isaac's questions, "Isaac did not recognize Jacob, because his hands were hairy like Esau's."

A study of the blessing Isaac offers the disguised Jacob also lends support to the opinion that Isaac is secretly aware of the deception. Blessings are a central theme of the Book of Genesis and in the lives of the patriarchs. From God's blessing the fish and birds to be fruitful and multiply to Jacob's death-bed blessing of his sons, the content of a Genesis blessing has great precision and significance. The complete blessing formula for the patriarchs always involves a promise of land and seed. For example, to Abraham, Jacob's grandfather, the Lord said, "Lift up your eyes and look northward and southward and eastward and westward, for all the land that you see, I will give it to you and to your seed forever. And I will make of your seed the dust of the earth."[290]

Isaac's blessing of Jacob-as-Esau does not promise him the land forever or infinite progeny, but rather prosperity and domination over his brother. Isaac blesses, "May God give you Of the dew of heaven and the fat of the earth…Be master over your brothers, And let your mother's sons bow to you…" Interestingly, it is only later, when Jacob is Jacob, as he embarks on his journey to a new land, that Isaac offers him the full patriarchal blessing. Isaac then says to Jacob, "God almighty bless you and make you fruitful and multiply you that you may be a multitude of peoples. And give you the blessing of Abraham, and to you and your seed that you may inherit the land in which you are sojourning which God has assigned to Abraham."[291]

If Isaac fully recognizes to which son he is speaking, as is suggested by this analysis, then more interesting psychological questions concerning the family drama and Isaac's character arise. Is Isaac searching for a way, an "easy out," to offer the blessing of Abraham to his younger son? Is he aware of the prophesy and preference expressed by God that the "older shall serve the younger"[292] expressed to Rebecca in the final trimester of her pregnancy? Is Isaac using his being a "victim" of this poorly-devised and thinly-disguised hoax as a way to renounce his own responsibility for blessing Jacob over Esau? Is this the reason why the blessing, clearly made on the basis of false pretenses, according to Isaac cannot be reversed? Are Isaac and Rebecca in league in this plot to circumvent Esau? Or Is Isaac merely playing the role assigned to him by his wife and that he chooses to play?

Rebecca, in the blessing narrative, is a tidal wave of will. She hurriedly and casually washes away Jacob's concerns about being found out by his father, and any of her own possible misgivings about deceiving her husband or betraying her older son. Isaac must bless Jacob, not Esau. For Rebecca, all other considerations are secondary or nonexistent. An indication of the nature of the Esau-Rebecca relationship is that throughout the passage, Esau is referred to as Isaac's son or Jacob's brother. Only once is Esau referred to as Rebecca's older son. On the contrary, in the brief biblical passage, Jacob's relationship with Rebecca is mentioned eight times.

Nothing is going to alter Rebecca's plan for Jacob. When Jacob raises the concern that, if their deception is discovered by his father that Jacob will be cursed, not blessed, Rebecca promises what she cannot promise—that the curse will be on her, not her forty-year-old son. Rebecca says to Jacob, "Upon me shall be your curse, my son. Just do as I say and go fetch the kids for me."

In the end, Rebecca is a tragic heroine, trapped within the drama she orchestrates. Days after Jacob steals Esau's blessing, in response to Esau's death threat against Jacob, lying to her husband about the true reason why Jacob should leave,[293] it is Rebecca who convinces Isaac to send her beloved Jacob away to her brother Laban's land. Jacob then spends twenty years in Laban's country, in exile. Mother and son never again see each other. After Jacob leaves her, Rebecca is never mentioned in the biblical text except to describe her burial place with her husband and son Jacob, among others, in the Cave of Machpelah.[294]

Jacob, in the blessing narrative, is a passive and sinful hero. At best, Jacob demonstrates blind obedience to his strong mother's wishes, following her lead to correct nature and grant him the blessing of the firstborn. In line with this interpretation of Jacob's character as overly dependent, the midrash describes Jacob, "distressed, bent and weeping," as he carried the kids to his mother for the hoax she designed and now institutes.[295]

At worst, Jacob is a ruthless and aggressive competitor, willing to deceive his father, betray his twin brother and even exploit the name of God to obtain what he craves. It is noteworthy, in this regard, that Jacob never raises a moral objection to his mother's plan, instead he worries about his being uncovered. After Rebecca tells him how he is going to deceive his father, Jacob says, "But Esau, my brother, is a hairy man and I am a smooth man. If my father touches me, I shall appear to him as a deceiver and bring upon myself a curse, not a blessing." And then, later, when Isaac questions how quickly his son has arrived with the meat, and adding moral insult to injury, Jacob uses the name of God in his deception. "Isaac said to his son, 'How did you find it so quickly, my son?' And Jacob said, 'Because the Lord, your God, brought it to me.'"

> In this text, more than in any other biblical narrative thus far, are we allowed to peek into, so intimately, the private lives, psyches and relationships of our ancient patriarchs, matriarchs and offspring. In this narrative, we are invited to witness an Isaac, only seemingly blind to, and impotent in the face of his wife's plans for her favored son. Here is an Isaac who blesses the son he chooses to, without taking responsibility for his wrenching decision. We are permitted to see Rebecca enlist Jacob to deceive and betray both her husband and her firstborn Esau. We perceive a forty-year-old Jacob, seemingly-swept away by the rush of his mother's scheme, worried about his being discovered and punished—never questioning the ethics of his participation in the plot or owning his own desire to carry it out. The Esau we are allowed to see in this biblical text is not the man of action, the cunning hunter, the "man's man," but the poignant pleading victim, betrayed by his own mother, twin brother and abandoned by Isaac. In this Genesis narrative, we discover a well-preserved, albeit distressing, psychological photograph of Jacob and his family.

The traditional setting for spiritual confrontation and transformation is the wilderness. It is in the wilderness that the eighty-year-old Moses encounters God's voice in the burning bush commanding him to return to Egypt and lead his people out of bondage.[296] It is into the wilderness that the children of Israel, runaway slaves, must escape in order to learn their mission and become a nation. It is in the wilderness, as well, that Jesus, after fasting for forty days and tempted by Satan, returns with his message more firm, "The kingdom of God is at hand; repent and believe in the gospel."[297] Six centuries later, it is in the wilderness that Muhammad receives his revelation that there is one true God, that He is a God of goodness and that the day of judgement is near.[298]

In Genesis Chapter 28, Isaac, now with "eyes open," blesses Jacob a second time and sends him off to Rebecca's brother's land. The journey to Laban's home involves significant danger. This journey requires that Jacob travel through the wilderness between Beer-Sheva and Haran. Interestingly, although Isaac is a wealthy man, Jacob travels without retinue or possessions, emphasizing the *spiritual* journey that Jacob has just begun.[299]

It is in the wilderness, alone, vulnerable and destitute, having only a stone for a pillow, franticly trying to escape from his brother, his past and himself, that Jacob dreams, and encounters God for the first time. Unlike Sigmund Freud and modern psychologically-minded men and women, who generally view dreams as the creation of an individual's unconscious wishes and fears, the biblical author understands the dream as a direct communication from God. A dream in the Bible is a "divine E-mail." What is evident from a careful examination of the spiritual masterpiece that is Jacob's wilderness dream, and the reaction to it, is that, while God offers Jacob a profoundly comforting message, Jacob, at this point in his character development, is *not* capable of hearing it.

> Jacob left Beer-Sheva, and went toward Haran. He came upon a certain place and remained there all night, for the sun had set. Taking one of the stones of that place, and using it as his pillow, Jacob laid down in that place to sleep. He had a dream; a ladder was set on the ground and its top reached to the heavens, and angels of God were going up and down on it. And the Lord was standing above it and He said, "I am the Lord, the God of your father Abraham and the God of Isaac: the ground on which you are lying I will assign to you and to your seed. Your descendants shall be as the dust of the earth; you shall spread out to the west and to the east, to the north and to the south. All the families of the earth shall bless themselves by you and your descendants. Behold, I am with you: I will protect you wherever you go and will bring you back to this land. I will not leave you until I have done what I have promised you." Jacob awoke from his sleep and said, "Surely the Lord is present in this place, and I knew it not!" Frightened, he said, "How awesome is this place!...Jacob then made a vow, saying, "If God will be with me, if He protects me on this journey that I am making, and gives me bread to eat and clothing to wear, and if I return to my father's house in peace—then the Lord shall be my God. And this stone, which I have set up as a pillar, shall be God's house; and of all that is given to me, I will give a tenth unto You."[300]

The dream graphically connects earth with heaven, Jacob with God and past with future. First, we see the angels going *up* and down on the earth-heaven ladder. The rabbis ask why the angels go up first. The answer they offer sets the tone for the dream as a whole—that Jacob, and perhaps all of us, are constantly surrounded by invisible angels who guard and protect us, not from a far-off heaven, but on the ground *with* us.[301] Thus the dream angels travel from earth where they live to heaven, not heaven to earth.

The dream includes a third blessing for Jacob. The first one, a partial blessing involving prosperity and dominance, was the one Jacob stole from Esau. The second one, involving land and seed, was invoked by his father as Jacob departed for Haran. This third blessing, also a full blessing involving land and progeny, is given by the Lord God Himself. In this third blessing, God first states that He is the God of Jacob's father and grandfather, and then reiterates the promise He had made to each of them—that the land will be Jacob's and his descendents, that his descendents will be too numerous to count, that all people will bless themselves by Jacob's children. Then God continues by making a set of powerful personal promises to Jacob—that He is with him, that He will protect him and bring him back to this land, that He will not leave him until all divine pledges are satisfied.

Although, in the dream, God offers blessings and assurances of great beauty, depth, complexity and comfort, it is clear from examining the final text in the passage, Jacob's vow, that Jacob, at this point in his life,[302] is psychologically unable to fully appreciate or contain God's message. In other words, Jacob just "doesn't get it." After God promises Jacob companionship and protection, today and in the future, Jacob distrusts the promise and begins the negotiation. Jacob says, "*If* God will be with me, *if* He protects me on this journey that I am making, and gives me bread to eat and clothing to wear, and *if* I return to my father's house in peace—*then* the Lord will be my God."

I imagine the Lord God, standing above the ladder, listening to Jacob's vow, asking Himself, "Jacob, my son, my chosen one, exactly what part of the dream I sent you did you not understand? And, by the way, who said anything about food and clothing?"

The Jewish and Christian biblical commentators are deeply troubled by the conditional nature of Jacob's vow—that only *if* God does this for him, *then* will the Lord be Jacob's God. Much midrashic ink is devoted to interpreting Jacob's vow in such a way to keep Jacob in a good spiritual light. For example, the Ramban argues that Jacob, here, is not casting doubts on God, but rather on himself. Jacob, according to this thirteenth century rabbi, is expressing his deep concern that he will sin so greatly in the foreign land to which he is traveling that he will not be able to make the Lord his God.[303] Others, both Rashi[304] and the Protestant American Standard Bible, combine the clauses in the passage to take the sting out of Jacob's words. They suggest that the verses of the vow should be translated, "If God will be with me,...and if I return to my father's house in peace, *and* the Lord shall be my God, *then* this stone…will be God's house and of all that is given to me, I will give a tenth unto You."

Rabbi Jonathan in the midrash on the Book of Genesis offers a particularly creative theory for understanding the content of Jacob's vow. He suggests that the Torah text here is in some disarray and that the vow was spoken before the dream. First Jacob asked God for His protection during this deeply troubling time and then, God responds to Jacob's request by offering him an answer in the form of the dream.[305]

Jacob's vow can best be understood psychologically. The vow is an expression of the characterological limitations of our hero, as he *is*, at the end of the first phase of his life. Here, as he stands in Bethel, between the forty years he spent in his parents' home and the twenty years of transformative exile, Jacob's vow is consistent with other disappointing aspects of his first four decades. Here stands a man who has manipulated Esau out of both his birthright and his blessing by exploiting his father's and brother's vulnerabilities as well as his intense relationship with his mother. Here stands a man who has lived by his cunning, deception and tricks. Jacob receives a powerful third blessing, this one from God Himself, and what is Jacob's response? Jacob, today, in the wilderness, a fugitive from his past, frightened for his future, cannot feel blessed or even appreciate the dream's significance. Instead, Jacob angles for more.

The question is often asked, given Jacob's less-than-auspicious beginning, why does God choose him for patriarch. Rabbi Samuel Karff wisely answers this question by suggesting that God has two choices, the only children Isaac had—an Esau, whose belly is his God, willing to forfeit his birthright for a bowl of lentils, or a Jacob, who uses all of his cunning to get what he wants. "God decides it is better to care too much than too little."[306] I would add that what God sees when He sees His Jacob on the road to Haran is not who Jacob *is*, but rather, who he *can be*.

In twenty years, when Jacob, the father of a large family, the leader of his people, returns to this wilderness and wrestles his demons, human and divine, it will be then that Jacob will contain God's message and feel blessed. How this transformation from self-absorption to maturity occurs is the focus of the next section.

What Changes Jacob

As we have seen, Jacob's first forty years are tainted by his overly-dependent relationship with his mother and his readiness to exploit the other, often resorting to deception to get his way. To be patriarch, other characteristics will be required.

But how does Jacob travel from trickster and "mama's boy" to father of a great people? The Book of Genesis, in its description of the next twenty years of Jacob's life, offers a three-fold answer to this question. Jacob's "therapy" entails a test of himself in a harsh hyper-masculine environment, a well-timed push from God and insight.

Jacob continues on his journey and arrives at the home of his mother's brother Laban. Laban first warmly welcomes Jacob. Over the next twenty years, however, when Jacob lives with Laban, Jacob discovers that his uncle is a domineering, dishonest and brutish man. The first hint that the Genesis text offers of Laban's character is the well-known story of the switch of Rachel and Leah. Jacob offers to work seven years for Laban without wages to marry Rachel, Laban's beautiful younger daughter. The two men agree to this contract. The text reads:

> And Jacob served seven years for Rachel. And they seemed unto him but a few days, for the love he had for her. And Jacob said unto Laban, Give me my wife, for my days are fulfilled, that I may go in unto her. And Laban gathered together all the men of the place, and made a feast. And it came to pass in the evening, that Laban took Leah his daughter, and brought her to Jacob. And Jacob went in unto Leah…And it came to pass in the morning that, behold, it was Leah. And Jacob said to Laban, What is this you have done to me? Did not I serve you for Rachel? Why have you deceived me? And Laban said, It is not the practice of our place, to give the younger before the first-born.[307]

In this passage, the trickster is tricked. Jacob, the younger brother who stole a blessing by disguising himself as the first-born, marries the first-born, disguised to be the younger. And, in case Jacob does not understand the moral of Laban's hoax, Laban points out to his victim that here, in this land, unlike the one from which Jacob comes, we honor the right of the elder.

Later, after marrying both Leah and Rachel, and having eleven sons and one daughter by his wives and concubines, Jacob wishes to return to his father's land. Jacob and Laban discuss the wages due Jacob for increasing Laban's flock. Jacob suggests that his wage should be all the speckled, spotted or black sheep and goats among the flock that day. Laban agrees, and then immediately steals the animals committed to Jacob and hides them within the flocks of Laban's sons. The text reads:

> And Jacob said unto Laban, You know how I have served you, and how your cattle have fared with me. For it was little which you had before I came, and it has increased to a multitude…And Laban said, What shall I give you? And Jacob said, Pay me nothing: if you will do this thing for me, I will continue to

feed your flock and guard it. I will pass through all your flock today, removing from it every speckled and spotted one, and every black one among the sheep, and the spotted and speckled among the goats: and this will be my pay...And Laban said, Behold, I agree. But Laban removed that very day the he-goats that were ringstreaked, and spotted, and all the she-goats that were speckled and spotted, every one that had white in it, and all the black ones among the sheep, and gave them into the hands of his sons.[308]

Jacob, in Laban, confronts a protagonist that Jacob had never encountered in his first four decades of life. To Jacob, his father Isaac was unaware and passive, and an easy dupe of Rebecca's and Jacob's cunning plots. Jacob's mother Rebecca was a dominating figure who got what she wanted, but always had to work undercover. Esau was a "man's man," like Laban, but Esau was so ruled by his appetite and impulses that he was easily manipulated. Laban is a different and significant force. He is masculine and harsh, yet cleverly deceitful. Jacob unhappily discovers during his twenty year exile with Laban that his uncle has no compunction whatsoever about making agreements and then changing them at will.

For Jacob to grow from who he *was* to who he was to *become*, it will be necessary for Jacob to survive his years with Laban and ultimately confront him and come to terms. The Book of Genesis describes this confrontation of man to man at the end of Chapter 31.

Now Jacob became enraged and confronted Laban,..."These twenty years I have spent in your service, your ewes and she-goats never miscarried, nor did I feast on rams from your flock. That which was torn by beasts I never brought to you; I myself made good the loss;...Often, scorching heat ravaged me by day and frost by night; and sleep fled from my eyes. Of the twenty years that I spent in your household, I served you fourteen years for your two daughters, and six years for your flocks; and you changed my wages ten times over. Had not the God of my father, the God of Abraham and the Fear of Isaac, been with me, you would have sent me away empty-handed. But God [not you] took notice of my plight and the toil of my hands.[309]

It is in response to Jacob's direct, honest and powerful confrontation of Laban that Laban establishes a covenant with his nephew. "And Laban said to Jacob, 'Here is this mound and here the pillar which I have set up between you and me: this mound shall be witness and this pillar shall be witness that I am not to cross to you past this mound, and that you are not to cross to me past this mound and this pillar, with hostile intent.'"[310]

Jacob, who was already considering leaving Laban's home and returning to the land of his birth, required a nudge. After all, not only would the wilderness journey itself have its own dangers and complexities—Jacob being chief of a large camp including two wives, two concubines, twelve children and countless number of servants and animals—but also, for Jacob, the destination was permeated with terror. Twenty years before, Jacob fled Beer-Sheva to escape from an enraged Esau who had threatened his life. Jacob's return to the land of his father meant that he would finally stop avoiding the inevitable, transcend his fears and face his brother.

It is God who provides Jacob the push he needs. "And the Lord said to Jacob, 'Return to the land of your fathers, and of your kindred, and I will be with you...I am the God of Bethel where you anointed the stone and made a vow to Me. Now, arise and leave this land and return to your native land.'"[311]

God's message helps Jacob take the dramatic and frightening step. So Jacob, at the head of a large caravan, comprised of all that is his, begins the pilgrimage back to his homeland.

An indication that Jacob's character has transformed during the travails and lessons of the last twenty years of exile, from arrogant and entitled manipulator to humble and grateful servant of God, is found in Jacob's prayer that he utters at the beginning of the journey home. Jacob, who has just learned that his brother Esau is riding toward Jacob's encampment with four hundred men, is shaken with terror. Jacob prays, "O God of my father Abraham, and God of my father Isaac, O Lord, who said to me, 'Return to the land of your country and of your kindred, and I will deal well with you'! *I am unworthy of all the mercy and truth that You have shown Your servant*: with my staff alone I crossed this Jordan...Deliver me, I pray, from the hand of my brother, from the hand of Esau; else, I fear, he may come and strike me down, and the mother with their children."[312]

That night, Jacob, twenty years after traveling through the same wilderness, again is alone, vulnerable and frightened. It is that very night that Jacob encounters a "man" who wrestles with him until dawn, and renames Jacob, "Israel."

> That same night Jacob arose, and taking his two wives, his two maidservants, and his eleven sons, he crossed the ford of the Jabbok. After taking them across the stream, Jacob sent across all his possessions. Jacob was left alone. And a man wrestled with Jacob until the break of dawn. When the man saw that he had not prevailed against Jacob, he wrenched Jacob's hip at its socket, so that the socket of Jacob's hip was out of joint as he wrestled with the man. Then the man said, "Let me go, for dawn is breaking." But Jacob answered, "I will not let you go, until you bless me." Said the other, "What is your name?"

He replied, "Jacob." Said the man, "Your name shall no longer be Jacob, but Israel, for you have struggled with beings, divine and human, and have prevailed." Jacob asked, "Pray tell me your name." But he said, "You must not ask my name!" And he took leave of Jacob there. So Jacob named the place Peni-El, meaning," I have seen a divine being face to face, yet my life has been preserved." The sun rose upon Jacob as he left Peni-El, limping on his hip.[313]

The dramatic culmination of Jacob's "therapy" is this wrestling "session." With the next daylight, Jacob will be facing the brother who swore to kill Jacob and whom he has not seen for twenty years. Jacob hopes that the gifts he has sent ahead to Esau might mitigate his brother's murderous rage and long-standing plans for revenge. And Jacob prays that God's promise to be with him and protect him is still remembered and honored.

Now, in the pitch black of this night, perhaps the final hours of his life, all alone, without family or possession, in the same wilderness where he began his spiritual journey twenty years before, Jacob faces himself. When Jacob wrestles with the "man," unrecognized and unnamed, what Jacob wrestles with is his own troubling history and character. Jacob wrestles with his contempt for his brother and his pleasure in triumphing over him. Jacob wrestles with his eagerness to follow his mother's cruel scheme. Jacob wrestles with the ease with which he deceived his blind father. Jacob wrestles with his ambition, unrestrained by considerations of family or morality. For the thirteenth century Cabalist, rabbi Yakov, this wrestling is the highest form of prayer and therefore one that God consistently answers. This wrestling/prayer involves "searching oneself, by becoming one's own opponent."[314]

There are four significant consequences for Jacob of the wrestling throughout the night. First, Jacob's name is changed by his opponent from Jacob to Israel. "Your name shall no longer be Jacob, but Israel (*Yisro-El*), for you have struggled with beings, divine and human, and have prevailed." As we have seen, names of God and men have great significance in the Bible. *Ya-akov*, the one who trips the other's heel, the supplanter, becomes *Yisro-El*, the one who contends with God and prevails.[315]

Second, although Jacob has been blessed many times before this night by both his heavenly and earthly fathers, it is this blessing, more than any of the others, that matters to Jacob. Jacob says to his opponent, "I will not let you go until you bless me." It is only this blessing that Jacob wins by his own honest force of will. Rashi, commenting on the blessing given to Jacob at the end of the wrestling vignette, and speaking directly to Jacob, writes, "Jacob, now it will no longer be said that the blessings came to you through deceit and trickery, but rather, with nobility and openness."[316]

Third, a physical consequence of the wrestling match is that Jacob is injured by his opponent. "When the man saw that he had not prevailed against Jacob, he wrenched Jacob's hip at its socket…The sun rose upon Jacob as he left Peni-El limping on his hip." The biblical author here understands that maturity and transformation cannot be achieved without some serious scarring. Sigmund Freud agrees. In a case history of Dora, a hysterical patient he treated in 1899, who greatly frustrated Freud by prematurely terminating her analysis, Freud draws on the Jacob wrestling narrative as metaphor without referring to the Genesis text explicitly. Freud wrote, "No one who, like me, conjures up the most evil of those half-tamed demons that inhabit the human breast, and seeks to wrestle with them, can expect to come through the struggle unscathed."[317]

Last, with morning, Jacob emerges from his all-night and all-out confrontation of himself with a renewed ability to face what and whom he was avoiding throughout his life. He limps away from his night and past and faces Esau. The text of Jacob's and Esau's encounter and reconciliation reads:

> And Jacob lifted up his eyes and saw Esau coming toward him with four hundred men. And Jacob, [frightened], divided the children among Leah, Rachel and the two handmaids…And Jacob went on ahead, and bowed himself seven times to the ground until he came near to his brother. And Esau ran to meet Jacob, and embraced him and falling on his neck, Esau kissed Jacob, and they both wept…And Esau asked Jacob, "What do you mean by all these gifts that I have met along the way?" And Jacob answered, "to gain my lord's favor." Esau said, "I have enough, my brother. Let what you have remain yours." But Jacob said, "No, I pray you, if now I have found favor in your sight then accept these gifts from me; for seeing your face is like seeing the face of God.[318]

Jacob, limping, terrified and transformed, approaches Esau not knowing whether he and his children will live or die. Esau, also transformed during the twenty years of separation, embraces his brother and kisses him. Together, the two brothers weep years of tears.

This morning, Jacob-Israel, no longer avoiding himself, his history or his brother, feels truly blessed. Finally, his own man, a father of his people, and a master of his own impulses and character, Jacob sees the "face of God." It is in the eyes of his compassionate and forgiving brother that Jacob ultimately finds the Divine.

Jacob as Israel

Immediately following Jacob's encounter with Esau, the climax of Jacob's twenty years of learning about and struggling with himself, the Genesis text confirms Jacob's achievement and state of mind. The text reads, "And Jacob came *whole*[319] to the city of Shechem which is in the land of Canaan."[320] Discussing this verse in the *Sfat Emet*, a nineteenth century Chasidic psychologically-sophisticated commentary on the Torah, Rabbi Yehudah Leib Alter writes that Jacob came from Laban's country into Canaan, changed by his experiences there and on the journey, possessing integrity and wholeness that he never possessed before.[321]

Sadly, for Jacob, this state of psychic integrity is not consistent nor complete throughout the remainder of the Book of Genesis. The biblical author provides us a hint to this in the way Jacob is referred to after the wrestling episode. By way of context, preceding Jacob's name change, a result of wrestling with the "man" until dawn, two other significant Genesis figures, Jacob's grandparents, known at that time in the text as Abram and Sarai, had their names changed as well. In the section of Genesis in which God announces that the elderly couple will have a child, God says to Abram, "As for Me, behold, My covenant is with you, and you shall be a father of many nations. Your name shall no longer be Abram, but Abraham, because a father of many nations have I made you."[322] Ten verses later, God says, "As for Sarai, your wife, you shall not call her name Sarai, but Sarah shall her name be. And I will bless her, and give you a son also of her: I will bless her and she shall be a mother of nations."[323] Significantly, after these name changes, never again in the Hebrew Bible is Abraham referred to as Abram or Sarah as Sarai.

However, this is not the case for Jacob-Israel. Surveying the eighteen chapters that follow Jacob's name change, through the final verses of the Book of Genesis, we find that Jacob-Israel is referred to as Israel forty-one times in the text and as Jacob in seventy-five instances. Why is there a shifting in the Genesis Jacob-Israel text from one name to another? Why does Abraham's and Sarah's name change "stick," and Israel's not? Is the biblical author trying to convey something of consequence concerning the inconsistency and instability of Jacob-Israel's transformation in the last half of his life? Is Jacob-Israel, in the remainder of the Book of Genesis, as the name statistics might imply, sometimes Israel, but mostly Jacob?

Jacob-Israel, in the eighty-seven years that elapse between his reconciliation with Esau to his death at age one hundred forty-seven, is more Jacob than Israel, and an unhappy man. What is the source of this dis-ease that washes over and colors Jacob's experience in the last half of Jacob's life?

First, as Genesis unambiguously depicts, Jacob is more a frightened victim and distant observer of events, than an active participant. This passivity begins in Shechem, where he settles with his family immediately following his reunion with Esau. As the Genesis text describes, after Jacob purchases the land upon which Jacob and his children settle from Hamor, the king of Shechem, Dinah, Jacob's only daughter, goes out to "visit the daughters of the land"[324] (possibly to serve as midwife to them[325]). Hamor's son sees Dinah, has sexual relations with her and falls in love. The text reads, "And when Shechem, the son of Hamor, the Hivite, prince of the land, saw Dinah, he took her and lay with her and defiled her. And the prince's soul clasped onto Dinah, the daughter of Jacob, and he loved the maiden and spoke gently to her."[326]

Although it is Jacob who hears first of Dinah's "defilement," at that point in this story, Jacob drops out and it is his sons who come forward to negotiate deceitfully with Hamor concerning the bride price. The sons offer a proposition to Hamor. If you and all the men of Shechem will be circumcised, then marriages between the children of Israel and the people of Shechem can take place. Otherwise, the marriage of Dinah and the prince of Shechem is impossible. The text reads, "And the sons of Jacob answered Shechem, [the prince], and Hamor, his father, with deceit because Shechem had defiled their sister…'Only on this condition can we consent. If only you are like we are, if all of your males be circumcised, then we will give our daughters to you, and we will take our daughters to us, and we will dwell with you, and we will become one people.'"[327]

The prince, because of his love for Dinah, quickly agrees and convinces all the men of Shechem to be circumcised as well. The story continues with a mass slaughter. The text reads, "And it came to pass, on the third day [after all the circumcisions took place] when the men of Shechem were in pain, that two of the sons of Jacob, Simeon and Levi,…slew all the males, and they slew Hamor and Shechem with the edge of their swords, and took Dinah out of the house of Shechem, and left."[328]

But where was Jacob-Israel, the patriarch, the confronter, the wrestler, the struggler, during this incident? The text states that Jacob knew what happened between the prince and Dinah, but was he involved in or aware of the duplicitous negotiations with Hamor concerning the bride price and circumcision? And where was he when two of his sons planned the vicious and total destruction of the city of Shechem?

The text offers us Jacob's first reaction to the news of what his sons have done. His words here are clearly more Jacob than Israel. Jacob, seemingly unconcerned about the injustice of the murder, worries about himself and the possibility of military retaliation. The text reads, "And Jacob said unto Simeon and Levi, 'You have troubled me and made me odious to the inhabitants of the land, the Canaanites and the Perrizites, and I, being few in number, they will gather themselves against me and kill me, and I shall be destroyed; I and my house.'"[329]

A second major example of Jacob's inconsistent achievement of Israel involves his lack of awareness that characterizes his differential relationships with his sons. Jacob's intense favoritism for Joseph, his twelfth child and eleventh son, but his beloved wife's firstborn, and his insensitivity to his other sons, all of whom are children of his less favored women, ultimately result in the loss of Joseph. It is this loss that is the greatest source of suffering in Jacob's later life, from which he only minimally recovers when father and son are reunited in Egypt many years later. It is this tragic drama, provoked by Jacob's own behavior, motivated by profound paternal favoritism, resulting in malignant sibling rivalry, that is the single psychological force that underlies the last quarter of the Book of Genesis.

Jacob's exclusive and intense affection for Joseph is explicit in the Bible. It is Jacob's blatant favoritism, as well as Joseph's airs in relation to his brothers, that the Book of Genesis understands as motivating the other sons' unbrotherly reactions. The text reads:

> Joseph, being seventeen years old, was feeding the flock with his brothers,...and Joseph brought evil reports concerning his brothers to his father. Now Israel loved Joseph more than his other children because Joseph was the son of his old age, and he made him a coat of many colors. And when Joseph's brothers saw that their father loved Joseph more than the other brothers, the brothers hated Joseph, and could not speak peaceably to him. And Joseph dreamed a dream [in which all his brothers' sheaves of grain bowed low to Joseph's sheaf, the only one standing upright], and Joseph told the dream to his brothers, and they hated Joseph even more.[330]

The text is explicit that it was Jacob who sent Joseph to his brothers the day they sold Joseph to a passing caravan and ultimately into Egyptian slavery. "And Israel said to Joseph, 'Do not your brothers feed their flocks in Shechem? Come and I will send you to them...Go and see if all goes well with them and the flock and then, bring me back word again.' So Israel sent Joseph out of the valley of Hebron and Joseph came to Shechem...And when Joseph's brothers saw Joseph at a distance, even before he had come near, they conspired against Joseph to slay him. And they said, one to another, 'Here comes that dreamer.'"[331]"

Should Jacob-Israel have known better than to express his favoritism for one son over the others? Lacking that, should Jacob-Israel been more aware of the exposed-nerve sensitivities and deep resentment of his other sons and therefore not sent Joseph into harm's way?

Certainly, Jacob would have known about his grandfather, Abraham, egged on by Jacob's grandmother, who banished his firstborn son into the wilderness so that the blessing and inheritance of his younger son, Jacob's father Isaac, would be secured.[332] Jacob, also, without doubt, would recall from his own childhood the distress he personally felt and the destruction visited on his family because of divided affections for the children—Isaac preferring the older twin and Rebecca preferring him.[333] Jacob might have even known about his distant and primordial ancestors, Cain and Abel, and how God's preferential treatment of the younger son's sacrifice was the context within which Cain's resentment and murderous rage festered.[334]

On the theological level, the choice of the later-born son over the firstborn, similar to the motive underlying the theme of infertility of the matriarchs (already discussed), conveys the message that those who are chosen are not determined by nature, in this case, by the fact of primogeniture. Chosenness, in the Book of Genesis, involves an active intervention of God, a "tampering" with what is natural and customary. God *chooses* Abraham's second-born to carry the blessing of Abraham. God *chooses Isaac's* second-born to father the twelve tribes of Israel. God *chooses* Jacob's eleventh son as that generation's patriarch, to save the children of Israel from famine and death and bring them into Egypt.

On the psychological level, however, the favoring and preferential treatment of the younger son over the firstborn, a practice that violates long-standing cultural traditions and morays, makes for intense sibling resentments, rivalries and fractured families. It is for this reason that in the same Torah, God explicitly commands the Israelites not to do what Jacob did—to favor the younger son of the beloved wife over the firstborn son of the less favored woman. In Deuteronomy, the law reads, "If a man has two wives, one beloved and the other unloved, and both wives have given him children, and if the firstborn is the son of the unloved wife, then it shall be, when the man wills his property to his sons, that the man must not put the son of the beloved wife before the son of the unloved one. But the firstborn, the son of the unloved wife, shall inherit a double portion of all the man has because this son is the first-fruit of his strength. The right of the firstborn is his."[335]

Even after Jacob-Israel's "struggle with beings, divine and human," his twenty years of wrestling with himself, his history, his uncle Laban and brother Esau, *even on his deathbed*, Jacob never learns the lesson, never transcends his "Jacobness" in relation to favoring the younger over the older. Against Joseph's wishes, the dying Jacob perpetuates the Genesis family tradition and blesses Joseph's younger Ephraim before Joseph's firstborn, Manasseh.[336]

Jacob, in the final analysis, because he never consistently and completely becomes Israel, lives an unhappy life. A poignantly self-reflective Torah passage in which Jacob's caustic bitterness is summarized is found in the text that follows Jacob's reunion with Joseph, when Jacob speaks with the Pharaoh. The text reads, "And Joseph brought in Jacob, his father, and set him before the Pharaoh. And Jacob blessed Pharaoh. And Pharaoh said to Jacob, 'How many are the days of your life?' And Jacob said to Pharaoh, 'The days of my life are one hundred and thirty years, *few and miserable*[337] have been the days of my life, nor do they reach my forefather's life spans.' Then Jacob blessed Pharaoh and left his presence."[338]

If the result of Jacob's transformation, all that "psychotherapeutic" hard work—his twenty years of struggling to become his own man in the harsh masculine land of Laban, his pushes from God to confront himself, his wrestling with himself, his history, his impulse to avoid the terrifying encounter with Esau—is judged only on the basis of Jacob's happiness or behavior in the remainder of his life, then we must conclude, based on the Genesis data, that Jacob's "therapy" was an unmitigated failure. However, this characterization of Jacob's struggles as worthless can only be maintained if one has a single generational perspective, that is, if one judges the impact of a psychological and spiritual struggle on a single life, and not the succeeding generation or generations. As we will examine, in the next chapter, one of the strengths of the religious over the psychological perspective is its appreciation of the multi-generational—that what happens in one generation, positives and negatives, has implications of great significance for future generations.

Within this multi-generational perspective, the Book of Genesis offers a solution to the Jacob-Israel problem. While it is clear that Jacob never becomes fully Israel in his life, his son Joseph does. We now turn to the final chapters of the Book of Genesis and examine how Joseph, as a beneficiary of Jacob's life struggles, *becomes* Israel.

Joseph: Genesis' Final Hero

Because Joseph surpasses and learns from his father's life, mistakes and struggles, because he masters and transcends his own and his father's characterological pressures toward entitlement, because he *completes Jacob and becomes Israel*, it is Joseph who is the spiritual and psychological apogee of the Book of Genesis. Joseph is Genesis' final form and ultimate hero. He is "the most complete pattern of genuine natural eloquence discovered in literature."[339] It is the story of Joseph, a complex tale of slavery and redemption of an individual, the figure responsible for bringing the Israelites into an Egypt that warmly welcomes them, that becomes the metaphor for, and bridge to Exodus, the next book of the Torah. Just as Joseph, at the end of Genesis, as an individual, is enslaved and then redeemed, so too is all Israel in Exodus, as a community, enslaved and then redeemed. Just as Joseph in Genesis saves the children of Israel from starvation and death in Canaan by bringing them into a temporary land of respite, so too does God in Exodus save the descendents of those same Israelites from a life of hardship, suffering and death, and lead them into the Promised Land. In this way, the Joseph Genesis novella serves both as a psycho-spiritual ideal and central organizing motif of Judaism.

The birth of Joseph has some, but not all, of the features common to the births of the two preceding patriarchs. Rachel, Joseph's mother, like Joseph's grandmother Rebecca and great-grandmother Sarah, spends long tormented years suffering with her infertility. Conception here again, in this generation, cannot be achieved naturally, but requires a special divine act. "And God remembered Rachel, and God listened to her, and God opened her womb. And Rachel conceived and delivered a son, and Rachel said, 'God has now taken away my disgrace,' and she called his name, Joseph."[340]

What is different about Joseph's birth than those of Isaac and Jacob is that in Joseph's case, while God opens Rachel's womb, He never states that Joseph is the one who will carry the blessing of Abraham. The choice of spiritual heir of Abraham, in Joseph's father's and grandfather's case is made explicit by God in the text.[341] In the story of Joseph, however, we do not read that God is specifically with Joseph until Joseph is at least seventeen years old and already a slave in Egypt. From this point on, through the end of Genesis, God's special relationship with Joseph—God's accompanying Joseph in his journey from slave to prisoner to Vice-Pharaoh, from betrayed orphan to head of a large extended family—is frequently referred to in the text. For example, the Torah reads, "And the Lord was with Joseph...and his master [Potiphar] saw that the Lord was with Joseph and that the Lord made everything that Joseph did prosper."[342] Later, when Joseph is placed into prison, an ancient victim of sexual harassment, the text again makes God's special connection with Joseph explicit. "And Joseph was in prison, but the Lord was with Joseph and showed kindness to him, and caused the guard to view Joseph with favor."[343]

It is the special relationship between God and Joseph that Joseph, himself, credits for his keen insight into the meaning of dreams. Pharaoh, speaking to Joseph who was just released from two years in the dungeon, says, "'I have dreamed a dream, and there is none so far that has been able to interpret it. I have heard that you can interpret dreams that are told to you.' And Joseph said to Pharaoh, 'Not me. It is God who will respond [to your dream through me].'"[344]

With Joseph's assertion that his acute insights into dreams are not really his to own, but that he is merely a vessel which temporarily contains and conveys God's wisdom, the Bible heralds and symbolizes a major shift in Joseph's character. After all, this is the same Joseph, exclusively favored and pampered by his father Jacob, who not only had grandiose dreams in his adolescence, but also was so self-absorbed and insensitive to the others' feelings as to unashamedly speak these dreams in public. In the first of these dreams, told to his brothers and offensive to them, Joseph represents himself and his brothers as sheaves of grain. Joseph says to his brothers, "Hear, please, this dream that I have dreamed. Behold, we were binding sheaves in the field and then, my sheaf arose and stood upright. And then your sheaves circled by sheaf and bowed low to it."[345] The second of Joseph's reported dreams, not only offended his brothers, but even his adoring father was hurt and taken aback by Joseph's frank narcissism. In this dream, all the heavenly bodies, the sun and the moon and the eleven stars bow down to Joseph. The text offers reactions to the dream's telling, "And Joseph told this dream to his father and to his brothers. And Jacob reprimanded Joseph and said to him, 'What is this dream you have dreamed? Should I and your mother and your brothers bow ourselves down to you to the ground?' And the brothers were envious of Joseph, but his father kept the incident in mind."[346]

With the shift from Joseph's unchecked entitlement and unedited self-absorption to his recognition that his talents are God working through him—a shift that is only hard won after slavery and facing death both in his brothers' pit and in the Pharaoh's dungeon—Joseph swims against the tide of his character, history and predisposition. In the process, *Joseph becomes Israel.*

Most poignant and of great significance, we see the signature of Israel in the conclusion of the Book of Genesis. After the death of Jacob, Joseph's terrified brothers worry about reprisals by Joseph for their behavior many years before. At this point, Joseph has a choice to make. Will Joseph perpetuate the multi-generational family history involving rivalry, envy and resentment of brother against brother; or shatter the vicious cycle by forgiving them for what they had done to him? Will Joseph be swept along by the impulse to get even with his brothers for their attempted murder of him and all of his suffering; or understand the arc of his life in a broader perspective in which his torment had a greater purpose? In the face of his brothers' vulnerability and dread, will Joseph choose to be Jacob or Israel? The text reads:

And when Joseph's brothers saw that their father was dead, they said, "It may be that Joseph hates us and will retaliate against us for all the wrong we did to him…And Joseph's brothers flung themselves to the ground in front of Joseph. And they said to Joseph, "Behold, we will be your slaves." And Joseph said to his brothers, "Don't be afraid. After all, am I God? **For even though you intended that I be harmed, God's intent was for good**; so that the [Jewish] people would survive [the famine in Canaan]. Now, therefore, do not fear. I will nourish you and your little ones." And Joseph comforted his brothers and spoke words of kindness to them.[347]

In this final chapter of the Book of Genesis, we are allowed to witness a majestic Joseph. Acutely aware of his own and his family's history, Joseph is a paragon of forgiveness and transformation. Fully cognoscente of the errors of the past, and having won the struggle against his own character, he takes steps to break the malignant cycle of sibling resentment and retaliation that had haunted his family for centuries; and had even bloodied the Bible's first brothers.

In Genesis' second generation, Cain is filled with rage and envy toward his younger brother Abel. God, aware of Cain's state, informs him that it is Cain's choice whether he will choose good or be ruled by sin. God tells Cain, "Surely, if you do good, there will be uplift. But if you do not do good, sin lurks at the door. It seeks you out. Yet you *can* master it."[348] Cain chooses. He kills Abel. Later, God asks Cain where is his brother. Cain's famous response is a question, "Am I my brother's keeper?"[349]

In the concluding chapter of the Book of Genesis, Joseph finally answers Cain's question, awaiting an affirmative response since the dark days of the biblical prehistory, more than two thousand years before. "Am I my brother's keeper?" Joseph's answer is a loud, clear and emphatic "Yes!"

Joseph completes the journey his father Jacob began, but never finished. As we have seen in this study of Joseph, *in only two generations*, Jacob *does* succeed. It is in Joseph that Jacob becomes Israel.

Judah: Genesis' Disadvantaged Hero

As we complete this study of Jacob's transformation, a second of Jacob's sons deserves our attention and respect. No investigation of the biblical view of how we change can ignore the narratives involving the figure of Judah. Judah, Jacob's fourth son, born to Leah, emerges in the last quarter of the Book of Genesis as a biblical model of repentance. Significantly, Judah is not Jacob's favorite son, nor is he the child of a favored wife, nor is he the firstborn. In addition, when compared with the biblical accounts describing the life of his younger half-brother Joseph, there are no Torah verses in which God's blessing or companionship is mentioned in relation to Judah.

And yet, it is Judah, without father's or God's specific blessing or support, who is able to turn his life around. It is Judah who does repentance, in Hebrew "*teshuvah.*"[350] Judah is, in fact, the only figure in the Book of Genesis that demonstrates such a significant transformation of character without any explicit parental and divine assistance.[351]

The first time the Bible describes Judah as an adult, we find him at the head of a hateful and murderous mob. Joseph, seventeen years old, adorned in the ornamented tunic, the token of his father's special love for him, approaches Dothan, where his ten older brothers tend their herds. As they see Joseph drawing near, the unnamed brothers conspire to kill him and throw his body into a pit. Jacob's firstborn son Reuben, attempting to save Joseph's life in the face of his brothers' murderous plans, argues with the mob. The text states, "But when Reuben heard it, he tried to deliver Joseph from their hands. He said, 'Let us not take his life…Shed no blood! Cast him into that pit in the wilderness, but do not touch him yourselves'—intending to deliver Joseph from the brothers' hands and return him to his father."[352] It is interesting to note in these verses that the biblical author leaves no doubt as to Reuben's benevolent motivation in suggesting the pit for Joseph—as a way to ultimately save Joseph from his brothers and restore him to Jacob.

The brothers strip Joseph of his coat and throw him into the desert pit, empty of food and water. With their young brother at the bottom of a pit—we assume hungry, thirsty and screaming—in a chillingly callous image, the text then states, "And the brothers sat down to eat bread."[353] At this point, a caravan of merchants approach on their way to Egypt.

Enter our "hero" Judah as new leader of the mob. It is Judah who suggests a way that the brothers can profit from Joseph's plight and, in addition, *not* have to bear the guilt of killing their own brother themselves. Judah says, "What do we gain by killing our brother and covering up his blood? Come, let us sell him to the Ishmaelites, but let not *our* hand be upon him."[354] Whereas, in Reuben's case, the text makes his benevolent motives explicit, no such explanation is offered for Judah. Reuben, when he returns to the pit to discover what Judah and his brothers have done in Reuben's absence, immediately rents his garment to repent and mourn.[355] The text describes no such behavior of contrition on the part of Judah or any of Joseph's other brothers.

The classical midrashic literature places most of the burden of responsibility for this despicable Joseph slavery incident squarely on the shoulders of Judah. According to this rabbinic literature, Jacob, not deceived by the story that is told him that Joseph was killed by a wild animal, suspects Judah as the murderer.[356] The midrash suggests that, instead of Judah carrying Joseph's blood-stained tunic to Jacob and lying to his father as to what happened in the wilderness, Judah should have carried an alive and healthy Joseph away from his brothers to his father.[357] According to another midrash, the brothers, seeing the depth of their father's grief for Joseph, deposed and banished Judah. The brothers said, "If Judah, our chief, had ordered us to bring Joseph home, we would have most certainly done so."[358]

Immediately following Joseph's sale into slavery in Egypt, the Bible offers us a seemingly disconnected narrative involving Judah and his daughter-in-law Tamar.[359] A deeper examination, however, reveals that this biblical account is the first of two portrayals of Judah's interest in and capacity for repentance.

In this first narrative, we learn that Judah has three sons. Judah's oldest son Er, married to Tamar, dies. Judah, consonant with biblical rules governing the levirate marriage,[360] commands his second son Onan to have sexual relations with Tamar, and by this method, provide offspring for his dead brother. Onan, resisting Judah's order, spills his seed, rather than grant his brother a child. Then Onan dies. At this point, Judah makes a false promise to Tamar. If she will return to her father's house, Judah's third son Shelah will be offered to her when he grows old enough to father a child.

Much later, after Judah's wife dies and Shelah is well grown, Tamar is informed that her father-in-law is coming to her village to shear his sheep. Tamar, desperate to have the child she was promised, covers her face and disguises herself as a harlot. Tamar seduces Judah. As a pledge for payment, Judah gives Tamar his signet, cord and staff. Tamar conceives.

It is three months later. Judah hears that Tamar is pregnant. Genesis states, "Judah was told, 'Your daughter-in-law Tamar has played the harlot; in fact, she is with child by harlotry.' [Judah, consistent with biblical law, commands,] 'Bring her out, and let her be burned.' As Tamar was being brought out, she sent this message to her father-in-law, 'I am with child by the man to whom these belong...Examine these: whose signet and cord and staff are these?'"[361]

At this point, the narrative forces Judah to make a decision. Will he admit publicly that it was he who, unaware, impregnated his own daughter-in-law? Will he have the strength of character to rescind the order of execution? Will he blame

Tamar for deceiving him? Or will Judah be capable of understanding why Tamar acted the way she did, and even see his own culpability within her predicament?

Genesis states, "Judah acknowledged his signet, cord and staff; and said, 'She is more righteous than I, inasmuch as I did not give her [as I promised] to my son Shelah.'"[362]

As we can see from this biblical passage, Judah passes the *teshuvah* test.

Tamar's pregnancy results in the birth of twins. Most significantly, one of them, Perez, is the ancestor of King David[363] and therefore, by both Jewish and Christian biblical traditions, the forefather of the messiah.[364]

The second Genesis portrait of Judah's *teshuvah* constitutes the emotional climax of the Joseph biblical "novella." Canaan, where Joseph's entire family lives, suffers with a great famine. Joseph's brothers, with the exception of Jacob's new favorite son Benjamin, come to Egypt to plead for food. Joseph is unrecognized by his brothers. Joseph, the second most powerful person in Egypt, subjects his brothers to a series of demanding tests to discern whether they have, over the many years that have elapsed, changed.

In one of these tests, Joseph demands that the youngest son be brought to Egypt. He refuses to give the brothers adequate food for the family unless this demand is met. In addition, to further intensify the test, he holds Simeon, his half-brother, in jail as ransom until the others return to Egypt with Benjamin.

Jacob, profoundly worried that he will lose Benjamin, as he has lost Joseph and Simeon, refuses, at first, to allow Benjamin to travel to Egypt. However, as the famine intensifies, Judah makes a pledge to his father that changes Jacob's mind. Judah promises that he will be security for Benjamin. Judah says to his father, "If I do not bring Benjamin back to you and set him before you, I shall bear your blame forever."[365]

When Benjamin and the brothers arrive in Egypt, and Simeon restored to them, Joseph, still unrecognized, dines with all of his eleven brothers in his home. Joseph then sends them away with the food that they require to save their families in Canaan. It is then that Joseph puts his brothers to the final and most excruciating of the tests. Joseph plants his special silver goblet in Benjamin's sack. Overtaking them on their route, Joseph informs the brothers that whoever is discovered to have taken the goblet will remain in Egypt and be Joseph's slave.

The drama of the biblical narrative is intense as the gear of each of the brothers, from oldest to youngest, is searched. When, in the last sac, that of Benjamin, the goblet is found, all the brothers rent their garments and throw themselves to the ground before Joseph. Joseph reaffirms that it is only Benjamin that will be enslaved in Egypt.

Joseph's test of the brothers is precise and bitter. Will they, yet again, eagerly, or even reluctantly sacrifice their younger brother, their father's now-favorite son? Will they leave Benjamin a slave in Egypt and return to Jacob in Canaan?

It is Judah who approaches Joseph. In what is the longest and most moving monologue in the Bible, Judah pleads for Joseph's mercy. He asks that Joseph have compassion on the old man who will surely die if Benjamin, like his other beloved son, is lost to him. And then, Judah offers himself as slave in Benjamin's place.

> Then Judah approached Joseph and said, "Please, my lord, let me, your ser-
> vant, speak a word in your ears, and do not be angry with your servant, You
> who are the equal of Pharaoh...My father said to us, 'My wife bore me two
> sons. But one is gone from me,...And I have not seen him since. If you take
> this one from me, too, and he meets with disaster, you will send my white
> head down to the grave in sorrow.' Now, if I come to my father and the boy is
> not with us—since his own life is so bound up with his—when he sees that
> the boy is not with us, he will die, and we will send the white head of our
> father down to the grave in grief...Therefore, please let me, I pray you, remain
> as a slave here to my lord instead of the boy, and let the boy go back with his
> brothers. For how can I go back to my father unless the boy is with me? Let
> me not be witness to the misery that would engulf my father!"[366]

Proved by this monologue, Judah, repentant and transformed, passes Joseph's test. Now finally convinced of Judah's and the brothers' change of heart, Joseph, weeping uncontrollably, announces to his astounded siblings, "I am Joseph."[367]

Without the benefit of blessing or preference by heavenly or earthly father, without the advantage of firstborn status or birth to a favored wife, it is Judah who becomes the undisputed leader of his generation. It is Judah who is the ancestor of the messiah. It is Judah who receives Jacob's most affirming deathbed blessing, "Judah, he who his brothers will praise,...and the royal scepter shall never depart from Judah,...and the homage of all people will be his."[368] It is Judah whose name will be remembered, throughout the centuries, in the religion of "*Juda*ism."

Judah is Genesis' hero of repentance. Because of this, with his brother Joseph, *Judah becomes Israel.*

As we have seen in these last two chapters, it is Abraham, Jacob, Joseph and Judah who call to us across the chasm of the millennia. Each of these ancient heroes of the Book of Genesis teaches *each of us* how to change.

PART III
Dialogue

This psychoanalytic journey to the sacred, like most journeys, ends where it began. It is 1954. I am walking down one of the oldest streets in Worcester, Massachusetts, where I was born and continued to live until leaving for college. My father holds my left hand and my zadie, his father, holds my right. I remember the bright red of the apples in one of the carts, a huge barrel of green pickles and a table with hundreds of men's and women's hats. The street was crowded with grownups' hurrying legs. My zadie, who had owned a small shoe repair shop in the neighborhood since he arrived from the tiny Polish village fifty years before, greeted most of the people we passed. He spoke a language I didn't know. I was surprised to hear my father speak to my zadie in that same language.

We came to one of the oldest buildings on this street of old buildings. My zadie opened the door without knocking. The murmuring of men's voices, darkness and the smell of ancient dust and food and books stunned me. The stairway was so narrow that I had to drop my father's hand. My zadie stood with me at the top of the steps until my eyes could see. It was a long flight of stairs, only dimly lit at the bottom. My zadie and I arrived at the basement floor in a room where twenty or so men, all looking more like zadie than my father, sat at tables, in front of open books, talking and laughing. My zadie brought me by the hand to each of the four or five tables and said something that included my name. Some of the men at the tables looked up from their books for a few moments and smiled at me.

We sat at an empty table in the corner and my father and zadie opened one of the big books and talked for a long time about what they read in it. For a few minutes, they got angry at each other. Zadie pointed at one page and started talking loudly. And then, my father grabbed the book from Zadie's hands and flipped the pages and pointed at the writing in the book. Then, all was calm again and they kept reading and talking about the book. I sat and ate the sticky pastry, filled with honey, raisins and nuts, that my father bought me that morning at one of the stalls on the way to zadie's.

Three years later, the night I learned that my zadie died, I dreamt that I returned to that basement room in that old building. There, among the men at the tables, was my zadie, smiling at me and studying Torah.

6

Character, Transformation and Meaning: What Is Said when the Modern and the Ancient Speak

There is a wickedness of human nature to think that we cannot praise one thing, without denouncing another.

—Henry Slonimsky

E.L. Doctorow, in his keynote lecture on the novel, *Moby-Dick*, said, "We are never in one place alone at any given minute. But in two. The present that is the past. Or on the land that is the sea. Or in the sea that is the soul. Or in the novel that is God's ineffable realm."[369]

It is the same for each of us. Each of us is never in one place alone at any given minute. Each of us is present and past. Each of us is individual, family and society. Each of us is flesh, psyche and soul. Each individual is a unique personality and, at the same minute and at all minutes, cultural delegate. Each of us is God, man and animal. Each of us is the person who is the subject of modern psychology and psychoanalysis. And each of us is the person who is, at the same time, the subject of the ancient and sacred text.

More than any specific conviction, doctrine or principle, what the biblical and psychological perspectives most intimately share are the questions. The ancient and the modern each thirsts to understand what is our essential nature. Each perspective struggles to know what makes characterological change possible and lasting. Each school of thought, separated from each other by centuries of ideology, history, culture and social complexity and structure, *together* considers what makes life worth living. It is to these questions which the ancient and the modern share that we now turn.

Who Are We?

When studying the principal Genesis narratives for what each says about the nature and essence of human experience, one distinctive theme emerges. In Genesis, who we are always involves the combination of two opposites. In the biblical, we are both Adam I and Adam II—divine image and also, simultaneously, more animal than angel. We are Abraham, a monotheist, struggling with our idolatry and our paganism. We are sometimes Jacob and sometimes Israel, sometimes the self-absorbed and deceitful manipulator, and sometimes the one who wrestles with our Jacobs, and prevails. We are both the glorious crown of God's creation,[370] and "one of the things that goes wrong in the world."[371]

Whereas the Genesis conception of who we are is a dual conception, understanding the essence of the human as a product of two clashing forces, the major contemporary classical psychoanalytic theories of who we are, that of Sigmund Freud and Carl Jung, trace the origin of human behavior and personality to different *single* factors.

Sigmund Freud (1856-1939), a physician, a philosopher, an Austrian, a Jew,[372] was the single most influential voice of the twentieth century. Although some of Freud's theories have recently been discovered to be wrong, imprecise or incomplete, requiring revision,[373] it was psychoanalysis, invented, developed and directed by Freud for its first four decades, that radically transformed the way the contemporary individual views himself. Never again could we, that is, post-Freudian men and women, feel so comfortable in our skins. Never again could we assert, without even a distant almost-silent whisper of ambivalence or question, that we are masters of our thoughts, feelings, behavior, choices or goals. The idea of the unconscious, as developed by Freud, and his commitment to the unfiltered inspection of its contents, reflected a profound truth—and deeply disturbed our sleep.

Cleverly presaging this deeper meaning of Freudian theory, Oscar Wilde, in response to a question put to him by Edward Carson, the prosecutor in Wilde's first decency trial in the Old Bailey, April 3, 1895, retorted to his relentless accuser, "It is only the shallow that know themselves."[374] Sigmund Freud would certainly agree.

Freud, perhaps more than any of his colleagues or contemporaries, was consistently and acutely aware of how his theories imbalanced the tenuous psychic equilibrium of the modern man and woman. In one of his essays, "A Difficulty in the Path of Psychoanalysis,"[375] Freud describes three narcissistic injuries that the contemporary individual is forced to suffer by virtue of being a modern. These are the cosmological, biological and psychological. For Freud, each of these wounding ideas challenges and ultimately shatters the contemporary person's comforting delusion of centrality, specialness and mastery.

First, Copernicus in the sixteenth century discovered that the earth was not the center of the universe, but rather more like all the other planets that revolved around a star. Freud wrote, "The central position of the earth was a token to him [humanity] of the dominating part played by it in the universe and appeared to fit in very well with his inclination to regard himself as lord of the world."

Second, Charles Darwin, fifty-seven years before Freud published this essay, discovered that man was not unique among the animals, but rather on a continuum with them. Freud wrote, "In the course of the development of civilization man acquired a dominating position over his fellow creatures in the animal kingdom. Not content with this supremacy, however, he began to place a gulf between his nature and theirs. He denied the possession of reason to them, and to himself he attributed an immortal soul, and made claims to a Divine descent which permitted him to break the bond of community between him and the animal kingdom."

The third, and according to Freud most wounding narcissistic injury to the modern individual was inflicted by Freud himself. The post-Freudian man and woman, unhappily inhabiting an outpost planet in an expanding and infinite universe, and uncomfortably seated so much closer to animal than angel, must now recognize that his behavior, thoughts and choices are not under his conscious control. Freud wrote, "…that the life of our sexual instincts cannot be wholly tamed, and that mental processes are in themselves unconscious and only reach the ego and come under its control through incomplete and untrustworthy perceptions—these two discoveries amount to a statement that the *ego is not master in its own house.*"

To these three narcissistic injuries suffered by the modern individual described by Freud, I would add a fourth—the moral wound. After the Nazi genocide, which was meticulously devised and efficiently executed by a society representing the pinnacle of the arts, literature and scholarship, post-Hitler man discovered that he could no longer afford to delude himself by thinking that sophistication, high culture and education can inoculate him against savagery.

In 1909, Freud traveled by ship to the United states (his only visit) to deliver a series of lectures at Clark University in Worcester, Massachusetts. His traveling companions were two psychoanalysts, Sandor Ferenczi and Carl Jung. Freud's writing on sex had won him some notoriety and admiration in New York where the ship was docking. The New York newspapers, unknown to Freud, had announced his arrival. Throngs of New Yorkers traveled to New York Harbor to greet the eminent and provocative Professor Freud. Freud, seeing the waiting crowds and realizing that they were there to greet him and always profoundly aware of the distressing implication of his theory of the unconscious, as he disembarked asked, "Carl, don't they realize that we're bringing them the plague?"[376]

Sigmund Freud was not the first to assert the existence of the unconscious. There is ample evidence that even the ancient rabbis, as well as the Chasidic masters of the eighteenth and nineteenth centuries, discussed and wrote about certain powerful aspects of the individual's personality, unknown to the individual himself.[377] Freud's unique contribution involved his positioning the unconscious in the center of his theoretical and therapeutic concerns. For the entire forty years of his life as a psychoanalyst, Freud investigated in minute detail the myriad implications for both the individual and societies of bearing long-hidden, disguised and disowned desires. Whether explaining the psychological differences between males and females, the evolution of religious ritual and belief, a specific dream image or the onset of a neurosis or psychosis, it was to the psychic force, unknown and almost unknowable to the individual, that Freud directed his attention. For Freud, the power of the unconscious to exert malevolent control over the individual or society was in direct proportion to how hidden it was from view. An unconscious fantasy, memory or wish, especially those entombed during childhood, like the well-buried canister of radioactive waste, not only stays largely intact, but also, from its hiding place, does significant psychological damage. Making the unconscious conscious became Freud's philosophical and psychotherapeutic *raison d'être*.

A demonstration of this attitude toward the unconscious is found in Freud's case of the "Rat Man." Early in this treatment, the patient asks Freud why uncovering memories and feelings will help. Freud tells his patient that everything conscious is subject to a process of wearing away, while those aspects that are unconscious are relatively unchangeable. Pointing to one of the archaeological artifacts with which Freud filled his office, Freud said, The destruction of Pompeii was only begun now that it had been dug up."[378] For Freud, unconscious desires remain intact and exert malignant influence only until they are discovered and unearthed.

Not only did Freud propose that there is an unconscious, but also what forces reside within its borders. For Freud, the deepest layers of the unconscious mind, the bedrock of human experience and motivation, from cradle to grave, were the baser instincts, the "elemental passions."[379] The newborn infant, a creature who is all id, is dominated by primitive sexual and aggressive impulses. As that infant grows into adulthood, he becomes more sophisticated in how he hides from others and himself his savage and hedonistic motivation. However, the primal desires never disappear. They are merely dressed in new costume so that the individual can come to terms with the demands of the social world. It is these primal passions of infancy that are seated at the control panel, behind the curtain, operating the levers that determine adult behavior, choices and attitudes.[380]

Freud even went so far as to characterize this deepest layer of the infant's motivation as "evil."[381] In his "Introductory Lectures on Psycho-analysis," Freud writes, "The strange impression of there being so much evil in people begins to diminish when we study the mental life of infants. This frightful evil is simply the initial, primitive, infantile part of mental life, which we can find in actual operation in children, but which, in part, we overlook in them on account of their small size, and which in part we do not take seriously since we do not expect any high ethical standard from children."[382]

Whereas for Freud, the single deepest level of the individual's motivation involves bestial desires, for Carl Jung (1875-1961) the unconscious is inhabited by higher motivations. Jung fully accepted Freud's assertions concerning the existence and the significance of the unconscious, but vehemently disagreed with his former mentor as to what constitutes its content. For Jung, the unconscious is more associated with revelation, the transcendent and even the voice of God-within, than with the savage.[383] In a series of lectures he delivered at Yale University in 1937, Jung argued, in opposition to Freud's motivational theory, "The unconscious mind is capable of assuming an intelligence and purposiveness which are superior to actual conscious insight. There is hardly any doubt that this fact is a basic religious phenomenon."[384] It was to emphasize that his concept of self was one which transcends the personal idiosyncratic ego that Jung always wrote self with a capital "S." Unlike the personal ego scrutinized by Freud, this Jungian "Self" had access to the spiritual realm.

Although disagreeing about what is psychological bedrock in the human, both Freud and Jung ascribe the foundation of human motivation to single factors. Genesis' narrative portrait of who we are is different. As we have seen in the previous chapters, in the Genesis accounts, the human being is *at his center both* savage and divine. He is *both* animal and angel. He is *both* heaven and earth. He is *both* merely dust and ashes and also, at the same time, the creature for whom God created the world. He is the composite individual described by *both* Freud and Jung.

As we saw in Chapters Two and Three of this volume, the Book of Genesis includes two separate narratives concerning the creation of humanity. Each of these distinct visions of how God formed mankind reflects conflicting aspects found in each of us. In the first of these accounts, God simultaneously created man and woman in His image. We are the only creature God forms that bears such a lofty manufacturer's logo. Just as God has no component parts or ingredients, this human creature's makeup is not described. For a recipe involving part God and part earth, one needs to turn to the second of the creation stories, the one set in the Garden of Eden. In this first creation account, this human image-of-God is only divine.

The transcendent nature of this first human pair is well captured by the midrash that taught that, when humanity was created, the angels were so dazzled by these creatures that they could not distinguish between man and God, "When the Holy One, blessed be He, created mankind, the ministering angels mistook him for a Divine being and wished to exclaim 'Holy' before him. What does this resemble? A king and a governor who sat in a chariot, and his subjects wished to say to the king, 'Domine!' [sovereign!] but they did not know which one was the king and which one was the governor."[385]

Humanity in this first creation account was also distinct from all other of God's living artworks in that it was God's final creature. In this narrative, man and woman are the glorious culmination of God's creativity. In the waning hours of God's long work week, only after the lavish banquet that is the world was prepared for him and her, did God announce, create and bless humanity.

In the second account of God's creation of man and woman, and of their Eden adventures, Genesis offers a sharply contrasting vision of who we are. Man, in this account, is formed fifteen verses before woman. *This* Adam is a composite creature. "And the Lord God formed man from the dust of the earth. He blew into man's nostrils the breath of life. And man became a living being."[386]

No divine image, Adam II is as much heaven as he is earth, as much animal as he is angel, as much fragile vessel as he is God's representative in the world. In this second biblical creation story, Adam II, a complex compound of dust and divine breath, is a decidedly ambivalent creature.

It is this creature's ambivalent nature that not only leads Adam and Eve inexorably to disobey God's command concerning the fruit, but to the greater sin of the Garden—the devastating renunciation of moral responsibility for their action. God asks Adam, "'Did you eat of the tree from which I had forbidden you to eat?' The man said, 'The woman You put at my side—she gave me of the tree, and I ate.' And the Lord God said to the woman, 'What is this you have done!' The woman replied, 'The serpent duped me, and I ate.'"[387]

In contradistinction to the motivational theory of Freud and Jung, the two biblical creation narratives taken together depict mankind as having *two* discrete and constant psychological pressures on the individual's behavior and personality. The Adam-I-within pushes us toward reason, the Divine and the transcendent. It calls us to moral action. It beckons us to create, like the one of whom we are an image. The Adam-II-within brings us face-to-face with our darker side. This Adam is an earthly creature, and like all other earthly creatures he is vulnerable and frightened. When he feels afraid, he hides. When he feels threatened, he attacks. In response to his fragility and his desperation, it is this Adam-II-within who abandons his reason and becomes enslaved by impulse and desire. The two creation accounts establish the biblical theory of human motivation that asserts that all of an individual's behavior and personality is a product of the ongoing struggle between Adam I and Adam II.

In Abraham's binding of Isaac (Chapter Four of this volume) and the Jacob-Israel novella (Chapter Five), we also see this two-factor biblical theory of human motivation embodied. Abraham is a tormented hero. Torn between the primordial deity who for millennia demanded child sacrifice as proof of worship and obedience, and a new God who values human life over all things, Abraham and Isaac ascend Mount Moriah. Once there, Abraham, enveloped by his pagan history and deafened by the archaic voice requiring human blood, prepares the altar for the slaughter of his precious and favorite son. The stage—upon which our struggle between the pagan and the monotheist, between the base and the transcendent, between the two Adams-within—is now set.

Abraham stands with knife in hand. Isaac is bound below him. The silence is forever shattered by a new voice from heaven. The angel of *YHWH* calls twice. The knife then falls to the ground.

The rabbis of the *Zohar* ask why the Lord's angel calls twice to Abraham on Mount Moriah. The *Zohar* answers because the second time Abraham hears his name called, only then has he been awoken and transformed, only then is he an "other," a man with a changed set of ears so that he can hear different words from his God.[388] At that moment of excruciating trial, Abraham passes the test by choosing the voice of *YHWH* over *Elohim*. *As we have seen, Abraham's struggle is our struggle. On that distant and lonely mountain, Abraham wrestles with the two colliding forces within him and within each of us—our idolatry vs. our monotheism, our escape to the empty ritual vs. the striving for the ethical, our valuing things and ideology more than human life—and emerges from the Akedah a psychological and spiritual hero.*

Abraham's grandson Jacob, in the first forty years of his life, is a troubled and troubling "hero." In the detailed biblical accounts of his birth, youth and adulthood, Jacob's baser personality traits are exclusively described. We see a Jacob who manipulates his hungry twin brother Esau out of his birthright. We see Jacob, allying with his domineering mother, deceiving his blind father and stealing a blessing that belongs to Esau. Even the biblical birth narrative is sullied by Jacob's ruthlessly ambitious character. "When Rebecca's time to give birth came, behold, there were twins in her womb. The first one emerged red, like a hairy garment all over; they named him Esau. And after that, his brother emerged, holding on to the heel (akev in Hebrew) of Esau; so they named him Jacob (*Ya-akov*)."[389]

It is not until after twenty years of exile, now sixty years old, that *Ya-akov*, the one who trips up his fellow's heel, the supplanter, is blessed with a new name to signify a more positive force within his character. Jacob and his large and complex family are traveling through the wilderness toward the land of his birth. The last time Jacob was there, twenty years before, Esau had threatened to kill Jacob for his betrayal. This night, Jacob had learned that his brother rides toward him with four hundred men. Frightened by blood-soaked images of what the morning may bring for him and his family, Jacob separates himself from all he owns and knows. Alone, in the most lonely and silent black of nights, Jacob wrestles.

"And a man wrestled with Jacob until the break of dawn…Then the man said, 'Let me go, for dawn is breaking.' But Jacob answered, 'I will not let you go, until you bless me.' 'What is your name?' asked the man. Jacob replied, '*Ya-akov*.' Said the man, 'Your name shall no longer be *Ya-akov*, but Israel (*Yisro-El*), for you have struggled with beings, divine and human, and have prevailed.'"[390]

In this dramatic culmination of Jacob's transformation of character, Jacob, sleepless and terrified, finally chooses to face himself. Jacob's past wrestles with his present and future. The deceiver and manipulator clashes with the struggler and confronter. Jacob's two Adams-within are locked in all-night and all-out battle and embrace. It is this night that Jacob becomes Israel.

Later, rabbinic Judaism, drawing on the Book of Genesis as its primary textual inspiration, developed a highly sophisticated dualistic theory of psychological motivation. For the rabbis of the *Talmud*, and the centuries of commentators that succeeded them, each individual is always uncomfortably teetering between his two inclinations or drives, between his two "*yetzers.*"[391]

The earliest talmudic reference to this rabbinic two-factor psychological theory centers around an explanation of why there is an extra letter in the Torah scroll when describing the creation of the Eden Adam. "And the Lord God **formed** (*va-yyitzer*) man from the dust of the earth. He blew into man's nostrils the breath of life. And man became a living being."[392] The rabbis of course noticed that there was an extra letter, "*yod,*" in the Hebrew word, "formed (*yitzer.*" The Talmud states, "Rabbi Nachman expounded: What is meant by the text, Then the Lord God formed (*va-yitzer*) man? The word, *va-yitzer* is written with two *yods*, to show us that God created two inclinations, one good (the *yetzer ha-tov*) and the other evil (the *yetzer ha-ra*)."[393]

For the rabbis of the *Talmud and* Midrash, the evil inclination refers to the appetites and passions, most of which are defining psycho-biological pressures of universal human nature and characteristic of the human condition. The rabbinic concept of the "*evil*" inclination is less harsh and sinful than the language implies; and less severe than Paul's interpretation of the same concept in the New Testament.[394] The rabbis appreciated that this inclination is a necessary prerequisite for much of what is positive in the world, and therefore not to be wholly suppressed. They argued that the world could not exist without the evil inclination[395] and "...that, but for the evil inclination a man would not build a house, nor take a wife, nor beget children."[396] Reflecting this same attitude, in two separate tractates of the *Talmud*, the rabbis taught that the greater the man, the greater his evil inclination.[397]

For the rabbis, the evil inclination, implanted in mankind by God Himself, is not to be fully suppressed. It should be instead mastered. This rabbinic psychology of motivation maintains that each element of human life is a battleground upon which our disposition toward self-absorption and our potential for transcendence meet and conflict. The question is one of relative weight of these psychological forces, and of making a choice. Therefore, as means to the unity of personality and the moral life, the rabbis recommended control, and not eradication of the evil inclination. This is explicitly expressed in the *Mishnah*. In the second century C.E., Simeon ben Zoma taught, "Who is he that is powerful? He who masters his evil inclination. As it is said (quoting the Book of Proverbs[398]), 'He that is slow to anger is better than the mighty; and he that rules his spirit more powerful than one who captures a city.'"[399]

As we have seen, whereas Freud and Jung each defined a single force that powered the unconscious and human motivation. The Book of Genesis and the rabbis proposed a dual conception. Who we are, for the ancient, is a product of the clash between the two Adams-within, the collision of pagan and monotheist, the struggle between Jacob and Israel, the incessant skirmish of *yetzer ha-tov* and *yetzer ha-ra*.

Interestingly, for both the modern and the ancient, that is, Freud, Jung and Genesis, what is advocated as the path to the good life is the same. Spiritual/psychological health according to each of these "personality theorists," separated from each other by scientific and religious assumptions, culture and the millennia, involves mastery and unity. Freud expressed the aim of psychological mastery when he described the goal of psychoanalytic treatment as providing therapeutic conditions so that, "Where id was, there ego shall be."[400] The goal of unity of the personality is expressed by Freud when he offered his other well-known description of the purpose of the therapeutic work—to make the unconscious conscious.

Mastery and unity is also the spiritual aim of the biblical. In the face of the duel between the two Adams, the Genesis "psychologist" reminds us that we can *choose* to master our baser impulses or to be mastered by them. In as early as the second biblical generation, we encounter Cain. Shattered by God's preference for his younger brother's sacrificial offering, Cain's "face falls." God, noticing Cain's black and dangerous mood, reminds him that he and each of us has a choice. Will the distressed and enraged Cain choose to control the lurking evil within him, or will he allow it to control him? God says to Cain, "Surely, if you do good, there will be uplift. But if you do not do good, sin lurks at the door. It seeks you out. Yet you *can* master it."[401] And just as the Genesis God is one, so too is the goal, for the individual and the world[402], to become one—to become whole, to become *shalom*.

But how can an individual develop this mastery and unity in his life? What does the dialogue of modern and ancient voices teach us about human transformation?

How Do We Change?

Adam and Eve, abruptly exposed by God as having eaten the forbidden fruit, show no sign of remorse or repentance. Our first parents choose instead to answer God's pointed inquiry into the matter by disastrously and embarrassingly renouncing all responsibility for their actions. Adam first blames Eve. Then Adam blames God who, after all, was the one who put Eve at Adam's side. Eve blames the serpent. Although they serve out the divine sentence—a lifetime of hard exile for themselves and all their descendents—Adam and Eve never admit what they had done nor plead for God's forgiveness. Adam and Eve are punished, but remain unchanged.

After Cain's murder of his brother, it is again God who has to deduce the crime. Cain never confesses. Sadly, it is Abel's blood, not Cain, that cries out to God. "And the Lord said to Cain, 'Where is Abel your brother?' And Cain said, 'I do not know. Am I my brother's keeper?' And the Lord said, 'What have you done? the voice of your brother's blood[403] cries out to me from the ground.'"[404]

At this point, God passes judgement. Cain will be exiled. He will live out is days east of Eden, a fugitive, without land or kin or protection. While never admitting his guilt nor asking his parents or God for forgiveness for his heinous crime, Cain, unlike his parents, throws himself on the mercy of the court. "And Cain said to the Lord, 'My punishment is greater than I can bear. Behold, you have driven me out this day from the face of the earth; and from your presence shall I be barred; and I shall be a fugitive and an outcast in the earth; and every one that comes upon me shall slay me.'"[405]

Although God shows mercy for the unrepentant murderer—promising vengeance on anyone who harms him and giving him a sign to protect him as he wanders through his life—Cain still never admits his crime or begs for divine or parental absolution. Cain, like his parents before him, lives out his life unchanged.

Each of these biblical figures has gone through a momentous transformation of fortune and circumstance. However, the first figure in the Book of Genesis who is described as having undergone a *transformation of character* is God. After regretting that He had created the world He declared as "very good" only six chapters before, God sends a cataclysmic flood to destroy His creation. All that live above the waters are to be drowned. The only ones to be saved are those who board a single ark—Noah, his family and the animals he selects to inhabit the boat with them.

Months later, once the small band of survivors had arrived back on land, and Noah had made a thanksgiving sacrifice to his Lord, the Bible describes God as having been altered by the recent experiences. "The Lord said to Himself [in His heart], 'I will never again curse the earth because of man...Neither will I ever again slaughter every living thing as I have done.'"[406] Interestingly, in this biblical and some ancient rabbinic sources[407], even God wrestles with Himself.

God then decides to "go public" with His newly-made resolution and, as a result, compels Himself to uphold the promise that He had already made privately. The chosen witness is not only Noah, but also his sons. "And God spoke to Noah and his sons with him, 'I establish my covenant with you and all your descendents to come, and with all living creatures...Never again shall all flesh be cut off by the waters of a flood. Never again shall there be a flood to destroy the earth.'"[408]

God, not wholly trusting Himself that He will be consistently able to maintain His promise, yet wanting to, creates a physical sign to remind Him of His covenant with all living flesh. God creates the rainbow. "And God said, 'This is a sign of the covenant which I make between me and you, and every living creature that is with you for all generations. I place my bow in the cloud, and it shall be a sign of a covenant between me and the earth. And when I bring clouds over the earth, and the bow appears [to me] in the clouds, then I will *remember* my covenant...and the waters shall never again destroy all flesh.'"[409]

Why does the Bible choose the rainbow as a symbol of God's non-aggression pact with His creatures? The Ramban, the highly-respected biblical commentator of the thirteenth century, offers an interesting answer. From God's heavenly perspective, looking down on the bow in the clouds, the ancient implement of war, the archer's bow, is turned so that the weapon is now rendered harmless. Just as the warrior, who wishes to signify that his intentions are peaceful, turns the bow inward, God, when He sees the bow with curve turned toward Him, reminds Himself that His intentions are peaceful toward the world.[410]

As we have seen, God of the Noah narrative is the first biblical figure to demonstrate a serious transformation of character. In His stages of repentance, first, God faces what He has done. Privately, within His own heart, God regrets having destroyed the world, and resolves never to do this again. He then makes this resolution public by establishing a unilateral covenant with Noah and his sons. Finally, to ensure that He remembers what He has struggled with within Himself and His resolve to act differently, God assigns the rainbow as a memory aid.

The principle characters of the remainder of the Book of Genesis—Abraham, Jacob, Joseph and Judah—follow God's lead. Each of these patriarchs wrestle with themselves and emerge transformed. Each of these heroes' stories clarify for us the biblical "theory" of psycho-spiritual transformation. And, in the process, each of their life narratives, found in the pages of Genesis, teaches *us* how *we* change.

So what *did* happen on Mount Moriah? Why did Abraham ascend the mountain, eager to prove his love for his God by slaughtering his precious son, and arrive at the very moment of the act only to drop the knife? How did Abraham acquire these "new set of ears"[411] that could only now discern this new voice of monotheism? How is it that our Abraham became a paragon of transformation?

As we saw in Chapter Four, Abraham accepts the command of *Elohim* to sacrifice his son without protest or comment. After a night of biblical silence, Abraham awakes early in the morning. Bearing the necessary sacrificial implements for a burnt offering, the ancient patriarch sets out on his religious pilgrimage, accompanied only by his son and two servants. The party travels for three days.

When Abraham sees the mountain on which the slaughter is to take place, he takes his son alone and they ascend the mountain together. Once they arrive at the top, Abraham immediately builds the altar. He then places wood upon it so that Isaac's bloody corpse could be wholly burned and the flames and smoke ascend toward the heavens.[412] Then Abraham binds his son and places him on the altar. Lifting his knife over the sacrifice, Abraham is now ready to prove his boundless faith in, and love for *Elohim*.

So far, Abraham's actions are no different from his pagan neighbors in the ancient Near East. A man, in fervent devotion to a particular god, might also, one night, hear his god telling him to sacrifice that which is most precious to him. He might also accept, in eerie silence, this divine command. The next morning, he might arise early, anxious to do his god's bidding.

This pagan neighbor, or even relative of our Abraham would offer the sacrifice, not in the mundane place in which he lives, but at a site believed to be sacred—perhaps atop a high and isolated mountain. He would prepare the altar. He would place wood upon it so that the odor and the smoke would ascend to the feared and beloved god. He would bind his precious son and then, he would take his knife and slaughter him.

Traditional commentators on the Akedah, Christian, Jewish and Muslim alike, praise Abraham's faith in God. They argue that it is Abraham's eagerness to serve his God, proved by his willingness to sacrifice Isaac, that makes Abraham worthy of fathering all three of these world religions. According to this view, Abraham should be emulated because he is a great "knight of faith."[413]

I disagree.

Yes. Abraham should be emulated, but not because he ascends Mount Moriah eager to sacrifice his son to his deity. Sadly, many zealots in his day and our own would do and have done the same. We should emulate Abraham because, when he descends the mountain, his hands are *not* blood-stained.

The ancient Abraham should be our model because on the top of Mount Moriah, with no human witness but his son looking on, Abraham heard a different divine voice. Abraham heard *YHWH*.

During the entire Akedah narrative, until the moment when Isaac was bound and readied to be slaughtered, it was *Elohim* who spoke to Abraham and issued the insistent sacrificial command. As we have already discussed,[414] *Elohim* is a generic term for God, also used in the Torah to mean pagan gods. *YHWH*, on the contrary, is the specific God of Judaism. *YHWH* never refers to any deity other than a monotheistic God.

It was precisely as Abraham raised his knife to kill his son that he heard, for the first time in the Akedah narrative, *YHWH*. The message that Abraham heard from *YHWH's* messenger was different from *Elohim's*. *YHWH's* message was that the ethical is more meaningful to God than is ritual obedience; that human life is not a means to an end, but an end in itself, and of greater import than a belief or an idea.

We *should* admire and emulate Abraham because, during the Akedah, Abraham changed. But what was it that made Abraham's change possible? What allowed Abraham to struggle with his pagan past and gods, and walk down

Moriah firm in his new-found ethical principles and beliefs? How did Abraham become a hero of transformation? Although Abraham's spiritual transformation is clear, we can only speculate as to the motive forces that catapult Abraham from pagan to monotheist. Unfortunately, these are not given voice in the biblical text.

I believe that there were two principle facets to Abraham's change of mind and heart. First, Abraham became exquisitely aware of himself. The three days of silent torment, his slow and excruciating pilgrimage to Moriah, was Abraham's transformative experience, his "self analysis." It was on this spiritually-grueling journey that Abraham's idolatrous unconscious was made conscious. For three long days, our pilgrim struggled with, agonized over, and ultimately faced himself

Second, before Moriah, I believe Abraham could not see beyond the instrumentality of Isaac, that is, could not see his son as anything but a useful object or symbol. To Abraham, Isaac was the fulfillment in flesh and blood that God had, in fact, a special relationship with the aged couple. Or, after Ishmael's banishment, Isaac was for Abraham the only one who would carry Abraham's name into the future. Or, of greatest spiritual import to Abraham, Isaac was Abraham's single hope for the survival of the patriarch's one-God vision of the world. In each of these ways that Abraham "valued" his son, Isaac is merely a means to Abraham's ends.

When Abraham bound his son on the altar, the father's and son's cheeks wet with the angels' bitter tears,[415] was this the first time in his son's young life that Abraham truly saw Isaac? Was this the first time that Abraham looked deep and long into Isaac's eyes—and in that looking, saw God?

In the Jacob novella in the Book of Genesis, not only do we have a more complete womb-to-tomb history of our subject than we do for Abraham, but also we have a more explicit account of what makes Jacob's character transformation possible. The story of Jacob's first forty years, in which he lived in his parents' home, is rife with narratives featuring our seriously-flawed ancestor. These distressing accounts begin with Jacob's failed attempt, *in utero*, to alter the birth order by holding back his twin brother's heel; and end, four decades later, with his participation in the plot to steal a blessing from his blind father that is meant for Esau.

Even Jacob's first interchange with God is disquieting. As Jacob flees from his brother's murderous rage, he stops for the night to sleep in the wilderness. Without possession, Jacob uses a stone for a pillow. This night, Jacob receives a dream from God that overflows with divine comfort and promise. What is Jacob's response to this dream? Jacob angles for more. The text reads:

> and God said [to Jacob in the dream], '…Your descendants shall be as the dust of the earth; you shall spread out to the west and to the east…Behold, I am with you: I will protect you wherever you go and will bring you back to this land. I will not leave you until I have done what I have promised you.' Jacob awoke from his sleep and said, 'If God will be with me, if He protects me on this journey that I am making, and gives me bread to eat and clothing to wear, and if I return to my father's house in peace—then the Lord shall be my God…'"[416]

While, in this dream, God did explicitly promise our disappointing hero expansive territory and innumerable descendents, in addition to divine protection and companionship, God failed to mention bread or clothing. Jacob, a biblical figure crying out for serious character transformation, at the dawn of his twenty years of exile, even strives here to manipulate God.

As we saw in Chapter five, for Jacob to develop from ruthless deceiver and manipulator to one who struggles with himself and confronts others face-to-face, Jacob will need to use his exile "therapeutically." How can the clever lier become patriarch? How can the man who hid behind his mother's ambitious schemes become a powerful man in his own right? How can the one who preferred disguises unmask himself? How can Jacob become Israel?

The Book of Genesis offers a three-fold answer to explain how Jacob becomes transformed. First, Jacob, coming from a household in which his father Isaac is passive and his mother Rebecca rules, finds himself in Rebecca's brother's home in which Laban is a brutish and deceptive man. In Laban, the trickster Jacob has met his match. The troubles begin early in their relationship with the switch of Leah with Rachel, and, as a result, Jacob marrying the undesired older daughter. The conflict of man-with-man continues for the entire twenty years that Jacob stays with Laban, with the older man stealing a portion of Jacob's flock after they come to an agreement concerning their separation.

For Jacob to grow from who he *was* to who he was to *become*, it will be necessary for Jacob to survive his years with Laban and ultimately confront him and come to terms. The Book of Genesis describes this confrontation of man-with-man as Jacob prepares to return to the land of his father. "Now Jacob became enraged and confronted Laban,…'These twenty years I have spent in your service, your ewes and she-goats never miscarried…Had not the God of my father,…been with me, you would have sent me away empty-handed. But God [not you] took notice of my plight and the toil of my hands.'"[417]

Second, Jacob, who is already considering the journey home, requires a psychic nudge. For Jacob, this is a terrifying pilgrimage. During the entire exile, Jacob has had no contact with his twin brother Esau who had sworn, twenty years before, to kill him. Going home, with his large retinue of wives, concubines and children, means that Jacob will not only have to confront Esau—but also himself.

It is God who offers Jacob the well-timed therapeutic push. "And the Lord said to Jacob, 'Return to the land of your fathers, and of your kindred, and I will be with you…*Now*, arise and leave this land and return to your native land.'"[418]

The third and final aspect of how Jacob's character becomes transformed is also the most dramatic. It is the culmination of Jacob's twenty year "psychotherapy." This night is the evening before Jacob is to encounter, for the first time, the brother he had deceived and had not seen for twenty years, Esau rides toward him with four hundred men. Jacob believes the morning will bring devastation to him and his family. It is on this night that Jacob separates himself from all he knows, and wrestles with a man throughout the night.

This wrestling contest is a compelling biblical metaphor for the kind of intrapsychic struggle that is an integral part of religious crises, the Jewish Day of Atonement, Christian and Jewish concepts of repentance, as well as psychoanalytic treatment. This night, in the wilderness that is Jacob's analytic couch, Jacob wrestles with his own troubling history and character. He wrestles with his contempt for his brother and his pleasure in triumphing over him. He wrestles with his eagerness to follow his mother's cruel scheme. Our struggling and transformed hero wrestles with the ease with which he deceived his blind father, and his ambition, unrestrained by considerations of family or morality.

Because he wrestles throughout the night and holds his own, Jacob achieves insight, and becomes Israel. As the sun rises, Israel, now limping and liberated, seeks his brother Esau.

But alas, Jacob's achievement of Israel is neither consistent nor continuous. In the remaining chapters of the Book of Genesis, it is two of Jacob's sons, Joseph and Judah, who are the focus of the transformational narratives.

Joseph, Jacob's clear favorite of his twelve sons and one daughter, is a spoiled and narcissistic teenager. Not only do his dreams reflect his sense of entitlement, but, even more so, does the fact that he reports these dreams to his brothers without a shred of self-consciousness. In the one which immediately precedes his being sold into slavery in Egypt by his brothers, all the natural world worships Joseph. "I dreamed…the sun and the moon and the eleven stars bowed low to me."[419] Even Jacob is troubled by the frank narcissism of his beloved son's dream.

In this dream, not only is there no room for brother, mother or father, but there is also no room for God. At age seventeen, before the pit and the dungeon, Joseph's ego has no bounds. His dream represents a clever reversal on idolatry—instead of

Joseph worshipping the sun, moon and stars, it is the heavenly bodies that prostrate themselves at the feet of the magnificent god Joseph.

Everything quickly changes for Joseph. First thrown into a pit to die by his envious brothers, and then sold into slavery in Egypt, Joseph's narcissistic world-view abruptly crumbles. What takes its place in Joseph's psyche and soul is a new-found and welcome humility, in which Joseph appreciates that his many and varied talents are not due to his own personal greatness, but to God's. An illustrative example of this occurs when Pharaoh releases Joseph from prison to explain two dreams that have troubled the Pharaoh and bewildered the wise men of Egypt. "The Pharaoh said to Joseph, 'I have dreamed a dream, and there is none so far that has been able to interpret it. I have heard that you can interpret dreams that are told to you.' And Joseph said to Pharaoh, [transcending his former narcissism], '*Not me*. It is God who will respond [to your dream through me].'"[420]

Although the biblical text does not explicitly describe what makes it possible for Joseph to change from center of the world to God's instrument, it is evident from the final narratives of the Book of Genesis that self-awareness plays a crucial role. We see the fruit of Joseph's self-awareness as he and his two sons sit by his father's deathbed. Jacob wishes to bless Joseph's sons. Two conclusions concerning the character of Jacob and Joseph can be drawn from this blessing narrative: Jacob has learned shockingly little in his life about the disastrous impact to a family of blessing the younger over the older; and Joseph has seriously considered his multigenerational familial history and struggles to break the pattern here and now. The text reads:

> And Jacob said to Joseph, 'Bring me your sons and I will bless them.'…And Joseph took them both close to his father, Ephraim [Joseph's younger son] in his right hand toward Israel's left, and Manasseh [Joseph's older son} in his left hand toward Israel's right…But Israel stretched out his right hand, and laid it upon Ephraim's head, although he was the younger; and placed his left hand upon Manasseh's head, guiding his hands knowingly…And when Joseph saw that his father laid his right hand upon the head of Ephraim [the younger], it annoy him greatly: and Joseph removed his father's hand, and placed it instead on Manasseh's head. And Joseph said to his father, 'Not so, my father: for this is the firstborn; put your right hand upon his head.' And his father refused, and said, 'I know [what I'm doing], my son, I know it: the elder also shall become a people, and he also shall be great: but truly his younger brother Ephraim shall be greater than Manasseh. and Ephraim's seed shall become a multitude of nations.'[421]

Most clearly, we see the result of Joseph's battle with himself, his past and his family history, and his attainment of penetrating insight in the literary and ethical climax of the Book of Genesis. Jacob is dead. Joseph's brothers are terrified that Joseph will now take revenge on them and their families for what they did to Joseph many years before. The brothers approach Joseph and beg for mercy. In return for their lives, they offer to be his slaves. Joseph has a choice. The moment is infused with the screaming voices of Cain and Abel, Isaac and Ishmael, Jacob and Esau and a teenage boy at the bottom of a desert pit.

Because Joseph knows himself and where he comes from, he chooses to smash the vicious unending cycle of malignant sibling rivalry that has driven and haunted his family for generations. Joseph answers his guilty and frightened brothers, "'Don't be afraid. After all, am I God? For even though you intended that I be harmed, God's intent was for good; so that the [Jewish] people would survive [the famine in Canaan]. Now, therefore, do not fear. I will nourish you and your little ones.' And Joseph comforted his brothers and spoke words of kindness to them."[422]

There are two separate and significant biblical transformational narratives involving another of Jacob's sons. Judah, Jacob's fourth child, the son of Jacob's less favored wife Leah, was the principle instigator of selling Joseph into slavery. And yet, whereas Joseph represents the biblical ideal of forgiveness, it is Judah who emerges as the archetype for repentance.

As we saw in Chapter Five, in the first of the Judah stories, Judah makes a promise to his daughter-in-law Tamar that he has no intention of keeping. This lie forces Tamar to live as a childless widow in her father's house for many years. Tamar takes the matter into her own hands. She dresses as a prostitute, covers her face, and seduces Judah. When she demands payment, Judah offers his staff and signet as pledge for a goat to be delivered the following day. When the goat is sent, the mysterious harlot is nowhere to be found.

Three months later, Judah hears his daughter-in-law is pregnant. He orders that Tamar be brought to him and burned as a harlot. At this dramatic point in the narrative, Tamar informs Judah that the father of her unborn baby is the man who gave her this staff and ring.

Judah makes a choice. He first publicly confesses that it is his child that Tamar is carrying. Then, he demonstrates his compassion for Tamar, and for the untenable position he himself had put her in, by declaring, "She is more righteous than I, inasmuch as I did not give her [as I promised] to my [youngest] son Shelah."[423]

The second Judah story is at the anguished heart of the strife between Joseph and his brothers. A prolonged and bitter famine has devastated Canaan where

Jacob and his children live. This natural calamity forces Jacob's sons to go down to Egypt and approach Joseph, unrecognized by his brothers, for food. Joseph, by means of clever and complex devices, has managed to get all eleven of his brothers, including Jacob's now-favorite son Benjamin, to Egypt.

Joseph has provided the brothers with enough food to feed their hungry families. Feeling successful on their mission, they ride off toward Canaan. Unbeknownst to the brothers, Joseph's silver goblet has been planted in Benjamin's sack. The brothers are brought back to Joseph's palace and Benjamin is arrested. The other brothers are free, but Benjamin is to stay in Egypt as a slave.

Joseph's test of the brothers is exact and brutal. Will they, yet again, eagerly, or even reluctantly sacrifice their younger brother, their father's now-favorite son? Will they leave Benjamin a slave in Egypt and return to the comfort of their land and family?

It is Judah, the leader of his generation, who comes forward. In a passionate plea, Judah, painting images of a heartbroken old man mourning the loss of yet another beloved son, offers himself as slave in Benjamin's place.[424]

Years ago, when taunted by design and circumstance to free himself from a brother his father adored and he envied, Judah sold Joseph into slavery. Now, when design and circumstance afforded him the identical opportunity—to abandon his father's favorite son Benjamin in Egypt—it was Judah who begged for Benjamin's freedom. Judah, repentant and transformed, reads the same old novel, but it is he who, through insight, years of suffering and sheer will, materially alters its ending.

What is common to all of these biblical heroes of psycho-spiritual transformation? Each of these individuals clashes with himself, battles *against* his impulses, character and history, wrestles beings, divine and human; and then ultimately prevails. It is the hero's self-awareness, a result of the arduous intrapsychic confrontation and conflict of the two Adams-within, that is the theme underlying the transformational narratives in the Book of Genesis.

For each of the five Genesis heroes of transformation, self-awareness is symbolized differently. God in the flood narrative considers what He has done privately, "within His heart," before publicly resolving never to destroy the world again. Abraham walks silent for three days to and up Mount Moriah to sacrifice his precious child. Alone, Jacob wrestles with a man or a demon or God or himself all through the darkness of the night. Joseph, abandoned in pit and dungeon by everyone but his God, emerges from both centered and benevolent. Judah, guilty and ashamed of his role in his brother's loss, even offers to sacrifice his own freedom to prevent it from happening again.

Sigmund Freud, who understood insight as the goal of psychoanalysis, also, like Genesis, argued that an individual's capacity to change is a function of his or her self-awareness. For Freud and the contemporary psychoanalyst, therefore, the major technique that helps the patient increase insight, and thereby change, is the interpretation. For Freud and his students, the interpretation alters the balance of the psychic forces of the patient, releasing the patient from ties to instinctual fixations and undoing repression. Freud wrote, "Our ultimate dynamic aim is the strengthening of the ego through the addition of instinctual energy, which has hitherto belonged to the unconscious. There can be no doubt that interpretation is our main pump in the draining of the therapeutic Zeider Zee."[425]

In answering the question of how we change, it is clear that the ancient biblical author and the contemporary psychoanalyst both conceptualize self-awareness as the primary element. However, as we have seen from the description of the various transformational narratives in Genesis, additional specified factors, crucial for change, are recognized by the biblical. The God of the Noah narrative, not only becomes aware of Himself, but also resolves to change, makes this resolution public and creates a sign to bind Him to His promise. Abraham, not only contemplates himself on that long lonely walk with Isaac, but also drops the knife and never again sheds human blood to prove his love for his God. Jacob, not only wrestles with himself throughout the night, but, as the day breaks, does what he has been avoiding for twenty years. That morning, Jacob faces Esau. Joseph, in pit and dungeon, not only scrutinizes his own narcissism and family history of sibling envy and retaliation, but also, when enticed to exact revenge on those brothers who had wronged him, transcends the impulse and the past. Joseph forgives his brothers and promises to protect their families. Judah, not only discerns with horror what he did to his brother Joseph, but also takes whatever steps are necessary so that the scenario is not repeated with Benjamin. By doing so, Judah makes a symbolic restitution to his father, so grievously wounded and betrayed by Judah and the brothers.

As we have seen, the Genesis "theory of personality change" always involves steps in addition to insight. Within this perspective, for change to occur, self-awareness is necessary, but not sufficient. Whereas Freud and his students generally understood insight as an end in itself, the Genesis "psychologist," in his characterization of the principle transformational heroes of his text, recognized insight as the essential condition *so that right action can be taken.* For the biblical, it is both self-awareness plus action that makes for lasting psycho-spiritual change.

In post-biblical Judaism, this action emphasis was most articulately elaborated and developed by Moses Maimonides, often referred to by his acronym, the

"Rambam." In his chapter on repentance in the *Mishneh Torah*[426] he wrote circa 1180, Maimonides describes the steps one must choose[427] to take to do *teshuvah*, that is, the actions required to "return," after sinning, to oneself and to God. Sin, for the Rambam, had a wide band, ranging from the relatively minor "missing the mark," in such sins as using words to hurt, gossip, a quick temper and elevating oneself, even in one's own mind, at the expense of the other; to the grievous sins of enticing a youth to a life of depravity or worshipping idols. An individual's or society's moral uprightness or turpitude is determined by the relative weight of merits and failings. Maimonides wisely suggests that each individual should assume each day that his merits and failings are of equal weight. Therefore, it is the next act that will tip the balance and determine if one is righteous or sinful. The individual's moral choices have broader ethical implications as well. With each turn toward goodness or away from it, the world's scale is nudged, ever-so-slightly, toward holiness or corruption.[428]

After 70 C.E., with the destruction of the Jerusalem Temple and of the cult of animal sacrifice that dominated religious practice there, repentance as a *psychological* process grew in importance. No longer could an individual who sinned bring a turtle dove or sheep to the Temple and be ritually cleansed of his sin. In the Diaspora, what one felt in one's heart of hearts, and how one made reparations to those who were wronged became increasingly significant. The Rambam, redacting and creatively elaborating the talmudic sages' teachings, characterized repentance as "the brightest gem of Judaism. For the ancient rabbis and Maimonides both, repentance is so crucial and primal a concept that it was one of the seven things that were made by God before He created the world.[429]

Maimonides identified four stages of repentance. Each of these stages is required for full *teshuvah*.[430] The first of these stages, that of **awareness**, will be enthusiastically endorsed seven centuries later by Sigmund Freud as well. In this first stage, referred to by Maimonides as, *hakaret ha'chet*, that is, awareness of how one has missed the mark, the individual searches his psyche—like the observant Jew looking into the smallest corners of his darkest closet for tiny bread crumbs the night before Passover—to discover in which ways he has fallen short.

Although looking inward is endorsed by the rabbis, and valued by God during *all* seasons,[431] in the Jewish liturgical calendar, the late summer and early autumn are especially devoted to self-awareness. During the month of Elul, a full four weeks before the first of the High Holidays of Rosh Hashanah (the Jewish New Year), the worshipper begins to prepare for the solemn penitential period. During the month of Elul, the ram's horn is blown each morning in the synagogue to remind the faithful that Yom Kippur, the Day of Atonement, is nigh. For one month before this highest of High Holidays, the Jew is prompted to interrogate his self. Then Rosh Hashanah arrives. This holiday carries the urgent message that Yom Kippur is only ten days away. The Jewish New Year introduces a contemplative period in which the individual is to scrutinize himself even harder and deeper. On Yom Kippur, when, for twenty-four hours, the penitent limits all distractions of food and sex and vanity, all that he is left with is himself and his God. Maimonides argues, in an earlier section of the *Mishneh Torah,* that in this painstaking self scrutiny, we emulate God who knows Himself perfectly.[432]

It is at the second stage of repentance that the modern and ancient "personality theorists" part company. Maimonides' second stage of repentance is *vidui,* that is, **confession**. Although some contemporary clinical writers[433] associate this stage with the "confession" of a patient in psychoanalysis to the psychoanalyst, this conceptual correlation misrepresents what the Rambam meant by this second stage, and robs this concept of its ethical power. For sins against god, the penitent can confess privately in prayer. For the sins against a fellow man, however, the confession must be public, and include the victim or the family of the victim. So central is confession to completing repentance that Maimonides argued that, even when a criminal is sentenced to death or whipping for his transgressions, even then, the transgressor must confess his sins directly to those he has wounded.

Maimonides writes, "Repentance and the Day of Atonement atone only for sins, such as eating a forbidden food, having prohibited sexual intercourse, et cetera, which are committed against God. Sins such as injuring, cursing, stealing, et cetera, which are committed against one's fellow man are never atoned for until one has paid any necessary fines to the person against whom one sinned, and *discussed it with him*. Even though one may have paid back any due money one still has to *discuss the sin with him* and ask for forgiveness."[434]

The third of the Rambam's stages involves the transgressor making an earnest **resolution** never to commit the sin again. This stage is graphically represented in the first transformational narrative in the Book of Genesis. After the flood, when God has allowed Himself to recognize what He has done, He first resolves in His heart never again to destroy the world. In the biblical account, God then takes the next step. God informs Noah and Noah's children of His newly-formed resolution. Finally, for God, the rainbow serves to "seal" the one-way covenant that He had just made by reminding Him of His promise to all people for all time.

For Maimonides, repentance remains incomplete unless the individual faces the old temptation and *chooses* not to repeat the transgression—in other words, unless the resolution "sticks." The Rambam asks, "What is complete repentance? That in which the former transgressor is afforded an opportunity of repeating his sin but stays his hand and refrains from doing so because he has repented, and not out of fear or due to incapacity."[435] Consistent with this Maimonidian assertion, and translating its main idea into a contemporary voice, I would suggest: Life gives each of us many opportunities to make the same mistakes we always make; but also, just as many opportunities to ultimately get it right.

The final stage of *teshuvah* for Maimonides involves **restitution**. In the case of an individual who wrongs his fellow man, after becoming keenly aware of his sin, confessing it openly to, at least, the one who was wronged, and resolving never again to repeat the transgression, the penitent must try to repair, as best he can, the damage he has done. As we saw in Chapter Five, Genesis' Judah is a poignant example of this fourth stage of the Rambam's theory. The biblical text tells us that the brothers hated Joseph primarily because he was their father's undisputed favorite. Judah, a leader in the family, also ruled by his intense feelings of sibling envy and resentment, seized opportunity when it presented itself to him, and sold Joseph into slavery. By taking this decisive and reprehensible action, Judah and the brothers rid themselves of "that dreamer," and what they discerned as the wedge in their relationship with their father. After many years of facing himself and his crime, and watching his father crumble under the weight of the suffering over Joseph's loss, Judah feels great remorse.

Genesis' plot then, of course, thickens and deepens. Joseph orchestrates the test with precision and guile. Will the brothers, confronting the identical temptation they had years before—to rid themselves of their father's favorite son, now Benjamin—choose to abandon him to slavery in Egypt, or attempt to repair the damage done by causing the same story to have a different ending? Dramatically, Judah at this point steps forward and offers himself as slave in Benjamin's place. While the biblical narrative never states that Judah confessed his heinous action to his father, evidently, Judah does fulfill the Rambam's other three stages of repentance. Judah becomes aware of himself and what he has done. He resolves never again to be mastered by his sibling resentment and envy. And, finally, Judah makes restitution for his past wrongs by offering himself to save his young brother's freedom and his aged father's life.

Whereas psychoanalytic theories of how people change emphasize the centrality of insight, the "theories" of the Bible and of Maimonides, after insight is achieved, accentuate certain proscribed actions necessary for a complete transformation of character to occur. For the ancient "psychologist," change occurs when we can know ourselves, recognize in what ways we are less than we should be, speak our faults out loud, resolve to do better and try, as best we can, to repair the damage we have done to others.

In contradistinction to the modern psychological view, For the ancient "personality theorist," as represented by Genesis and Maimonides, *teshuvah* is not primarily or merely a psychologically-healthy course of character "therapy." Because the biblical perspective takes for granted an intimate and continuous connection between heaven and earth, that the modern psychological perspective does not share, *teshuvah* for the ancient has momentous ethical and theological implications. On the level of ethics, when a transgressor repents, the entire world is gently shifted toward justice and unity. One tiny, but perhaps critical fragment of this fractured planet is repaired. On the theological level, because God cares about His children, He hopes that we will choose to act better. For the ancient, therefore, when the transgressor repents, God smiles broadly.

As we have seen in this and the previous chapters, for the ancient "psychologist," repentance, as well as many other behaviors and experiences, are understood within a sweeping landscape involving both God and community. It is this observation that directly leads us to consider what the ancient and the modern voices say to us about life's meaning.

What is Our Purpose?

Sigmund Freud enjoyed "spiritually jabbing" his close friend, the Swiss Protestant pastor and psychoanalyst, Oscar Pfister. In 1918, Freud wrote to Pfister, "Incidentally, why was it that none of all the pious ever discovered psychoanalysis? Why did it have to wait for a completely *godless Jew*?" Pfister replies that Freud is neither godless nor a Jew. Pfister writes, addressing the first point, "For he who lives in truth lives in God," and addressing the second, "A better Christian there never was."[436] Although Freud found amusing Pfister's mischaracterization of him as Christian, Freud was moved by Pfister's appreciation that Freud was doing God's work by seeking truth.

Some authors have criticized psychoanalysis as being devoid of an ethical foundation, and of providing its adherents with little by way of purpose. For example, Carl Goldberg describes psychoanalysis as demonstrating indifference to issues of social and moral responsibility. He then goes even further and places much of the blame for the deterioration in our contemporary society's moral fabric squarely at Freud's feet. Goldberg writes, "As the most influential contemporary theory of American society, psychoanalysis must be held accountable for its substantial impact on society's malaise…My thesis is that Freud's lack of responsiveness to the importance of community and social responsibility of analytic patients has prevented psychoanalysis from developing a theory of moral imperatives for human behavior. Moreover, this insufficiency has not only hindered analysands from their moral and social responsibilities for others, it also has had a subversive effect on American society as well."[437]

While Erich Fromm does not share Goldberg's view that psychoanalysis is to blame for the vast majority of our societal and moral ills—Fromm having a more complex social analysis than Goldberg—Fromm does criticize psychoanalytic theory for its cynical attitude toward higher human values. According to Fromm, because Freud was more interested in positioning psychoanalysis as a natural science, and not as a modern discipline within the long-standing philosophical traditions of humanism, Freud de-emphasized values and ethics in his theory and practice. The major philosophers of the Enlightenment had taught that people should trust their reason as guide to valid ethical norms. These nineteenth century thinkers argued that man and woman should rely more on themselves to discern good and evil, and less on any revelation from heaven or church authority. For Fromm, Freud and the majority of psychoanalysts undermine the progress made during the Enlightenment of freeing man from the chains of narrow religious beliefs and institutions by arguing that human reason and values too are nothing more than symptoms of psychic forces that are beyond man's control. Fromm writes, "But while psychoanalysis has tremendously increased our knowledge of man, it has not increased our knowledge about how man ought to live and what he ought to do. Its main function has been that of 'debunking,' of demonstrating that value judgements and ethical norms are the rationalized expressions of irrational and often unconscious desires and fears; and they therefore have no claims to objective validity."[438]

While it is accurate to say that Freud and most of his intellectual descendents demonstrate considerable reluctance in teaching ethical principles and social responsibility to those being analyzed, the practice of psychoanalysis itself expresses a highly-developed ethic. First and foremost, Freud, far more than to any other value, was committed to truth. It was the search for truth wherever it might lead that originally attracted Freud to Oedipus as a tragic ideal. It was the deciphering of truth in his patients that impelled Freud to perceive, struggle with and ultimately interpret dreams, resistances and the transference. Freud adamantly recommended that each analyst, to be an analyst, should be analyzed himself so that the patient's truth not be lost in the clinician's distorted filter.

For Freud, the search for truth even took on a moral dimension. Freud writes, "He who has successfully accomplished the education of being truthful towards himself is lastingly protected from the danger of immorality."[439] And even more boldly, in his 1914 paper, "The History of the Psychoanalytic Movement," Freud described truth-seeking and truth-knowing in messianic and utopian terms. In this paper, Freud asserts that, if enough people became adherents of analytic self-scrutiny, then society would be transformed from a hostile, fearful place to a world in which good-will and reason prevail.[440]

A second aspect of psychoanalysis' ethic is its celebration of all human life by investigating one person, in detail and over an extended period of time. No other contemporary psychological discipline elevates the human being to such a lofty status as does psychoanalysis. By developing the psychotherapeutic treatment that he did, Freud positioned the individual, his life and its nuances, his fantasies, experiences and motivations at the precise center of the inquiry. Psychoanalysis' implicit moral message is that a single human life, with all its complexity, conflicts, struggles, achievements and failings, *deserves* attention. Consistent with this ethical value, the philosopher and psychoanalyst Jonathan Lear wondered *not* whether, in our present society, psychoanalysis has become obsolete; but whether the individual has.[441]

Freud's relentless search for truth and his meticulous focus on the psychic life of the individual have practical applications that also embody human values. The aim of psychoanalysis, as a treatment for emotional dis-ease and distress, is to fortify the patient, by means of increasing insight. Aspects of the unconscious, now conscious allow the patient a freedom from his past, his fears and his impulses, each of which served as the individual's harsh jailer before treatment. Now emotionally released, the individual can love and work with renewed creativity. The goal of the treatment Freud invented is to increase human life. This is clinical psychoanalysis' ultimate goal and most essential ethic of care.

As we have seen, psychoanalysis *does* have a basis in human values and ethics. However, what psychoanalysis and other contemporary psychological models lack is a theory that locates the individual within a broader context, and that can provide us meaning. The glory of psychoanalysis is its painstaking and exclusive focus on the single life. The individual is not only the subject of the psychoanalytic inquiry, but also its only goal. In an attempt to legitimize psychoanalysis as an objective science, Freud severed all conceptual ties to the long-standing religious and philosophical traditions that involved God, community and social responsibility. Freud's integrated human being, after his successful analysis was completed, loved and worked in a world in which he is existentially alone. Perhaps this is what is at the basis of Freud's pessimistic observation that the goal of psychoanalysis is to transform neurotic misery into ordinary human unhappiness.[442]

The Book of Genesis offers us something different. As we have seen, the individual in the biblical text is critically important, but he or she is *not* the goal of the text. In Genesis and the other books of the Bible, the individual always reposes within the intricately-woven nest of community, family heritage and the Divine. In the Hebrew and Christian Bibles and Koran, each individual is an instrument of God's plan or purpose, or an obstacle to it. Each individual is profoundly affected by the spiritual successes or failings of the previous generations. Similarly, the choices made by each individual in one generation makes the deepest of impacts on the lives his children and grandchildren live. *In Genesis, each character's life has purpose because it is lived out within a sweeping multigenerational landscape involving heaven and earth.*

The profoundly intimate connection between heaven and earth is demonstrated throughout the Bible, but never so graphically as in Jacob's first dream. "…A ladder was set on the ground and its top reached to the heavens, and angels of God were going up and down on it. And the Lord was standing above it and He said, 'I am the Lord, the God of your father Abraham and the God of Isaac.'…Then, Jacob awoke from his sleep and said, 'Surely the Lord is present in this place, and I knew it not!'"[443]

In this dream, not only do we have a dramatic and explicit biblical depiction of the link between heaven and earth in the ladder, but we also have the image of the angels, who travel freely between the two spheres of this single reality. Jacob, unaware that the "whole earth is filled with God's glory,"[444] is astonished to wake from this dream and appreciate, for the first time, that God and angel are with him in the wilderness. Even here, heaven and earth are in constant contact. *Even here, man is not alone.*

Significantly, the angels in Jacob's dream go up the ladder before they come down. This symbolism affirms the Genesis view that the angels are here with us on earth. They are messengers to us. They encircle and protect us as we travel our paths. They are ladders who continually link earth with heaven and us with God. The angels remind us what the Book of Genesis wants us to know—that *each of us is always in a divine context.*

In the Genesis account of Joseph's life, soul and psyche, we discover a second answer to the biblical understanding of human purpose. As we saw in Chapter Five, Jacob, Joseph's father, is a hero who, from his birth and for forty years afterwards, is ruled by his impulse to triumph over his brother. The text depicts Jacob as ruthless in his drive to gain the birthright and blessing that belong to Esau. Others' vulnerabilities, his brother's impulsivity, his father Isaac's blindness, are merely Jacob's props in his morally reprehensible schemes. As Jacob flees his brother's homicidal rage and the parents that were incapable of controlling him at his worst, Jacob is a hero who requires a radical character "make-over."

Jacob has this psycho-spiritual transformation over the next two decades. It culminates with the wrestling match which results in Jacob's name change to Israel. However, as we saw in some detail in the previous chapter, Jacob's transformation is neither complete nor consistent. This wavering of Jacob's psychological state is best indicated by Genesis' inconsistent use of the name, "Israel," to refer to Jacob. Jacob, in the remaining chapters of Genesis, is sometimes Israel, but mostly still referred to as "Jacob."

It is in the figure of Joseph that Jacob's journey to Israel is completed. It is Joseph who *knows*, perhaps more firmly than his father ever could, that God is with him and guiding him. It is Joseph who understands, certainly more than his father ever did, the absolute psychological devastation and havoc that a father's preference for one son over the other can wreak on a family and the future. It is Joseph, after Jacob's death, who definitively rejects his family tradition of retaliation when he promises his brothers, in the final chapter of the Book of Genesis, that he will care for them and their children. It is at that moment, in only two generations, as we gently close the biblical book we've studied in such detail, that Jacob becomes Israel. We see in this Jacob novella that we can and should begin our journeys, but that sometimes, if we make our choices wisely, it will be our beloved Josephs that complete them.

This poignant and inspirational story of Joseph teaches us the second biblical moral concerning human purpose. Not only does each of us, as we saw in Jacob's dream, inhabit a world that is heavily populated by God and angels, but each of us, as well, lives within a communal and multigenerational nexus. For Genesis, no generation is a vacuum. Adam and Eve affect Cain, Abel and Seth. Abraham and Sarah affect Isaac and Ishmael. Isaac and Rebecca affect Jacob and Esau. And Jacob and his wives and concubines affect their twelve sons and one daughter. How one generation chooses to act, for good or for evil, has a momentous impact on those who follow. For the Genesis "author," just as there is no individual who is alone, there is no individual who can ignore his responsibility to the community and future. Jacob's obligation was to struggle with himself so that he could, at least partially, achieve Israel; so that Joseph could save his brothers. Joseph needed to find his way to humility and forgiveness in pit and dungeon; so that the descendents of these people of Genesis could ultimately find their way to Sinai and the Promised Land.

Unlike the psychoanalytic perspective, the biblical asserts that each of us has a meaningful role to play in the present and the future. According to Genesis, the survival and integrity of this world depend on each of us and how we act.

The genius of Genesis is its depiction through multi-layered narratives of a clarion philosophy of human purpose. Most simply put: Genesis teaches us that each of our lives, in this brief time we have, should demonstrate gratitude toward all things past, service toward all things present, and responsibility toward all things future.[445]

The Bible is our culture's literary soul. Throughout the past two millennia, for those seeking spiritual comfort and meaning, it is the Bible to which they have and still turn. For those searching for ethical and ritual rules to live by, it is the Bible that is scrutinized and then re-scrutinized to discover the law. For those seeking a history of the Jewish people or of the monotheistic principles, legends and traditions that are the foundational stone of Judaism, Christianity, Islam, Western literature and institutions, it is yet again the Bible that both scholars and the faithful study and contemplate.

As we have seen, in addition to these purposes for the Canon, the Bible is also a masterpiece of psychological genius. In its myriad narratives, we have unearthed ancient wisdom concerning the complexity of human experience. We have seen in our study that the Bible is not merely a book reflecting the origin and adventures of an ancient and alien people, separated from us by the millennia, belief, culture and experience. Nor is the Bible merely the record of our God, the Promised Land or our great religious heroes and ancestors. We have seen that the Bible is *our* story. In its pages, it has been we who have been revealed.

Genesis, more than any other single book of the Bible, includes the greatest number of these narratives of psychological insight, and therefore constitutes the largest part of this ancient library of psychological wisdom literature. What we have concluded from this modern excavation of this ancient library is that the Book of Genesis is, remarkably and consistently, the latest insights from the distant past.

From this survey of the psychological genius of the Book of Genesis, we have discovered that each of us is the first man and woman, dazzling and resplendent, formed in our God's image; and each of us is Adam and Eve, fragile, frightened and forever barred from the Garden. Each of us is Abraham, all too ready to sacrifice our ethical principles and life purpose; and each of us is Abraham, needing to invent monotheism time and again and, in the process, elevating human life to the sacred. Each of us is Jacob, eagerly deceiving others and ourselves; and each of us is Jacob, when forced to confront ourselves, who struggles with angels and demons, and sometimes emerges transformed, but limping. It is this voice of Genesis, still miraculously audible over the chasm of the forty centuries, that speaks to each one of us today through the narrative contours of our lives.

Bibliography

Arafat, K.W. (1990). *Classical Zeus: A Study in Art and Literature*. Oxford, Great Britain: Clarendon Press.

Augustine. (1949). *The Confessions of saint augustine*. New York: Modern Library.

Baeck, L. (1948). *The Essence of Judaism*. New York: Schocken Books.

Barnes, T.D. (1971). *Tertullian: A Historical and Literary Study*. Oxford, Great Britain: Clarendon Press.

Bemporad, J. (1964). Dimensions of Jewish ethics. *Judaism, 14*: 133-148.

Bergmann, M.S. (1992). *In the Shadow of Moloch: The Sacrifice of Children and Its Relation to Western Religions*. New York: Columbia University Press.

Birnbaum, P. (1949). *Daily Prayer Book*. New York: Hebrew Publishing Company.

Bornstein, R.F., & Masling, J.M. (Eds.). (1998). *Empirical Studies on the Psychoanalytic Unconscious*. Washington, D.C.: American Psychological Association.

Braun, M.A. (1999). *The Sfas Emes: The Life and Teachings of Rabbi Yehudah Aryeh Leib Alter*. Northvale, NJ: Jason Aronson Publisher.

Brown, F., Driver, S., & Briggs, C. (1996). *The Brown-Driver-Briggs Hebrew Lexicon*. New York: Hendrickson Publishers.

Buber, M. (1957). *Eclipse of God: Studies in the Relation Between Religion and Philosophy*. New York: Harper.

Buber, M. (1961). *Tales of the Hasidim: The Later Masters*. New York: Schocken Books.

Calvin, J. (2001). *Genesis*. New York: Crossway Books.

Carmi, T. (1981). *The Penguin Book of Hebrew Verse*. New York: Viking Press.

Cassuto, U. (1978) *From Adam to Noah: A Commentary on Genesis*. New York: Eisenbrauns.

Cassuto, U. (1983) *The Documentary Hypothesis and the Composition of the Pentateuch: Eight Lectures*. New York: Magnes Press.

Cohen, H. (1971). *Reason and Hope: Selections from the Jewish Writing of Hermann Cohen*. New York: W.W. Norton.

Cohen, H. (1995). *Religion of Reason: Out of the Sources of Judaism*. New York: American Academy of Religion.

Cook, A.B. (1925). *Zeus: A Study in Ancient Religion*. Cambridge, Great Britain: Cambridge University Press.

Cooper, D.A. (1998). *God is a Verb: Kabbalah and the Practice of Mystical Judaism*. New York: Riverhead Press.

de Vecchi, P. (1990). *Michelangelo*. New York: Konecky & Konecky, Inc.

Diamant, A. (1998). *The Red Tent*. New York: Picador Press.

Eliade, M. (1974). *Gods, Goddesses and Myths of Creation*. New York: Harper and Row.

Euripides. (1981). *Ten Plays*. New York: Bantum Books.

Fishbane, M. (1989). *Biblical Interpretation in Ancient Israel*. New York: Clarendon Press.

Fosshage, J.L. (1997). The organizing functions of dream mentation. *Contemporary Psychoanalysis, 33:* 429-458.

Fox, E. (1995). *The Five Books of Moses: Genesis, Exodus, Leviticus, Numbers, Deuteronomy (a new translation with introduction, commentaries and notes)*. New York: Schocken Books.

Frankel, E. (1998). Repentance, psychotherapy, and healing through a Jewish lens. *The American Behavioral Scientist, 41:* 814-833.

Freud, S. (1893-1895). Studies of hysteria. *The Complete Psychological Works of Sigmund Freud, Vol. II*. London: Hogarth Press.

Freud, S. (1900). The interpretation of dreams. *The Complete Psychological Works of Sigmund Freud, Vol. IV-V*. London: Hogarth Press.

Freud, S. (1905a). Fragment of an analysis of a case of hysteria. *The Complete Psychological Works of Sigmund Freud, Vol. VII*. London: Hogarth Press.

Freud, S. (1905b). Three essays on the theory of sexuality. *The Complete Psychological Works of Sigmund Freud, Vol. VII*. London: Hogarth Press.

Freud, S. (1907). Obsessive actions and religious practices. *The Complete Psychological Works of Sigmund Freud, Vol. IX*. London: Hogarth Press.

Freud, S. (1909). Notes upon a case of obsessional neurosis. *The Complete Psychological Works of Sigmund Freud, Vol. X*. London: Hogarth Press.

Freud, S. (1912). Recommendations to physicians practicing psychoanalysis. *The Complete Psychological Works of Sigmund Freud, Vol. XII*. London: Hogarth Press.

Freud, S. (1914). The history of the psychoanalytic movement. *The Complete Psychological Works of Sigmund Freud, Vol. XIV*. London: Hogarth Press.

Freud, S. (1915a). Introductory lectures on psycho-analysis. *The Complete Psychological Works of Sigmund Freud, Vol. XIV*. London: Hogarth Press.

Freud, S. (1915b). Instincts and their vicissitudes. *The Complete Psychological Works of Sigmund Freud, Vol. XIV*. London: Hogarth Press.

Freud, S. (1917). A difficulty in the path of psycho-analysis. *The Complete Psychological Works of Sigmund Freud, Vol. XVII*. London: Hogarth Press.

Freud, S. (1933). New introductory lectures on psycho-analysis. *The Complete Psychological Works of Sigmund Freud, Vol. XXII*. London: Hogarth Press.

Friedman, R.E. (1997). *Who Wrote the Bible*. San Francisco, CA: Harper.

Fromm, E. (1947). *Man for Himself*. New York: Rinehart.

Fromm, E. (1957). *The Forgotten Language: An Introduction to the Understanding of Dreams, Fairy Tales and Myths*. New York: Grove Press.

Fromm, E. (1966). *You Shall Be as Gods: A Radical Interpretation of the Old Testament and Its Traditions.* New York: H. Holt & Co.

Gay, P. (1987). *A Godless Jew: Freud, Atheism and the Making of Psychoanalysis.* New Haven, CT: Yale University Press.

Gill, C. (1999). *Plato: The Symposium.* New York: Penguin Classics.

Ginzberg, L. (1998). *The Legends of the Jews: From the Creation to Jacob.* Baltimore, MD: Johns Hopkins University Press.

Goldberg, C. (1998). The indifference of psychoanalytic practice to social and moral responsibility. *International Journal of Psychotherapy, 3*: 221-230.

Guthrie, W.K.C. (1993). *Orpheus and Greek Religion.* Princeton, NJ: Princeton University Press.

Heidel, A. (1951). *The Babylonian Genesis (Enuma Elish): The Story of the Creation.* Chicago, IL: University of Chicago Press.

Henry, M. (1999).) *Matthew Henry's Commentary.* New York: Zondervan Publishing House.

Herdt, G.H. (1999). *Sambia Sexual Culture: Essays from the Field.* Chicago, IL: University of Chicago Press.

Hertz, J.H. (Ed.). (1960). *The Pentateuch and Haftoras.* New York: soncino Press.

Heschel, A.J. (1952). *The Sabbath: Its Meaning to Modern Man.* New York: Farrar, Straus and Giroux.

Heschel, A.J. (1983). *I Asked for Wonder: A Spiritual Anthology.* New York: Herder and Herder.

Hesiod. (1953). *Hesiod's Theogony.* Indianapolis, IN: Bobbs-Merrill Publishers.

Hunter, S. (1989). *George Segal.* New York: Rizzoli.

Ibn Ezra, A.. (1988). *Ibn Ezra's Commentary on the Pentateuch.* New York: Menorah Press.

Jonas, H. (1963). *The Gnostic Religion: The Message of the Alien God and the Beginnings of Christianity*. Boston, MA: Beacon Press.

Josephus, F. (1960). *Complete Works*. Grand Rapids, MI: Kregel Publications.

Jung. C.G. (1938). *Psychology and Religion*. New Haven, CT: Yale University Press.

Jung, C.G. (1960). *Answer to Job*. New York: Meridian Press.

Kant, I. (1979). *The Conflict of the Faculties*. New York: Abaris Books.

Kaplan, M. (1964). *The Purpose and Meaning of Jewish Existence: A People in the Image of god*. Philadelphia, PA: Jewish Publication Society Press.

Kaufmann, Y. (1972). *The Religion of Israel: From Its Beginning to the Babylonian Exile*. New York: Schocken Books.

Kessler, E. (2000). Art leading the story: The Akedah in the early synagogue from Dura to Sepphoris. *Journal of Roman Archaeology*. *40*: 77-93.

Keyes, R. (1996). *The Wit and Wisdom of Oscar Wilde: A Treasury of Quotations, Anecdotes, and Repartee*. New York: Harper Collins.

Kierkegaard, S. (1954). *Fear and Trembling, and the Sickness unto Death*. Garden City, NY: Doubleday.

King, L.W. (Ed.). (1999). *Creation: The Babylonian and Assyrian Legends Concerning the Creation of the World and of Mankind*. New York: Book Tree Publishers.

Kohut, H. (1976). *The Restoration of the Self*. New York: International Universities Press.

Kohut, H. (1982). The semi-circle of mental health. *International Journal of Psychoanalysis*. *63*: 395-407.

Kravitz, L.S. (1997). *Abraham, the rabbis and us: Torah commentary on Parashat Lech Lecha (November 8)*. UAHC Torat Hayim Webpage, http://uahc.org/torah/issue/971102.shtml.

Kugel, J.L. (1997). *The Bible as It Was*. Cambridge, MA: Harvard University Press.

Kugel, J.L. (1999). *Traditions of the bible: A Guide to the bible as It Was at the Start of the common Era*. Cambridge, MA: Harvard university press.

Lacan, J. (1977). *Écrits: A Selection*. New York: Norton.

Langdon, H. (1999). *Caravaggio: A Life*. New York: Farrar, Straus and Giroux.

Langdon, S. (1923). *The Babylonian Epic of Creation from the Recently Restored Tablets of Assur*. Oxford, Great Britain: Claredon Press.

Lear, J. (1999), *Love and Its Place in Nature. A Philosophical Interpretation of Freudian Psychoanalysis*. New Haven, CT: Yale University Press.

Leiber, D.L., & Harlow, J. (2001). *Etz Hayim: Torah and Commentary*. New York: The Rabbinic Assembly of America.

Leibowitz, N. (1976). *New Studies in Bereshit: Genesis in the Context of Ancient and Modern Commentary*. Jerusalem, Israel: World Zionist Organization Department for Torah Education and Culture.

Lerner, M. (1994). *Jewish Renewal: A Path to Healing and Transformation*. New York: G.P. Putnam and Sons.

Levenson, J.D. (1998). Abusing Abraham: Traditions, religious histories and modern misinterpretations. *Judaism. 47*: 259-277.

Lowden, J. (1997). *Early Christian and Byzantine Art*. London, England: Phaidon.

Maccoby, Y. (1983). *The Sacred Executioner: Human Sacrifice and the Legacy of Guilt*. London, England: Thames & Hudson.

MacIsaac, S. (1974). *Freud and Original Sin*. New York: Paulist Press.

Maimonides, M. (1963). *The Guide of the Perplexed*. Chicago, IL: University of Chicago Press.

Maimonides, M. (1970). *Mishneh Torah: Maimonides' Code of Jewish Law and Ethics*. New York: Hebrew Publication Co.

Maimonides, M. (1983). *The Book of Knowledge: From the Mishneh Torah of Maimonides*. New York: Ktav Publishers.

Meng, E. & Freud, E.L. (Eds.). (1963). *Psychoanalysis and Faith: The Letters of Sigmund Freud and Oscar Pfister*. New York: Basic Books.

Meyer, M. (1992). *The Gospel of Thomas: The Hidden Sayings of Jesus*. San Francisco, CA: Harper.

Michener, J. (1965). *The Source*. New York: Random House.

Miles, J. (1995). *God: A Biography*. New York: Alfred A. Knopf.

Milton, J. (1935). *Paradise Lost*. Garden City, NY: Doubleday.

Nachmanides, M. (2001). *Commentary on the Torah*. New York: Shilo Publishing.

Neiman, S. (2002). *Evil: An Alternative History of Philosophy in Modern Thought*. Princeton, NJ: Princeton University Press.

Omdahl, B.L. (1995). *Cognitive Appraisal, Emotion and Empathy*. Northvale, NJ: Lawrence Erlbaum & Associates.

Owens, W. (1988). *Poems*. Oxford, England: Oxford University Press.

Philo. (1993). *The Works of Philo: Complete and Unabridged*. New York: Hendrickson Publishers Inc.

Plaut, W.G. (1981). *The Torah: A Modern Commentary*. New York: Union of American Hebrew Congregations.

Pritchard, J.B. (Ed.). (1969). *Ancient Near Eastern Texts Relating to the Old Testament with Supplement*. Princeton, NJ: Princeton University Press.

Racker, H. (1966). Ethics and Psycho-analysis and the psycho-analysis of ethics. *International Journal of Psychoanalysis, 47*: 63-80.

Rank, O. (1991). *The Incest theme in Literature and Legend: Fundamentals of a Psychology of Literary Creation*. Baltimore, MD: Johns Hopkins University Press.

Rashi. (1972). *Pentateuch with Targum Onkelos, Haphtaroth and Rashi's Commentary: Genesis*. New York: Routledge and Kegan Paul.

Reik, T. (1964). *Pagan Rites in Judaism*. New York: Noonday Press.

Rembrandt. (1990). *Rembrandt and the Bible: Stories from the Old and New Testament*. Weert, Netherlands: Magna Books.

Rice, E. (1990). *Freud and Moses: The Long Journey Home*. Albany, NY: State of New York Press.

Rives, J.B. (1995). Human sacrifice among Pagans and Christians. *Journal of Roman Studies. 85*: 65-85.

Rogers, C.R. (1951). *Client-Centered Therapy: Its Current Practice, Implications and Theory*. New York: Houghton Mifflin College Books.

Sandell, R. (2001). Can psychoanalysis become empirically supported? *International Forum of Psychoanalysis, 10*: 184-190.

Sandars, N.K. (1969). *Poems of Heaven and Hell from Ancient Mesopotamia*. Princeton, NJ: Princeton University Press.

Sartre, J.P. (1905). *Being and Nothingness*. New York: Gramercy Books.

Scheindlin, R. (1999). *The Book of Job*. New York: W.W. Norton.

Scherman, N. (1984). *The Complete ArtScroll Siddur*. New York: Mesorah Publications.

Shatz, D., Waxman, C.I., & Diament, N.J. (Eds.). (1997). *Tikkun Olam: Social Responsibility in Jewish Thought and Law*. Northvale, NJ: Jason Aronson Publisher.

Shulman, D.G. (1990) The investigation of psychoanalytic theory by means of the experimental method. *The International Journal of Psychoanalysis, 71*: 487-498.

Shulman, D.G. (1992) The quantitative investigation of psychoanalytic theory and therapy: A bibliography 1986-1992. *Psychoanalytic Psychology, 9*: 529-542.

Shulman, D.G. (in press). Clinical psychoanalysis as midrash. *CCAR Journal: A Reform Jewish Quarterly*.

Slipp, S. (2000). Subliminal stimulation research and its implications for psychoanalytic theory and treatment. *Journal of the American Academy of Psychoanalysis, 28*: 305-320.

Smith, W.R. (1972). *Lectures on the Religion of the Semites: Second and Third Series*. London, Great Britain: Sheffield Academic Press.

Soloveitchik, J.D. (1996). *The Lonely Man of faith*. Hillsdale, NJ: Jason Aronson Press.

Sophocles. (1994). *Oedipus the King*. New York: Pocket Books.

Spiegel, S. (1967). *The Last Trial*. New York: Pantheon.

Stanton, E.C. (1999). *The Woman's Bible*. New York: Prometheus Books.

Strong, J. (1997). *The New Strong's Exhaustive Concordance of the Bible*. New York: Thomas Nelson.

Telushkin, J. (2000). *The Book of Jewish Values: A Day-By-Day Guide to Ethical Living*. New York: Bell Tower Press.

Trible, Ph. (1973). From depatriarchalizing in Biblical interpretation. *Journal of the American Academy of Religion. 41*: 30-48.

Twain, M. (1996). *The Bible According to Mark Twain: Irreverent Writings on Eden, Heaven and the Flood by America's Master Satirist*. New York: Simon and Schuster.

Urbach, E.E. (1987). *The Sages: Their Concepts and Beliefs*. Cambridge, MA: Harvard University Press.

Vermes, G. (1996). New light on the sacrifice of Isaac from 4Q225. *Journal of Jewish Studies. 47:* 140-146.

Visotzky, B.L. (1996). *The Genesis of Ethics*. New York: Crown Publishing.

Wellhausen, J. (1994). *Prolegomena to the History of Israel*. New York: Scholars Press.

Wesley, J. (1990). *John Wesley's Commentary on the Bible*. New York: Zondervan Publishing House.

Yerushalmi, Y.H. (1991). *Freud's Moses: Judaism Terminable and Interminable*. New Haven, CT: Yale University Press.

Zlotowitz, B.M. (1975). The Torah and Haftarah readings for the High Holy Days. *CCAR Journal.* 93-105.

Zlotowitz, M. & Scherman, N. (Eds.). (1995). *Bereishis: Genesis/A New Translation with a Commentary Anthologized from Talmudic, Midrashic and Rabbinic Sources (Volume 1A).* New York, NY: Mesorah Publications.

Zornberg, A.G. (1995) *Genesis: The Beginning of Desire.* Philadelphia, PA: Jewish Publication Society.

About the Author

Rabbi Dennis G. Shulman, Ph.D. is a clinical psychologist-psychoanalyst with private practices in Manhattan and Bergen County, New Jersey. For almost thirty years, he has treated individuals and couples, and taught and supervised mental health professionals throughout the United States and Europe. Dennis Shulman is on the Kollel faculty of the Hebrew Union College-Jewish Institute of Religion (the Reform rabbinic seminary in New York City; and a member of the senior faculty, a training analyst and clinical supervisor at psychoanalytic institutes in New York, Minnesota and Missouri. In May, 2003, he received rabbinic ordination.

Dennis Shulman is a frequent and popular lecturer at universities, psychoanalytic training institutes, synagogues and churches. His lectures on psychopathology are featured in the nationally-televised PBS series, "The World of Abnormal Psychology."

Dennis Shulman received his B.A. from Brandeis University in 1972, his Ph.D. from Harvard University four years later, and his postdoctoral psychoanalytic certificate from the National Institute for the Psychotherapies in 1980.

Dennis Shulman lives in New Jersey with his wife, an obstetrician, and their two daughters. Saturday mornings, he leads Shabbat services at Chavurah Beth Shalom in Alpine, NJ.

Endnotes

1. For a comprehensive discussion of Sigmund Freud's relationship to his Judaism, see my journal article, "Clinical Psychoanalysis as Midrash," (Shulman, in press). Also, see Yerushalmi (1991) and Rice (1990).

2. Freud (1907).

3. Freud (1912).

4. Mishnah Avot 5:22.

5. Freud (1900) p. 514.

6. For a discussion of the relationship between clinical psychoanalysis and the midrashic method of the rabbis, see Shulman (in press).

7. Job 38:39-39:29. This passage was translated by Raymond Scheindlin (1999).

8. *Bereshit* is the first Hebrew word in the Bible. It means, "In the beginning of." This term is often used to refer to this first creation narrative, as well as the entire section of the Torah from creation to the generation of Noah.

9. The translation of the *Enuma Elish* quoted in this chapter is from N.K. Sandars (1989). For the history and alternative translations of the text of the *Enuma Elish*, see Heidel (1951); King (1999); S. Langdon (1923) & Pritchard (1969).

10. For additional similarities between the Babylonian and Israelite creation narratives, see Shalom M. Paul's article, "Creation and Cosmogony," in the *encyclopedia Judaica* and King (1999).

11. For the distinction between pagan and monotheistic creation narratives, I am indebted to Yehezkel Kaufmann (1889-1963), for his outstanding scholarly review of comparative pagan cosmogonies. See especially Chapter Two in *The Religion of Israel: From Its Beginnings to the Babylonian Exile* (1972).

12. Kaufmann (1972) especially pp. 24-29.

13. Guthrie (1993).

14. Kaufmann (1972) p. 22.

15. See Hesiod (1953. For a discussion of mythology centering around Zeus and his family, see Cook (1925) and Arafat (1990).

16. See Gilbert Herdt's (1999) excellent ethnographic study on the "Sambia," who live in the highlands of New Guinea.

17. See especially Eliade (1974).

18. Genesis 1:1 27.

19. Jonas (1963).

20. *Genesis Rabbah* I:3.

21. See Rashi's (1972) comment on Genesis 1:5 and Note 29.

22. See the Preamble to the *Mishneh Torah, translated and abridged by Philip Birnbaum (Maimonides, 1970).*

23. The names of God used in these biblical texts are, in fact, different (*Elohim, YHWH-Elohim, YHWH*). This point will be examined in Chapters Three and Four. The "character" of God does develop in the Hebrew Bible, from His introduction to us in Genesis to His closing words in the Book of Job. For a more complete treatment of this, see Jack Miles' (1995) *God: A Biography.*

24. Cassuto (1978) p. 3.

25. Birnbaum (1949) p. 135.

26. Kaplan (1964) p. 302.

27. For outstanding essays on the psychological and spiritual aspects of the Shabbat (the Sabbath), see Abraham Joshua Heschel's *The Sabbath: Its Meaning for Modern Man* (1952); and pp. 41-49 in Erich Fromm's The *Forgotten Language: An Introduction to the Understanding of Dreams, Fairy Tales, and Myths.*

28. For William Robertson Smith's discussion of the Hebrew Bible's sui generis universal focus of its creation narrative, see especially Smith (1972), "Lecture Three: The Gods and the World."

29. *Genesis Rabbah* I:2.

30. This quotation is attributed to Joseph Al-Bashir, the eleventh century Karaite scholar of Talmud, Muslim philosophy and languages.

31. *Baruch she-amar va-hayah ha-olam.* This phrase is used in the morning prayers in the synagogue. Also see Urbach (1987).

32. This quotation is attributed to the architect-philosopher, R. Buckminster Fuller. Also see Cooper (1998).

33. Genesis 1:1-3. My choices concerning the English translation of the first three Hebrew verses of Genesis draw on the commentaries of Everett Fox (1995), Rashi (1972) and Abraham ibn Ezra (1988). Umberto Cassuto (1978), because of the verb form used in Genesis 1:2, argues against treating Genesis 1:1 as a subordinate clause to Verses 2 and 3 as I do in this excerpt. When preparing my translation of Genesis, however, I did draw on Cassuto's linguistic analysis and insight to translate *ruach* as "spirit" and *ma-ra-chefet as* "hovers over."

34. Genesis 1:26-27. In my decision to translate "*adam*" as "humanity" I am guided by Everett Fox's (1995) similar translation of this verse. Also see Strong (1997) and Brown, Driver & Briggs (1996) for the understanding of *adam* as the species of humanity, rather than the narrow meaning, "man."

35. The English Bibles that translate "*bereshit*" as "in the beginning" include the King James bible, the Revised Standard Version, the JPS Tanakh published in 1917, the Soncino Torah, the J.H. Hertz Torah and the Darby Bible. The Young's Literal Bible, the JPS Tanakh (1985), the Stone Chumash and the Everett Fox translation of the Schocken Five Books of Moses, on the other hand, translate the first verse of Genesis in a way that is consistent with Rashi's and ibn Ezra's insight.

36. For a philosophical discussion of the continuity of creation, see Hermann Cohen (1995). This point is also examined by Avivah Gottlieb Zornberg in her chapter on Bereshit in *Genesis: The Beginning of Desire* (1995).

37. Maimonides (1963) pp. 349-350.

38. *Genesis Rabbah* III:7.

39. The "*Yotzeir Ma-orot*," Birnbaum (1949) p. 74.

40. For an excellent overview, see Louis F. Hartman's article, "Names of God," in the *Encyclopedia Judaica*.

41. For biblical examples of "*adon*" used to mean human lord, see Genesis 19:2, 23:6, 42:30.

42. Genesis 20:13.

43. Exodus 20:3.

44. 1 Samuel 7:3.

45. Psalms 96:5.

46. 1 Kings 11:5.

47. For an examination of the differences between *YHWH* and *Elohim*, as well as a discussion of the Documentary Hypothesis, the modern biblical theory that asserts that the two creation texts are products of different literary traditions within ancient Israel, with divergent heritages involving the names of God, see the conclusion of Chapter Three.

48. Genesis 1:3-24.

49. Many have argued about the meaning of the plural in this verse, "Let *Us* make man in *Our* image." For an excellent description of various points of view on this subject and a critique of the midrashic understanding of it as reflecting consultation with a Divine angelic court, see Umberto Cassuto's (1978) comment on Genesis 1:26. For the classical midrashic discussion of this verse, see *Genesis Rabbah* VIII:3-4 & 8-9.

50. Genesis 1:26.

51. *Genesis Rabbah* VIII:6. For a similar description of how God would not create man until the world was first prepared for him, see Philo (1993) p. 12.

52. *Genesis Rabbah* VIII:10.

53. Psalms 8:3-9.

54. I am indebted to Huston Smith for this beautiful midrashic image, which he describes in his interview in the segment about Judaism, "The Wisdom of Faith: A Bill Moyers Special," televised in 1996 and produced by WNET-TV.

55. Maimonides (1963) & Cohen (1971) p. 132.

56. See *adam* in Strong (1997) and Brown, Driver & Briggs (1996); and Leiber and Harlow's (2001) comment on Genesis 1:27. (

57. Genesis 5:1-2.

58. *Disputatio Nova Contra Mulieres Qua Probatur Eas Non Esse* was probably written by Acidalius Valens. The original document, as well as the earliest English translation (1677), can be found in the Oxford University library.

59. See *Genesis Rabbah* VIII:1, BT Erubin 18a, BT Berachot 61a. Also see Rashi's (1972) comment on Genesis 1:27.

60. For Plato's *Symposium*, see Gill (1999).

61. See the Hebrew roots for *zachar* and *n'kayvah* in Strong (1997) and Brown, Driver & Briggs (1996).

62. Baeck (1948) p. 152.

63. See Kugel (1997; 1999).

64. For an examination of how interpretation of biblical texts is evident even within the Hebrew Bible itself, for example, Jeremiah explicitly interpreting Deuteronomy, see Fishbane (1989).

65. 2 Chronicles 29:12.

66. Isaiah 51:3.

67. Ezekiel 36:33-36.

68. For a discussion of whether these biblical verses refer to Adam, the person, or *adam* meaning humanity, see Marvin H. Pope's article on "Adam" in the *Encyclopedia Judaica*.

69. 1 Chronicles 1:1.

70. Deuteronomy 32:7-9.

71. Job 31:33-35.

72. Although generally the English translations of the Christian Bibles tend to strengthen the association between the Hebrew word, "*adam*," and the person Adam from the Garden of Eden for theological reasons, Hosea 6:7 is translated by the King James Bible, "But they like *men* [not Adam] have transgressed the covenant…"

73. Hosea 6:6-7.

74. 2 Esdras 3:21.

75. Wisdom of Solomon 2:23-24.

76. 2 Esdras 7:48.

77. Romans 5:11-14.

78. 1 Corinthians 15:21-22.

79. 1 Corinthians 15:45.

80. ABC News. *U.S. Adults Skeptical About Evolution.* http://abc-news.go.com/sections/science/DailyNews/evolutionviews990816.html

81. Genesis 2:7.

82. For an examination of the differences between *YHWH* and *Elohim*, as well as a discussion of the documentary hypothesis, see the conclusion of this chapter. The documentary hypothesis asserts that the two creation texts are products of different literary traditions within ancient Israel, with divergent heritages involving the names of God,

83. Genesis 2:18-24.

84. Stanton (1999), p. 18.

85. See BT Sanhedrin 39a and Genesis Rabbah XVII.

86. Genesis Rabbah XVII.

87. See Radak quoted in Zlotowitz's and Scherman's (1995) comment on Genesis 2:18; and J.H. Hertz's (1960) comment on Genesis 2:21.

88. See especially Abarbanel quoted in Zlotowitz's and Scherman's (1995) comment on Genesis 2:21.

89. Examples of Mother-goddess Earth giving birth to the culture's hero are Ishtar in Babylonia, Isis in Egypt, Aphrodite in Greece and Venus in Rome. See Reik (1964), p. 69

90. Rank (1991).

91. This point was also made by Phyllis Trible (1973).

92. See Rashi's (1972) comment on Genesis 2:18.

93. Genesis 3:1-7.

94. See W.G. Plaut's (1981) comment on Genesis 3:1.

95. Surah 20:116-123.

96. See especially Genesis Rabbah VIII:5.

97. Revelation 12:9-10.

98. Revelation 20:1-3.

99. See Calvin's (2001) comment on Genesis 3.

100. Milton (1935).

101. See Urbach (1987).

102. Abraham ibn Ezra (1988).

103. See Cassuto's (1978) comment on Genesis 3:1.

104. Kugel (1998) p. 78; Avot de-Rebbi Natan; and Genesis Rabbah IXX:3.

105. Leiber & Harlow (2001) p. 18.

106. Leiber & Harlow (2001) p. 20.

107. Twain (1996).

108. Genesis 3:8-22.

109. Augustine (1949).

110. Barnes (1971).

111. Genesis Rabbah XIX:3.

112. Rashi (1972). Also see Genesis Rabbah XVIII:6.

113. See Genesis Rabbah IXX:6; and J.H. Hertz's (1960) and Leiber's & Harlow's (2001) comments on Genesis 3:7.

114. Eliade (1972).

115. Micah 4:1-5.

116. See especially Zechariah 14:9 which is quoted in the Aleinu prayer.

117. Isaiah 2:2-5.

118. Isaiah 11:1-8.

119. This vision of the messianic is also found in Maimonides' (1970) *Mishneh Torah, Hilkhot Melakhim* (Laws of Governments), especially Chapters 11 & 12.

120. Fromm (1957). p. 246.

121. This quotation is attributed to the philosopher, W.P. Montague.

122. Micah 6:8.

123. Kaplan (1964).

124. See Erich Fromm's (1957) chapter on the Sabbath ritual, pp. 241-249.

125. Cohen (1971; 1995).

126. See the rabbinic interpretation of Shabbat "work," that is, the 39 categories of activities prohibited on the Shabbat (BT Shabbat 73a).

127. BT Shabbat 119b.

128. See Rashi's (1972) comment and notes on Genesis 2:8.

129. See de Vecchi (1990).

130. For a more comprehensive examination of the discrepancies between Creation I and II, and some recommendations concerning the harmonizing of these two texts, see Cassuto (1978), especially his introduction to the second creation narrative.

131. Genesis 1:11-13.

132. Genesis 2:5-7.

133. Genesis 1:20-26.

134. Genesis 2:18-19.

135. Genesis 1:27.

136. Genesis 2:22.

137. Genesis 3:1-5.

138. Wellhausen (1994). For a contemporary review of the documentary hypothesis, see Friedman (1997).

139. For an examination and critique of the documentary hypothesis as it has been applied to the Genesis creation accounts, see Cassuto (1978), especially the introduction to the section concerning Eden; and Cassuto (1983).

140. Although I disagree with his descriptions of Adam I and II, the Orthodox rabbi, Joseph Dov Soloveitchik (1996) also analyzes the two creation narratives in a nontraditional way, as reflecting distinct aspects of the human.

141. Genesis 2:4.

142. Genesis Rabbah XII:15.

143. See Cassuto (1978), especially the introduction to the second creation account.

144. Cassuto (1978) p. 132-135.

145. This text is from the "*Yotzeir Or*," the benediction recited in the morning prayer service in most synagogues. See the ArtScroll Prayer Book, Scherman (1984) p. 87. The same theme can be found in the similar pre-Shema benediction, "*Ma'ariv Aravim*," recited in the evening service. In this and the next passage, I translated "*HaShem*" back to "*YHWH.*"

146. This text is from the "Ahavah Rabbah," the benediction recited in the morning prayer service in most synagogues. See the ArtScroll Prayer Book, Scherman (1984) p. 89-91. The same theme can be found in the similar pre-Shema benediction, "*Ahavah Olam*," recited in the evening service.

147. This interpretation of Adam I and Adam II as human ideal and reality respectively is also seen in the Gospel of Thomas, only discovered in 1945. See Meyer (1992).

148. Bemporad (1964).

149. Kaplan (1964).

150. Buber (1961) p. 250; and Telushkin (2000) p. 185.

151. Kessler (2000).

152. Romans 8:32.

153. Lowden (1997).

154. H. Langdon (1999).

155. Rembrandt (1990).

156. Owens (1988).

157. Hunter (1989).

158. Kant (1979) footnote to p. 115.

159. Kierkegaard (1954).

160. Kierkegaard (1954) p. 122.

161. For an interesting and scholarly examination of the rabbinic choice to read the Akedah on the second day of Rosh Hashanah, see Zlotowitz (1975).

162. BT Rosh Hashanah 17a. Also see Genesis Rabbah LVI:9.

163. Birnbaum (1949) pp. 22-24.

164. See 2 Chronicles 3:1.

165. Koran, Surah 37:100-111.

166. For midrashim concerning Isaac as willing sacrifice, see Genesis Rabbah LVI:8 and Ginzberg (1998).

167. Josephus (1960); *Antiquities of the Jews*, Book I, Chapter 13:4.

168. Vermes (1996).

169. According to some older Muslim sources, Muhammad believed that the son Abraham almost sacrificed, described in this Koran text, was Isaac, not Ishmael (see H. Hirschberg's *Encyclopedia Judaica*, article on "Isaac").

170. James Michener (1965) pp. 111-112. A similar scenario is described by Martin Bergmann (1992).

171. Leviticus 20:2-5.

172. 2 Kings 23:10.

173. Jeremiah 7:30-31.

174. See especially Ezekiel 16:21, 20:31, 23:37; and Isaiah 57:5. Also see Psalms 106:37-38 & Micah 6:7.

175. Rives (1995).

176. Euripides (1981).

177. See Heinz Kohut (1982) in which he argues that Freud overemphasized inter-generational conflict and under-emphasized intergenerational support in Freud's reading of the Greek classics and in his analysis of psychodynamics.

178. Sophocles (1994).

179. For a more comprehensive comparison of Freud's and Sophocles' Oedipus, see Erich Fromm (1957).

180. For an excellent critical discussion of the "Laius Complex" and some of its theoretical and clinical implications, see Bergmann (1992).

181. Genesis 12:1.

182. For variations of this legend concerning the birth of Abraham and the origins of his faith in a "prime mover" God, see Ginzberg (1998).

183. Exodus 2:5-8.

184. Matthew 2:2.

185. Matthew 2:16-18.

186. Genesis 16:1-2.

187. For a discussion of this Genesis pattern of blessing the younger over the older, see Chapter Five.

188. Genesis 17:19-21.

189. Genesis 21:14.

190. Genesis 18:23-32.

191. This characterization of the Jewish God as "constitutional monarch" is developed by Fromm (1966).

192. See especially Zohar I, 106a, 215b, Chadash 23a; and Genesis Rabbah XLIX:9-10.

193. Zohar I, 215b.

194. Fox's (1995) comment on genesis 22.

195. Genesis 22:1-19.

196. Calvin's (2001) comment on Genesis 22:1.

197. Compare this aggadic talmudic text concerning Abraham's banquet and Job 1:6-12 & 2:1-7.

198. BT Sanhedrin 89b. Similar stories are found in Genesis Rabbah LV:4 and the Dead sea Scroll Book of Jubilees in which a version of the Akedah is included (Vermes, 1996).

199. Genesis Rabbah LV:4. See also BT Sanhedrin 89b.

200. Isaiah 56:7.

201. BT Berachot 7a.

202. Exodus 20:3.

203. See Maccoby (1983).

204. Rashi's (1972) comment on Genesis 22:2. Also see Genesis Rabbah LV:7.

205. Matthew Henry's (1999) comment on Genesis 22:2. Also see the similar comments on the same biblical verse by John Wesley (1990) and John Calvin (2001).

206. John Wesley's (1990) comment on Genesis 22:2.

207. Genesis 12:1.

208. Genesis 8:20.

209. Exodus 20:24.

210. Amos 5:22.

211. Genesis Rabbah LVI:8. Also see Rashi's (1972) comment on Genesis 22:2.

212. Genesis 21:14.

213. Genesis 14:11.

214. BT Pesachim 4a.

215. John Calvin's (2001) comment on Genesis 22:3.

216. For a critique of the contemporary commentaries on the Akedah, see J. Levenson (1998).

217. Kant (1979) Footnote to p. 115.

218. Micah 6:8.

219. Buber (1957).

220. Lerner (1994) p. 45.

221. Visotzky (1996).

222. Josephus asserts that Sarah was most certainly unaware of Abraham's plan. See Josephus (1960) Book I, Chapter 13:2.

223. Genesis Rabbah LV:6 and Ginzberg (1998).

224. For a discussion of the aloneness of the hero, see Kierkegaard (1954).

225. Genesis Rabbah LV:6.

226. Also see Tanhuma 22.

227. For a series of legends involving Satan attempting to challenge Abraham's equanimity on his three-day pilgrimage, see Genesis Rabbah LVI:4, BT Sanhedrin 89b and Ginzberg (1998).

228. See especially Genesis Rabbah LVI:8. Josephus (1960) maintains that Isaac was twenty-five years old at the time of the Akedah (Book I, Chapter 13:2).

229. Genesis Rabbah LVIII:6.

230. See Genesis 17:17.

231. For a critique of the rabbinic idea that Isaac was thirty-seven years old, see Abraham ibn Ezra's (1988) comment on Genesis 22.

232. See Brown-Driver-Briggs (1996) & Strong (1997).

233. Kierkegaard (1954) pp. 45-46.

234. For midrashic elaborations of the altar scene, see Genesis Rabbah LVI.5, the Dead Sea Scroll version of the Akedah text (Vermes 1996), Ginzberg (1998) and the Zohar 120a.

235. Zohar 120b. I am appreciative to Avivah Gottlieb Zornberg who drew my attention to this Zohar text in her Akedah talk at the William Allanson White Institute, May, 2002.

236. Genesis Rabbah LV:8.

237. Genesis LV:8.

238. Ginzberg (1998).

239. Carmi (1981) p. 373.

240. Spiegel (1967).

241. Leiber and Harlow (2001) p. 118.

242. 2 Kings 4:32-35.

243. See Kravitz (1997).

244. This is a paraphrase of a quotation attributed to the philosopher W.P. Montague.

245. Plaut's (1981) comment on Genesis 22.

246. Inscription on the shrine to Apollo in Delphi.

247. John 8:32.

248. Maimonides (1970).

249. Freud (1915a).

250. Sartre (1905).

251. See especially Omdahl (1995).

252. Rogers (1951).

253. Kohut (1976).

254. BT Sanhedrin 37a and Koran Surah 5:32.

255. Genesis 1:27.

256. Heschel (1983).

257. Genesis 22:7.

258. Genesis 23:19.

259. Genesis 24:1-7.

260. Genesis 24:15-20.

261. Genesis 24:67.

262. See Footnote 1, Genesis Rabbah LX:16, Soncino Edition.

263. Rashi's (1972) comment on Genesis 24:67.

264. Calvin's (2001) comment on Genesis 24,67.

265. Genesis 25:21.

266. Genesis 30:22.

267. Genesis 26:18.

268. A similar understanding of Isaac's personality is found in Fox's (1995) comment on Genesis 24-25.

269. Genesis 25:22. Often the Hebrew verb is translated as "struggled," however, ratsats has a more aggressive connotation. (See Brown, Driver and Briggs, 1996; & Strong, 1997).

270. Genesis Rabbah LXIII:6 and Rashi's (1972) comment on Genesis 25:22.

271. Genesis 36:1.

272. See Genesis Rabbah LXV:21 and TJ Ta'anit 4:8.

273. BT Shabbat 89b.

274. Genesis 25:24.

275. Compare Genesis 38:27.

276. See Rashi's (1972) comment on Genesis 25:24 and also, Genesis Rabbah LXIII:8.

277. Genesis 25:19-28:9.

278. Malachi 1:2-4.

279. Genesis 25:22-24.

280. John Calvin (2001), in his comment on Genesis 25:23, emphasizes the "election" of the younger son over the older one to justify Christianity's supplanting of Judaism.

281. See Genesis 25:26.

282. See Genesis 27:36, Jeremiah 9:3 and Hosea 12:4.

283. Nahum Sarna points out that the name, Ya-akov, predates the Israelites and therefore, the connection of Ya-akov with heel is a biblical word play.

284. Genesis 25:27-28.

285. Deuteronomy 21:17.

286. Genesis 25:29-34.

287. Genesis 27:1-36.

288. Ginzberg (1998).

289. See Ginzberg (1998) and Genesis Rabbah LXV:10.

290. Genesis 13:14-16.

291. Genesis 28:3-4.

292. Genesis 25:23.

293. Compare Genesis 27:41-45 and Genesis 27:46.

294. Genesis 49:31.

295. See Leibowitz (1976).

296. Exodus 3:1-10.

297. Mark 1:14.

298. Koran Surah 44, 74 and 97.

299. An interesting alternative explanation from the midrash for Jacob's traveling to Laban's land without possessions implicates Esau's oldest son Eliphaz who set upon Jacob and his retinue, leaving him without servants and possessions, but alive. (See Rashi's (1972) comment on Genesis 28).

300. Genesis 28:10-22.

301. Genesis Rabbah LXVIII:12.

302. Jacob refers to this wilderness dream more than one hundred years later on his deathbed. (See Genesis 48:3-4.)

303. See Nachmanides' (2001) comment on Genesis 28:20.

304. Rashi's (1972) comment on Genesis 28:20.

305. Genesis Rabbah LXX:4.

306. Samuel Karff, quoted in Plaut (1981) p. 195.

307. Genesis 29:20-26.

308. Genesis 30:29-35.

309. Genesis 31:36-42.

310. Genesis 31:51-52.

311. Genesis 31:3,13.

312. Genesis 32:10-12.

313. Genesis 32:23-31.

314. Rabbi Yakov b. Yakov Ha-Cohen quoted in Plaut (1981) p. 219.

315. See Brown, Driver and Briggs (1997) and Strong (1996).

316. Rashi's (1972) comment on Genesis 32:27.

317. Freud (1905a) p. 109.

318. Genesis 33:1-10.

319. The Hebrew is *shalaym*, which can be translated as peace, but has more of the connotation of possessing integrity or completeness. (See Strong, 1997; and Brown, Driver & Briggs, 1996.)

320. Genesis 33:18.

321. See Braun (1999).

322. Genesis 17:5.

323. Genesis 17:15.

324. Genesis 34:1.

325. For an excellent contemporary book-length midrash on the Dinah Genesis text, see Anita Diamant's *The Red Tent* (1998).

326. Genesis 34:2-3.

327. Genesis 34:13-16.

328. Genesis 34:25-26.

329. Genesis 34:30.

330. Genesis 37:2-5.

331. Genesis 37:13-19.

332. See especially Genesis 21:10.

333. Genesis 25:28.

334. See Genesis 4:1-8.

335. Deuteronomy 21:15-18.

336. See Genesis 48:17-20.

337. *Ma'at va-ra'im* in Hebrew. For connotation of *ra* as "miserable," see Strong (1997) and Brown, Driver & Briggs (1996).

338. Genesis 47:7-10.

339. This quotation concerning Joseph is attributed to Sir Walter Scott.

340. Genesis 30:22-24.

341. Compare Genesis 17:19 and 25:23. In both of these verses (involving Isaac and Jacob), God makes His choice of patriarch explicit.

342. Genesis 39:2-3.

343. Genesis 39:20-21.

344. Genesis 41:15-16.

345. Genesis 37:5-7.

346. Genesis 37:10-11.

347. Genesis 50:15-21.

348. Genesis 4:7.

349. Genesis 4:9.

350. *Teshuvah* is a Hebrew word that literally means to return. It has come to mean repentance.

351. The only other possible figure in the Book of Genesis who, like Judah, demonstrated transformation without benefit of support of God or of father is Esau. Esau, Jacob's twin brother, swears to kill Jacob for the betrayal and then, twenty years later, weeps with his brother and forgives him. However, in the case of Esau, the Torah offers no narrative as to what led to Esau's transformation. The fact that four hundred of his men accompany Esau in his reunion with Jacob may imply that Esau rode

toward his brother with malice, but had a change of heart when he actually encountered him.

352. Genesis 37:21-22.

353. Genesis 37:25.

354. Genesis 37:26-27.

355. Genesis 37:29.

356. Genesis Rabbah XCV:1.

357. Genesis Rabbah LXXXV·4

358. Exodus Rabbah XLII.

359. See Genesis Chapter 38.

360. Deuteronomy 25:6.

361. Genesis 38:24-25.

362. Genesis 38:26.

363. See Ruth 4:1821.

364. See Isaiah 11:1 and Matthew 1:1.

365. Genesis 43:9.

366. Genesis 44:18-34.

367. Genesis 45:3.

368. Genesis 49:8-10.

369. The keynote speech at the *Moby-Dick* 2001 conference to commemorate the 150th anniversary of Herman Melville's publication of the novel, Hofstra University Cultural Center, November 24, 2001.

370. Psalm 8:5.

371. Susan Neiman (2002) p. 91

372. For an examination of the relationship between Freud's psychoanalytic worldview and the method of midrash developed by the rabbis, see Shulman (in press).

373. For contemporary empirical evaluations of specific tenets of Freud's theory see especially Bornstein & Masling (1998); Fosshage (1997); Sandell (2001); Shulman (1990, 1992); and Slipp (2000).

374. Keyes (1996).

375. Freud (1917).

376. For an analysis of a version of this incident, see Lacan (1977) p. 116.

377. For a discussion of how the ancient rabbis and more recent chasidic masters understood the unconscious, see Steinsaltz's (1988) essay, "Chasidism and Psychoanalysis." For an example of Chasidic awareness of the unconscious, see especially the Sfat Emet's comment on Genesis 18:12-16 in which Sarah laughs when she learns that she is to have a child (Braun, 1999).

378. Freud (1909) p. 166.

379. Freud (1905b).

380. For Freud's descriptions of the primitive content of the unconscious of the infant and the adult, see "Instincts and Their Vicissitudes" (1915b) and "Three Essays on the Theory of Sexuality" (1905b).

381. The characterization of the infant's mental life as evil by Freud has encouraged some scholars to associate psychoanalytic instinct theory with the Christian doctrine of original sin. See especially MacIsaac (1974).

382. Freud (1915a) p. 210.

383. See Jung's (1960) *Answer to Job*, p. 16.

384. Jung (1938) p. 45.

385. *Genesis Rabbah* VIII:10.

386. Genesis 2:7.

387. Genesis 3:11-13.

388. Zohar 120b. I am appreciative to Avivah Gottlieb Zornberg who drew my attention to this Zohar text in her Akedah talk at the William Allanson White Institute, May, 2002.

389. Genesis 25:24-26.

390. Genesis 32:24-28.

391. The Hebrew word, *"yetzer,"* has come to mean inclination. This word derives from the verb root, *"yatzar,"* which means "to form," "to squeeze into shape," or more figuratively, "to determine." (Strong, 1997; Brown, Driver & Briggs, 1996)

392. Genesis 2:7.

393. BT Berachot 61a.

394. See especially Romans 6:23 & 7:22-24.

395. BT Yoma 69b.

396. Genesis Rabbah IX:7.

397. BT Sukkah 52a & Kiddushin 81a.

398. Proverbs 16:32.

399. Mishnah Avot 4:1.

400. "The Dissection of the Psychical Personality," in Freud (1933) p. 80.

401. Genesis 4:7.

402. The repair of the incomplete and fractured world is what is meant by the originally Kabalistic concept of "*tikkun ha-olam*." See especially Shatz, Waxman & Diament (1997).

403. The word, "blood," is actually in the plural. The verse is more accurately translated, "The voice of your brother's *bloods* cry out to me from the ground." This verse is the basis of the talmudic warning to witnesses in a capital case to take their responsibility seriously when testifying against a defendant facing execution. When anyone is killed, like Abel, all his "bloods," that is, all his potential for descendents are also killed with him. (BT Sanhedrin 37a)

404. Genesis 4:9-10.

405. Genesis 4:13-14.

406. Genesis 8:21.

407. See Chapter Four and BT Berachot 7a.

408. Genesis 9:9-11.

409. Genesis 9:12-15.

410. Nachmanides' (2001) comment on Genesis 9:12.

411. Zohar 120b.

412. The Hebrew word for this form of sacrifice is *olah*, a burnt offering, a "holocaust." See Chapter Four.

413. Kierkegaard (1954).

414. The name, *Elohim* in contrast with *YHWH* is discussed in Chapters Two, Three and Four.

415. For heartbreaking midrashic descriptions of how the angels of *YHWH* suffered and protested when Abraham readied the sacrifice, see especially Genesis Rabbah LVI:5; Ginzberg (1998); and the Zohar 120a.

416. Genesis 28:10-22.

417. Genesis 31:36-42.

418. Genesis 31:3,13.

419. Genesis 37:9.

420. Genesis 41:15-16.

421. Genesis 48:9-20.

422. Genesis 50:19-21.

423. Genesis 38:26.

424. See Genesis 44:18-34.

425. Freud (1933) p. 106.

426. Maimonides (1983) "*Hilkhot Teshuvah*," (Laws of Repentance).

427. Maimonides was a passionate advocate of free will. He characterized those who believed that all things were fated by God at birth as "stupid gentiles and idiots of Israel." (Maimonides (1983) "*Hilkhot Teshuvah*," (Laws of Repentance), 5:2.

428. Maimonides (1983) "*Hilkhot Teshuvah*," (Laws of Repentance), Chapter Three.

429. BT. Pesachim 54a; Maimonides (1983) "*Hilkhot Teshuvah*," (Laws of Repentance), Chapter One.

430. For a discussion of these stages of *teshuvah*, see especially Chapter Two in Maimonides (1983) "*Hilkhot Teshuvah*," (Laws of Repentance). These four stages of repentance are examined in the context of psychotherapeutic principles by Estel Frankel (1998).

431. See Urbach (1987).

432. Maimonides (1983) "Foundations of Torah," 2:10.

433. See especially Frankel (1998).

434. Maimonides (1983) "*Hilkhot Teshuvah*," (Laws of Repentance), 2:9.

435. Maimonides (1983) "*Hilkhot Teshuvah*," (Laws of Repentance), 2:1.

436. See Meng and E.L. Freud (1963); & Gay (1987) p. 81.

437. Goldberg (1998) pp. 221-222.

438. Fromm (1947) p. 16.

439. Freud quoted in Racker (1966).

440. Freud (1914).

441. Lear (1999).

442. Freud's actual words were directed to his hysterical patient who questioned the point of subjecting herself to an analysis. Freud said to her, "…much will be gained if we succeed in transforming your hysterical misery into common unhappiness." (Freud, 1893-1895, p. 305).

443. Genesis 28:10-16.

444. Isaiah 6:3.

445. Huston Smith, defining Zen, in "The Wisdom of Faith: A Bill Moyers Special," televised in 1996 and produced by WNET-TV. I consider this statement an extremely apt description of the best that the Book of Genesis offers as its goals for human purpose; and the best of other religions as well.

0-595-28025-0